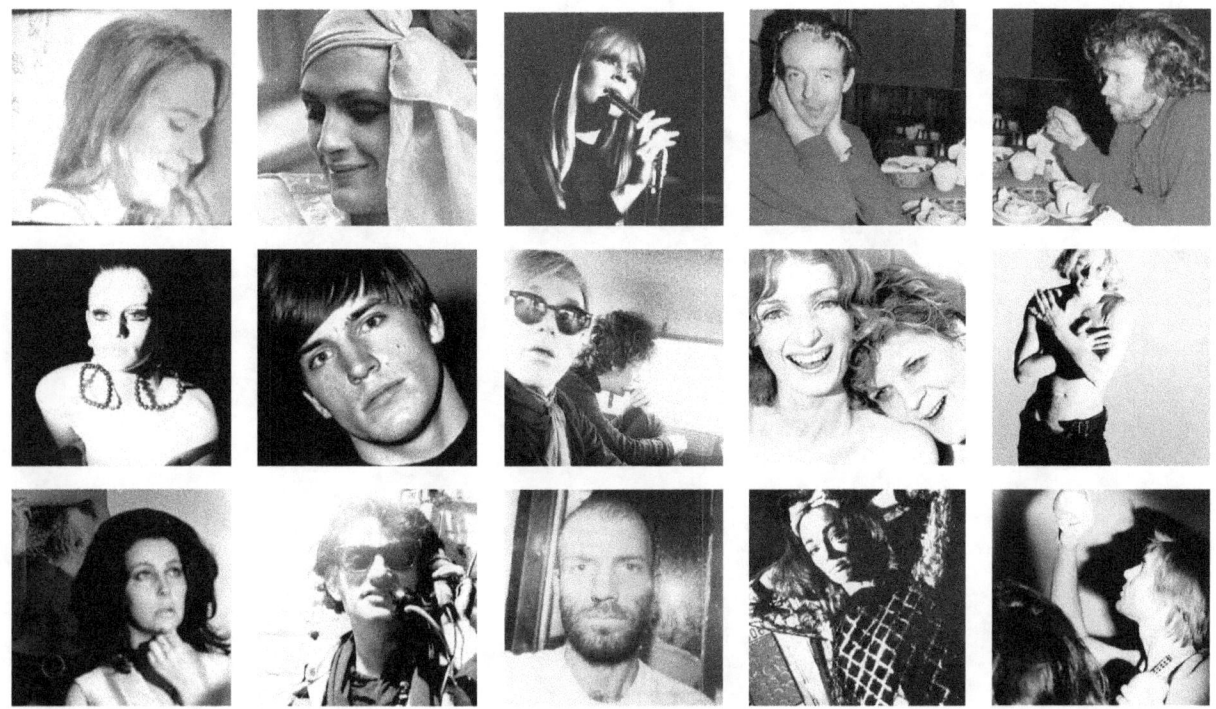

Andy Warhol's Factory People

Inside the 1960's Silver Factory . . . an Oral History

Book III Your 15 Minutes Are Up

Cover Photo and Portrait Montage on preceding page by Billy Name.
L. to R., from top: Mary Woronov, Candy Darling, Nico, Taylor
Mead, Louis Waldon, Susan Bottomly (International Velvet), Joe
Dallesandro, Andy Warhol and Paul Morrissey, Viva and Brigid
Berlin, Eric Emerson, Ultra Violet, Ondine, Billy Name, Ivy
Nicholson, and Allen Midgette

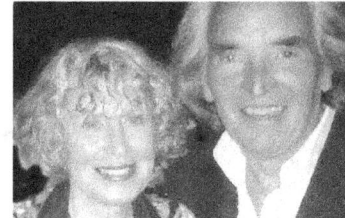

Poster Design by Tom & Leo, Paris.

At right: Catherine and husband Patrick Nagle, producer of 'Factory
People', photographed in L.A. by Matthew Smiley, 2013

Published by Planet Group Entertainment Ltd.

BOOK III

YOUR 15 MINUTES ARE UP

Dying is the most embarrassing thing that can happen to you,
because someone's got to take care of all your details.
—Andy Warhol, 1928-1987

For Patrick . . .

Thanks, partner. You took care of
all the details, and made it happen.

CONTENTS

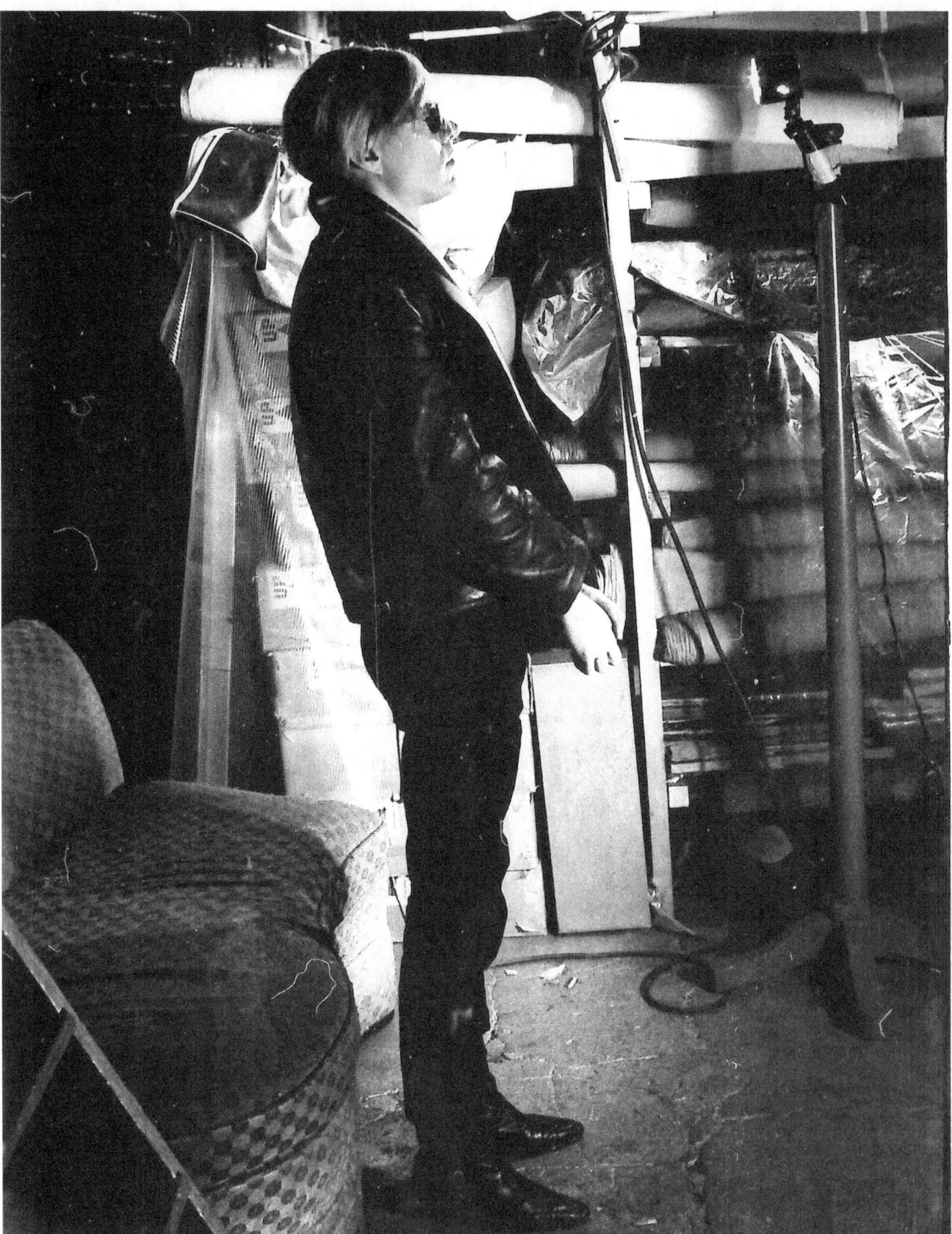

"Everyone will be famous for 15 minutes." On the 50th Anniversary of the Silver Factory, that hoary saying has become ubiquitous. Even Warhol tired of the expression, claiming, "I'm bored with that line." Our Factory People thought so too, except for Ultra Violet, who cleverly entitled her memoir: 'Famous For 15 Minutes'. This, undoubtedly, did not endear her to many other writers with ties to the Factory, who would have killed for it. Anyway, once again, we incorporated intros for this last episode of the TV series. Though most of our subjects were familiar by now, new characters were constantly being added to further flavor the simmering Silver Factory stew. Unfortunately, as with any favorite dish, too many cooks in the kitchen can ultimately destroy it. . .

Warhol was looking for, not so much for extraordinary ideas, but things that had never been done, so why not do a film for twenty-four hours?
—**Ultra Violet: Socialite, Artist, Warhol Superstar**

He seems to prefer to do filmmaking to painting.
—**Leo Castelli: Famed Art Dealer, Owner of Castelli's, Warhol's Gallery**

The only acting experience I got with Andy was impersonating him, by request, on college tours. And these people knew nothing about Warhol.
—**Allen Midgette: Actor, Warhol Superstar**

He was the one who had the guts to save the Velvet Underground from poverty and misery.
—**Nico: Warhol Icon, Velvet Underground Star**

They hated the music. They couldn't get past the one track. I had one engineer that said, "They don't pay me enough to listen to this shit."
—**Lou Reed: Rock Legend, Founder, Velvet Underground**

Everyone's jumping ship. Edie wasn't there anymore, and by spring of '67, the Velvets weren't there anymore.
—**Gerard Malanga: Warhol Factory 'Prime Minister', Poet**

Andy came to La Jolla, California, when he was shooting 'San Diego Surf', and the police could hardly wait to bust him
—**Vincent Fremont: Founding Director, Andy Warhol Foundation for the Visual Arts**

The last movie we made was 'San Diego Surf', and on the plane back, Andy said I would be next Superstar. Two days after we got back he was shot.
—Taylor Mead: Poet, Downtown Personality, Warhol Star

People were stealing his work left and right. We even knew them! I didn't know what to do, because I was afraid.
—David Croland: Publisher LID Magazine, young member Warhol 'family

Edie was getting too stoned to do anything. The dealers had a lot to do with it. Edie was losing her sense of balance. She couldn't even stand up without tipping over. At the end there, it was very sad.
—Danny Fields: Edie Sedgwick confidant, Music Entrepreneur (The Ramones)

Warhol really fucked up a great many young people's lives. I was a good target. I bloomed into a healthy young drug addict.
—Edie Sedgwick: Warhol Icon, Girl of the Year, 1965

Edie had burned down her apartment (at the Chelsea Hotel). She left candles everywhere, and they burned down her place, and that era was over.
—Bibbe Hansen: Warhol Actress, Youngest Member of Warhol family

I knew Andy was mad at me, because he doesn't like to give *anyone* money. That's not true—he would give these crazy transvestites a hundred dollars once in a while, but me, no. We weren't paid.
—Mary Woronov: Writer, Artist, Actress, Warhol Star

Jackie (Curtis) devised this plan: "Why don't we just go to Max's (Kansas City) and sign Andy's name. . ." And Andy got all the bills.
—Holly Woodlawn: Drag Queen, Warhol Superstar ('Flesh', 'Trash')

I'm only a woman . . . only a facade.
—Candy Darling: Drag Queen, Superstar ('Women In Revolt')

These pioneer female impersonators were so gifted, and so funny, and had such a hard time, making very little money.
—Paul Morrissey: Warhol Co-Director, Filmmaker, 'Women in Revolt'

They would put on five pairs at least, of false eyelashes at the same time, so when they blinked their eyes, it was *awnings* going up and down!
—'Leee' Black Childers: Factory Acolyte, Photographer, Former Mgr. David Bowie

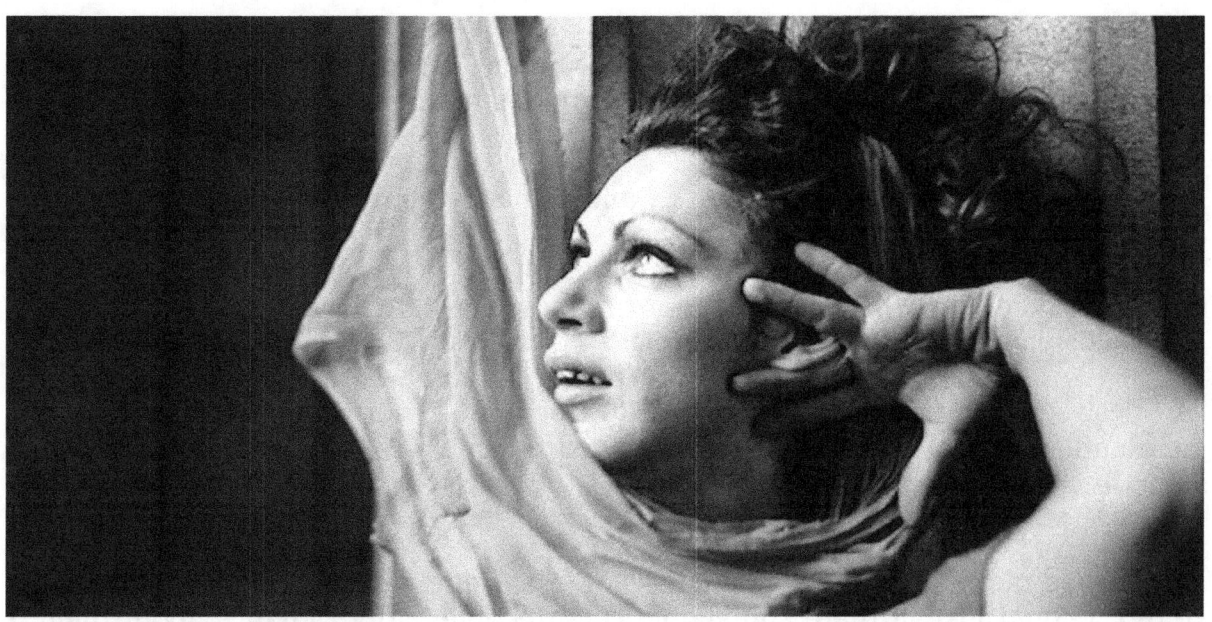

"Only a fascade." In the pale light of dawn, Holly Woodlawn could almost convince as a 1940s Grecian goddess. (Photo: 'Leee' Black Childers)

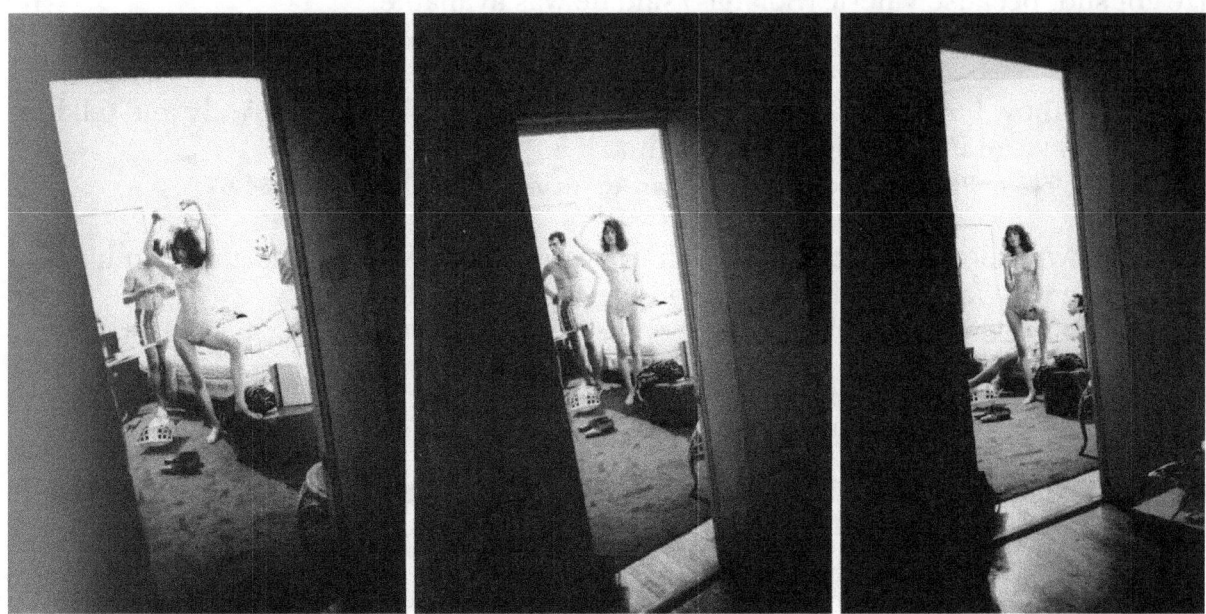

Triptych of Ivy Nicholson, in her fabulously flimsy underwear. The truculent star of 'I, A Man' shares a small room, barely, with Tom Baker. (Photo: Billy Name)

9

When I left, Andy said he had to replace me with drag queens. Well, Paul didn't want me around. I had a fiery temper. I almost broke the camera in 'I, A Man'.
—**Ivy Nicholson: Warhol Superstar**

After I saw 'I, A Man', I went up to Andy and demanded to be in the next movie.
—**Viva: Warhol Superstar, Artist**

Oh, people like Viva, (*mimicking*) *"He owes me money; he never paid me!"*
—**Brigid Berlin: Warhol Muse, Movie Character and Confidante**

In 'Flesh', I was going to be married to Joe Dallesandro and have this lesbian girlfriend. I improvised it all. . . Andy loved to collect colorful characters that had something special about them.
—**Geraldine Smith: Warhol Star ('Flesh', 'Trash'), one of 'Andy's kids**

Andy asked me to do pictures for 'Interview' Magazine. Max's back room was like a studio. I could just sit there and shoot. These people had a radiance about them. I didn't have to use a flash; they would just light up the picture.
—**Anton Perich: Photographer, Filmmaker, Painter**

I was in the dark room, I heard a bang, and there was Andy lying in a pool of blood. He got shot because Valerie (Solanas) said he was available.
—**Billy Name: Warhol Photographer, Factory Foreman, 'Gate-keeper'**

Well, you know how Valerie got there, don't you? I said, "I will call Andy and tell him that you have an interesting script for him."
—**Nat Finkelstein: Photojournalist, Black Star Agency, Warhol Chronicler, 64-67**

I never saw (Valerie) personally, but there were many people in his circle, in his film world. He was dealing with curious and eccentric subject matter.
—**Ivan Karp: Longtime Warhol Art Dealer**

50-50 at this stage. There is a team upstairs . . . operating.
—**Warhol's surgeon, Columbus Hospital, 1968**

Andy said, *"I died, Louis. The light at the end of the tunnel went out."*
—**Louis Waldon: Actor, 'Artist', Warhol Star**

He wouldn't fall asleep until dawn cracked, because if you fall asleep at night you're not quite sure of waking up again. . . Andy probably has his own idea about Hell.
—**Henry Geldzahler: Art Critic, Curator, Metropolitan Museum of Art**

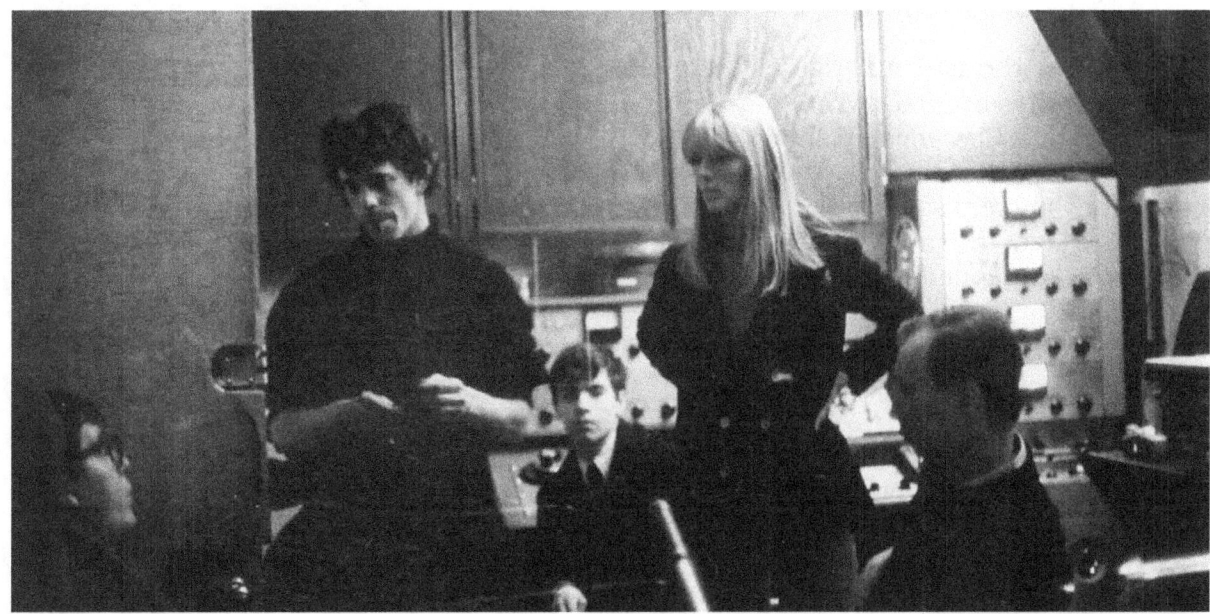

"There are no rules. . ." The Velvet Underground recordng "one of the 10 most influential albums of all time." Lou Reed, who helped shape rock for 50 years, died in 2013. (Photo: Nat Finkelstein)

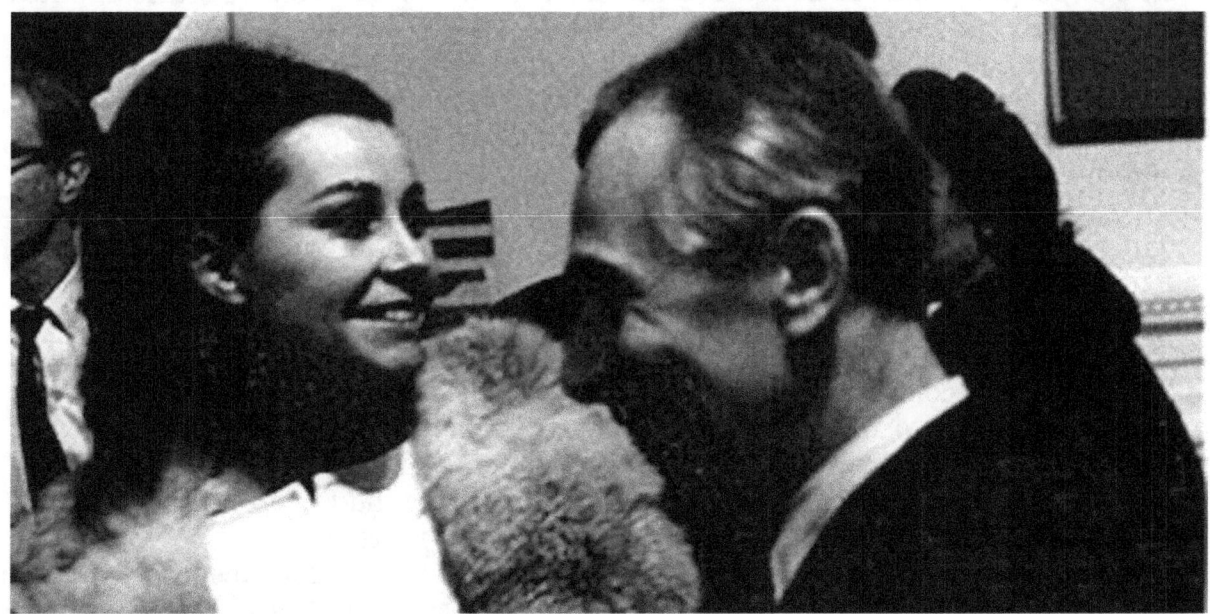

Busy, busy Ultra Violet ("They are blind, blind in the art world.") meets with uber art dealer Leo Castelli. 50 years later, in May of 2014, aristocratic Ultra (aka Mlle. Isabelle Collin Dufresne), still has her 15 minutes, with her own Pop art retrospective at the Dillon gallery in Chelsea. (Photo: Billy Name)

Andy was at the cutting edge of the age that we live in now. We will not want our fifteen minutes of fame. We'll pay dearly for our anonymity.
—Robert Heide: Playwright, Warhol Confidant

Later, newspapers said, "Oh, he destroyed people; some of them committed suicide." No, no! Maybe the only happy moments they had were in the Factory.
—Jonas Mekas: Founder, Film-Makers' Cinematheque, Anthology Film Archives

Don't pay any attention to what they write about you. Just measure it in inches.
—Andy Warhol

Because Warhol deliberately obscured his origins, few outside of academic circles know that his family came from Rurethania, in the Carpathian Mountains near the borders of Russia and Poland, which happens to be the home of the real Count Dracula, otherwise known as 'Vladimir the Impaler'. Ondine bestowed on Warhol the endearing name of 'Drella', a combination of Dracula and Cinderella. Lou Reed wrote 'Songs for Drella' in tribute. Everyone wore black and favored the night life. Warhol evidently related to his family's infamous neighbor. One of his early ('64) movies, the aforementioned funfest known as 'Batman/Dracula' starred influential camp filmmaker Jack Smith as the Count, with his group of thespians, along with Warhol's people, which included Naomi Levine, Baby Jane Holzer, Mario Montez (also a Smith star), Gerard Malanga, Taylor Mead, Robert Heide, Allen Midgette, Henry Geldzahler, Philip Fagan, Rufus Collins, Ivy Nicholson, and Darius de Polean, her son by a French Viscount. Whew! No wonder I didn't list them before! The film, which took months to make, was endless and often gruelling to watch, with moments of erotic brilliance, but our blood had long since been siphoned out of us. 'Batman/Dracula' was never released, so thank you, Warhol Museum, for that singular experience. . . Going over our own footage, I wondered if we would ever get our film released, either. We had too much material! By the time we'd reached the end of our exhaustive interviews, and our exhausted interviewees, we'd sensed a note of melancholy stealing into the amusing anecdotes and titillating oft-told tales. Warhol's former confidants and co-workers, boyfriends and beauty queens, were coming once again to the end of their time with the man who had, for better or worse, changed their lives forever. Though some would be considered damaged goods, for a brief moment in history, the Factory Family had been lucky enough to have lived, as Ivy remembers, "a fairy tale period." Others were not so charitable, blaming Warhol for the escalating mental meltdowns. But as Lou Reed once stated, "The Factory is not a mental hospital." So no one, least of all Warhol, was about to help the floundering souls who found themselves losing touch with reality.

FACTORY LIFE . . . LATE SIXTIES

Andy, what is the most difficult thing for you?
—Victor Bockris

Getting through the day.
—Andy Warhol

Victor Bockris: Billy Name put it really well in my biography of Andy: "To be in the Factory you must be able to stand up in front of those people and take it, you had to have confidence in yourself. Your self-image has to be really strong." Because you were going to be put to the test, constantly. Your ego is being attacked, constantly. Can you take it, can you stand it. Are you really one of us?

Nat Finkelstein: And here was this permissive father image—again, kindergarten leader image—who gave them a place to play. These people were really very, very bright, and they could really inflict hurt. And they inflicted hurt to the extent that Danny Williams, who was his lover, committed suicide. Danny was the person who set up the light shows, who did the strobe lighting, but once Morrissey and that group learned how to do it, he knew he was expendable.

13

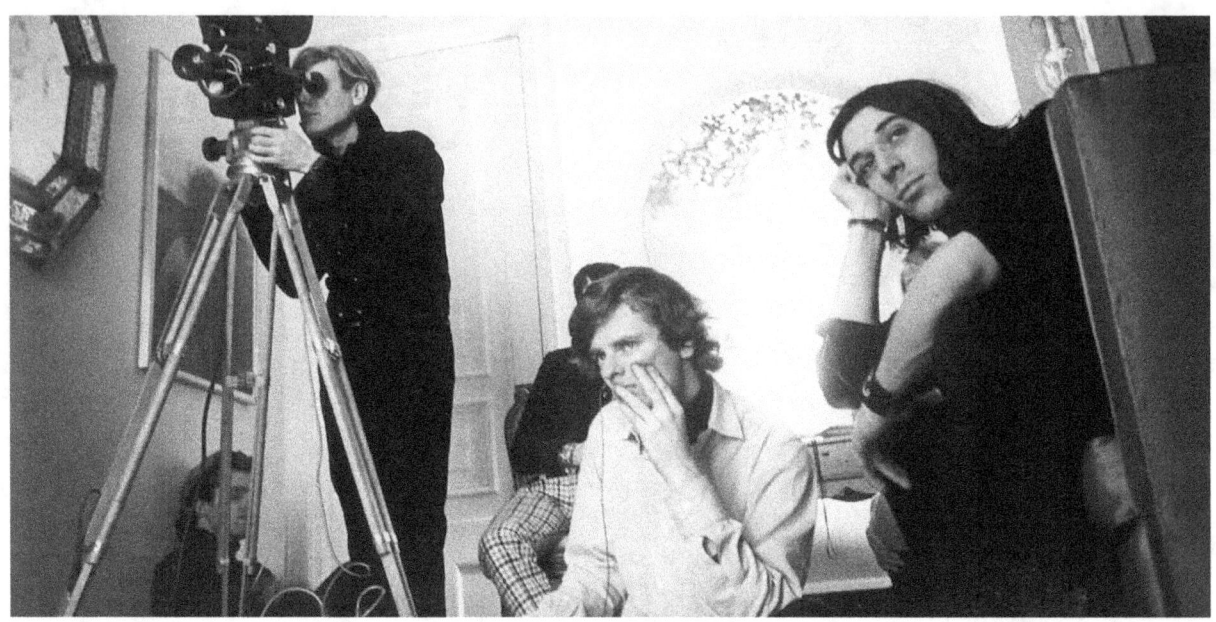

Andy filming with Paul Morrissey, who had his own ideas about filmmaking. Gerard is on floor at left, John Cale at right. (Photo: Nat Finkelstein)

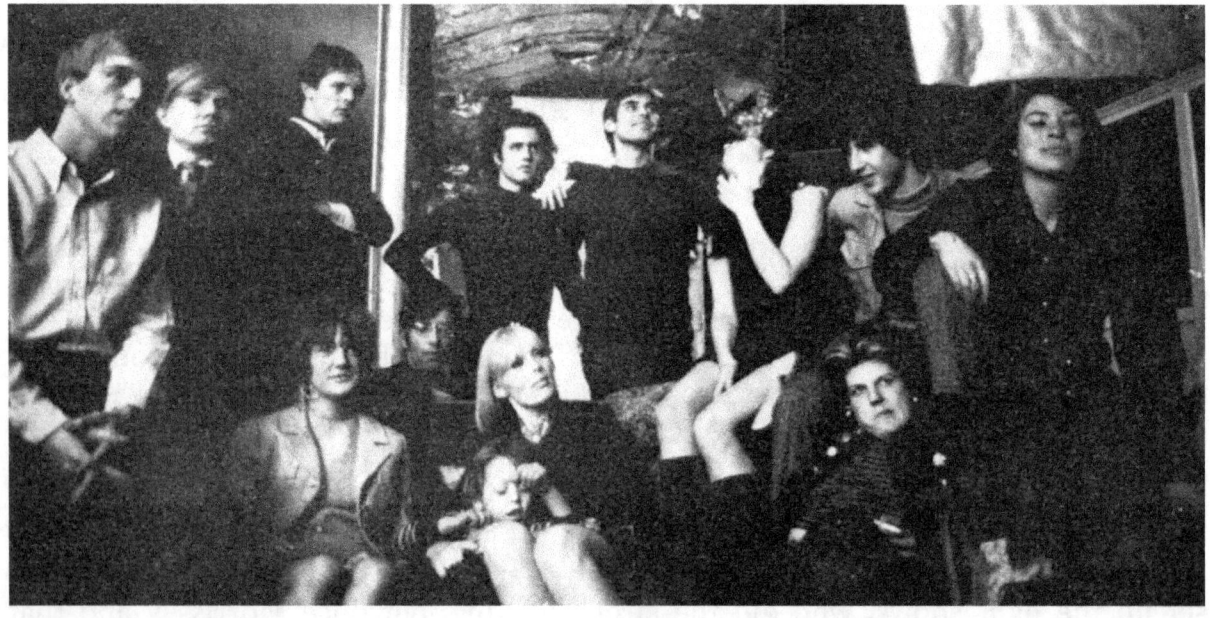

The gang's not all here, but most of them show up for a fun, out-of-focus but who cares, family portrait. Allen Midgette, in the middle, smiles, David and Susan laugh, and everyone else grins and bears it, while Nico's son Ari just wants to go to bed. (Photo: Billy Name)

Photojournalist Nat Finkelstein, who took photographs of the Factory folk from 1964 until 1967, was considered to be the 'court' photographer, present for the special 'state' occasions that Warhol wanted publicized, such as the meetings with Marcel Duchamps and Bob Dylan. As Nat told us, his first impression of the Factory was: "My God, people here are crazy! The music is great, the art is fantastic! This is really the rotten underbelly of the American bourgeoisie." Nat was also looking for love, but had to settle for sex. . .

Nat Finkelstein: They were vicious people. There was no "peace and love" there. They weren't there to help. Help or utilize? Andy utilized them, but who would you think they would help? Okay, maybe I'm an outlaw, but we have this thing: "You use your friends but you don't abuse them." They abused. As for Gerard, he got a royal screwing, and in some sort of ways I can understand why he stole, because he was stolen from, but he shouldn't have done it to me, because I was his friend.

Gerard Malanga: There was a lot of talent out there that could be utilized in terms of just being helpful, or being creative, helpful to Andy's work. You'd catch Andy and me silk screening; you'd catch Billy playing opera records and talking to Ondine, and some friends seated on the couch chatting away.

'Leee' Black Childers: So I got to where I was going there every day. Sometimes I would get little jobs from Andy, photographic jobs that he would pay me for. And there was a guy at the Chelsea Hotel that, whenever the check was from Andy Warhol, he'd give you an extra twenty-five dollars if he could buy it, because he wanted the autographs. Andy couldn't lose, because he would write us a check, but it never got cashed, so Andy wasn't out the money. And we got our money and twenty-five dollars extra for a check we would have just lost or peed on. I don't know what the guy at the Chelsea Hotel ever did, but he was doing a big business in Andy Warhol checks.

Billy Name: He valued people if they could participate in the creation of something that was going to impact people, but it will be known as a Warhol work. . . We had this case of Coca-Cola small bottles and their wooden cases. So one night, I took them all out, put them on the floor and sprayed them silver, and just left them there for Andy to see when he came in the next day. I would always do surprises like that for him. We were talking about this idea of using them as perfume bottles, and having a line of 'parfum', and it would be called "Your-In" by Andy Warhol. So we got some cheap cologne, and then filled the Coke bottles and got those little rubber >

stoppers with the rubber sealers, and we made these bottles of . . . 'urine' *(laughs)*. I think they're collectable, but the thing is that the cologne inside of the bottles made the paint drip and come off on whoever was wearing it, so they were like a fiasco, but a fantastic idea! Your-In.

Billy Name, the omnipresent Factory foreman and essential gatekeeper, lived in the Factory. He thus was able to chronicle with his camera literally everything going on during and after hours, making him, according to Victor Bockris, "One of the great photographers of the sixties in terms of capturing the atmosphere of that scene."

Ivy Nicholson: Billy Name's photos are more like paintings. There is something so magical about them. He wasn't obvious. He was almost invisible, and now I see all these photos he was taking. "Where were you Billy? Were you hanging from the ceiling?" His photos just shine. The lighting is like silver, very strange. Billy had all these people to photograph. Lucky for him; his models were always there. Each one of us had our own dramatic personalities, even though I wasn't really into the drugs thing.

Ultra Violet: I don't know if it was my background, but I always knew that drugs were dangerous. Andy and the whole group, they were willing to give you drugs, they thought it was okay. They each had their own thing. Taylor Mead was on Quaalude, and still is. Andy wanted to lose weight at one time, and he was given a pill (Obetrol). He said it worked, so he took a bit more, and a bit more, then more. But the dog was not on drugs, and the cat was not on drugs. And I was not on drugs!

Ultra Violet, health food aficionada extrordinaire, never intentionally took so much as an aspirin, but as she mentioned earlier, there was that interlude when we all readily accepted Doctor Feelgood's needle of 'vitamin elixir' as the source of eternal energy. It seemed to be healthy, if not exactly nutritious, since one forgot to eat for days. We were astounded when the good doctor was arrested! He was addicted himself, after all, and believed in his product, so there you were. We all wound up in rehab of one form or another, which I wrote about for an organic health and lifestyle magazine, as one does. . .

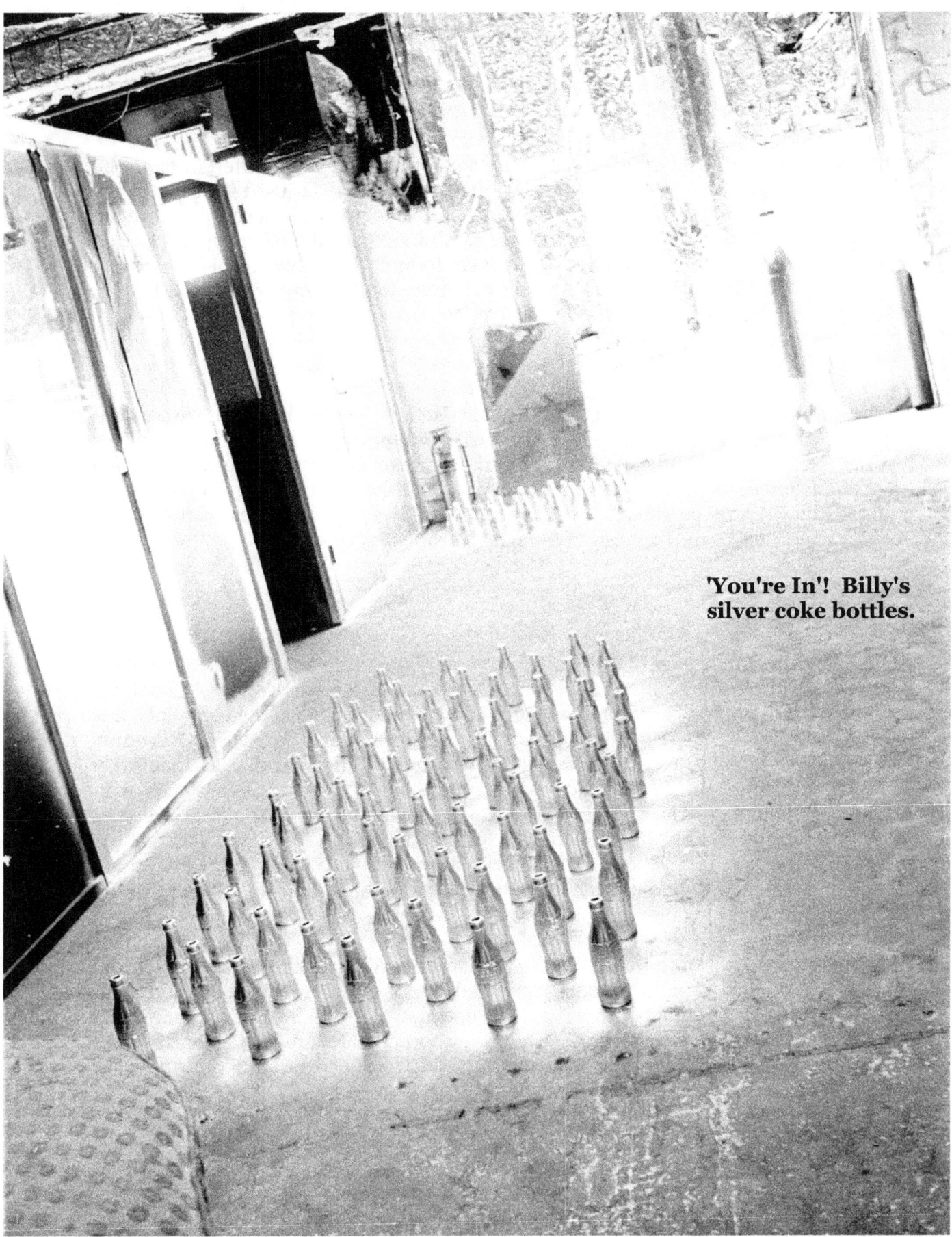

'You're In'! Billy's silver coke bottles.

Mary Woronov: With Warhol, you always look for a niche that's different from the rest. My niche was not to be this stoned, fabulous star who is just teetering on the border of, you know, *death*. Which was mostly Edie Sedgwick and a couple of others. No, mine was different. I did not want to be feminine. I acted like a guy, and I fitted really well with all the guys who were being very feminine. With Warhol it was like a circus. You had to think of something to be effective, so that was my thing. . .
Well, that and drugs.

Mary Woronov fared better than many of her Factory friends, because she was flat out told by her doctor that she had "no liver left," and promptly quit. Mary may have lost her liver, but she never lost her looks, like some of the boys, or her mind, like a lot of the women. So, the murderous Amazon we all loved in 'Eating Raoul' will no doubt outlive everyone. Interesting, that the word 'liver' kind of goes with the verb 'to live'. . . Louis Waldon was another Factoryite adept at suvival. . .

Louis Waldon: Andy said, "Let's go, I'll buy everybody dinner." Okay, everybody is happy about that. We go in, and as we're approaching the bar he says, "Louis, we can't go in. We don't have enough women. They won't let gay people come into this bar." I said, "Andy, they're gonna let you in here." He knew the owner! But Andy hid his homosexuality, for a long time. It was not until the seventies that Andy started coming out. He used to hold hands under the table at Max's Kansas City with his boyfriends, but he wouldn't announce it. They were all nervous about it, except Billy Name—Billy and his Silver Factory, all those rolls of tin foil. He never wanted anything, never lived off you. He was always successful with himself, always on the scene, always happy when I'd come up to the Factory. But when I left, when I didn't take over, and Paul took over, he was angry.

Billy Name: In the late years, Paul Morrissey started cutting out people from coming around, like Ondine, because Andy had shot so many reels with Ondine that were nothing. All the money from Andy's painting was going into developing these reels, but it's like panning for gold, attempting to cull a few nuggets. So it didn't work, Andy's wanting to be a powerful impresario. You need capital, and Andy was so far out there that investors were fearful.

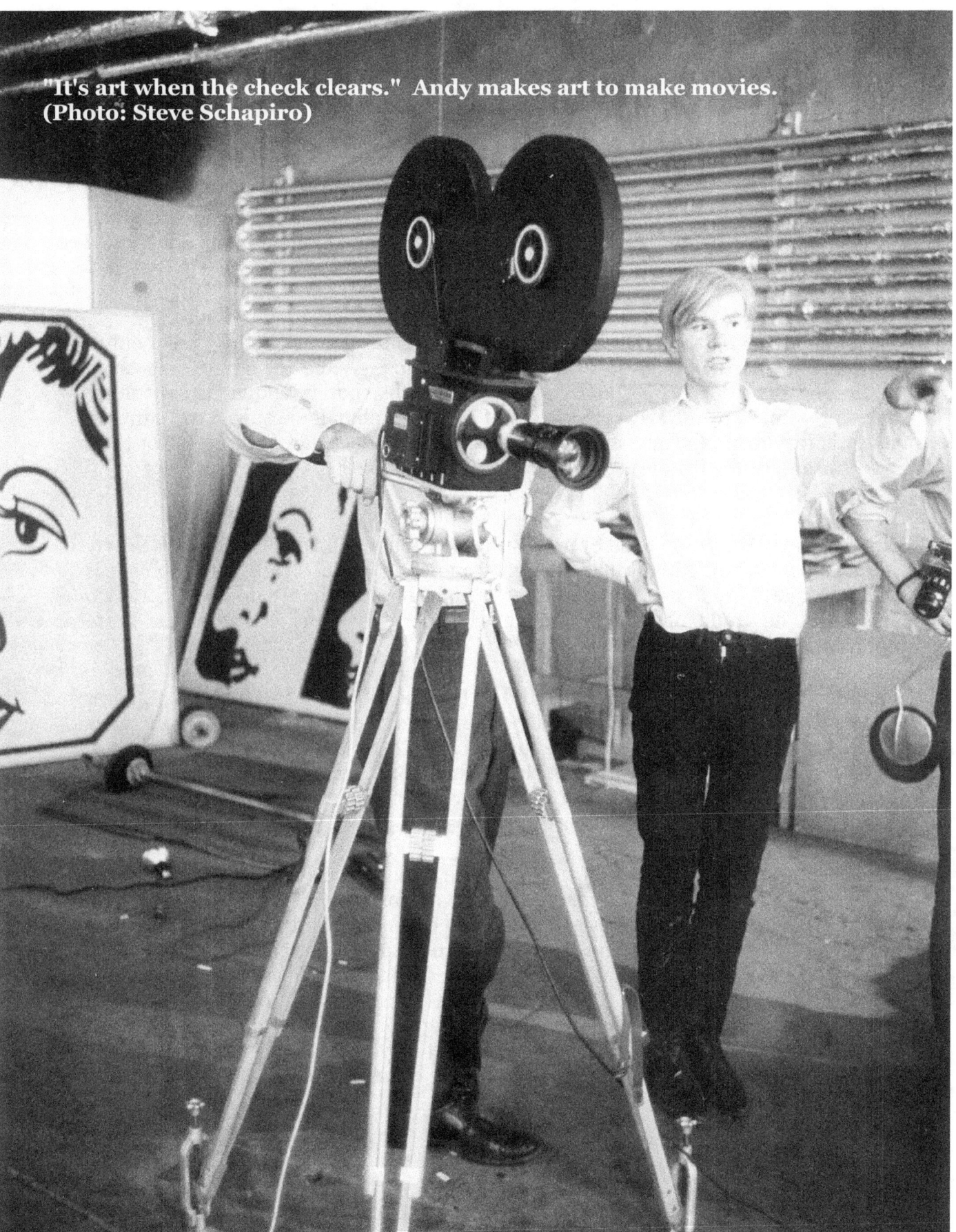

"It's art when the check clears." Andy makes art to make movies.
(Photo: Steve Schapiro)

Billy Name: I remember an actual bomb casing which we had in the Factory for some reason—Andy sprayed it silver, so it was posing as a Warhol sculpture *(laugh).* And the New York Post ran a contest to name something about a Warhol thing and he would "win" the bomb. This guy who won it just sold it at auction for I don't know how many hundred thousand dollars.

According to Billy, Warhol despised the New York Times for its shoddy treatment of him, but enjoyed the attention of the New York Post. While the Times was tartly questioning his talent as an artist and mocking his motley clique of subculture Superstars, the Post—New York's answer to the tabloids—would give him an audience, maybe not the one he wanted, since they were (still are) notorious for their gruesome and titillating tales of city mayhem.

Brigid Berlin: Andy used to sit every day on the window sill with The Post. He'd say *(mimicking)*, "Briiiiig, this would be a good movie." I said, "Andy, the problem is you'll never get to Hollywood because there's no beginning, there's no middle, and no end." And he could never seem to get that. He thought dialogue was more important.

Jonas Mekas: The scripts came in, and they became more and more complex. After 'Chelsea Girls', some producers approached Andy and thought that maybe he's ready for something that could play for wider audiences. There was a lot of press of course, and he made three or four films. But they didn't work, because they were no longer Andy's films. They didn't have much action, or anything else attractive enough to be booked across the country, even on a small scale.

David Croland: After 'Chelsea Girls', Andy did a big film called 'Four Stars', which was a group of films all put together. That was very long, too. I did one called 'Three Boys and A Girl in Bed', which was me and two other guys and Susan (Bottomly) in bed. I said, "What are we supposed to do?" Andy said, "Just get in bed, come on, just do it; it's going to be fun." We kept our underpants on. At least I did. . . The best film was called 'Makeup'—forty minutes of me telling Susan how great she was, which is what I did in real life. Andy kept saying, "Oh just ignore him." Susan did this elaborate makeup. She looked like she was thirty, and she was seventeen. But the people who kept filming were not afraid of the camera. They loved it. Those girls loved being filmed.

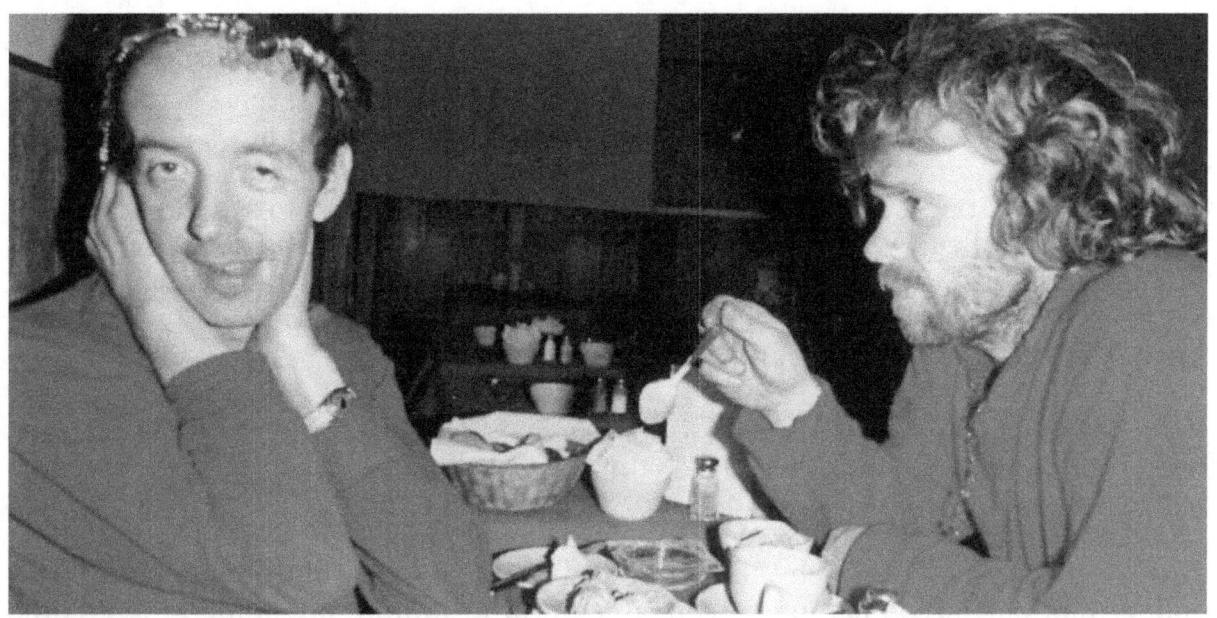

Two boys walk into a bar. A gay (as in happy) Taylor Mead and a grizzled Louis Waldon meet up at Max's Kansas City, gathering spot for poets, artists, actors, musicians and drag queens.

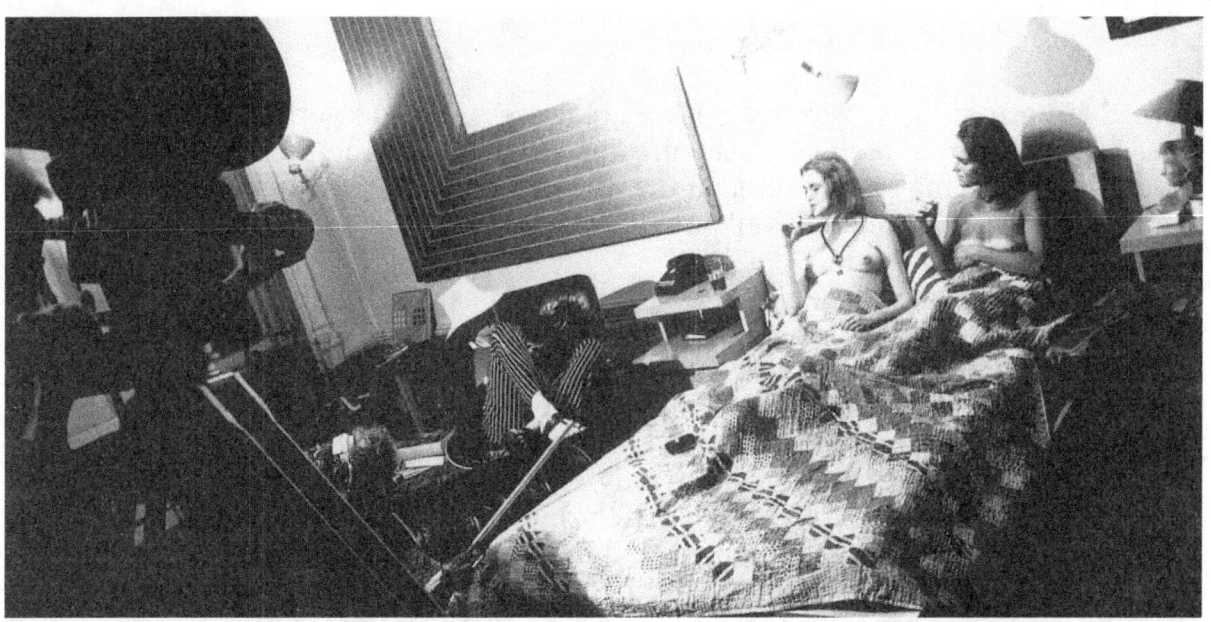

Two girls get into a bed, while Andy films, patiently waiting for something to happen. Ingrid Superstar on left. (Photos: Billy Name)

Robert Heide: I had been walking down 4th Street. Someone was cleaning up a mess, and I saw all this blood and big chunks of white, what must have been *brain*. I was so out of it that I thought, "Oh, that must be somebody I know," and kept on walking. Apparently what happened was that Freddie (Herko) took some LSD and did a ballet leap out the window. . . So, Andy came, and wanted to see the exact spot where he had fallen. We walked over to 5 Cornelius Street, and he looked up at the window and said, "Gee, if Edie kills herself I hope she lets us know, so we can film it."

Andy Warhol: I don't think of myself as evil, just realistic.

Bob Heide had been telling us lots of funny stories about life with Warhol. This was not one of them. But he was quick not to lay any blame at Warhol's feet, brain-splattered though they were. We used sepia-toned archive footage to follow them through the fabled Greenwich Village of the sixties, remembering why the downtown underground art scene had once seemed a world of infinite possibility. . . Freddie Herko was a talented gay misfit, too campy and outrageous to appeal to the legitimate Broadway theater. Of Herko, Warhol wrote: "The people I loved were the ones like Freddie, the leftovers of show business, turned down at auditions all over town. They were too gifted to lead regular lives, but also too unsure of themselves to ever become real professionals."

Gerard Malanga: Andy was not getting great press. He was getting a lot of negative press about his art as well as on the movies, even though the press coverage on the movies was more interesting than on the art. Pop art was still very much favorite day in a way. Things that we took for common could be art, like a Marilyn photo.

David Croland: Andy came to our apartment and said, "Oh, this is a Christmas gift for you and Susan." It was a Marilyn Monroe, a big one. He signed it, and I said, "Oh, what should we do with this?" Paul (Morrissey) said, "Just tack it up over your fireplace. It's a poster." So I did, right in front of Andy. He didn't say anything. He just, well, it was the only time I had ever seen him react. We took it all over Europe with us, just rolled this 'poster' up. Andy also did a beautiful drawing of me with hearts on it. That was stolen immediately by the speed freaks that were around. Andy knew who had taken my drawing but didn't want to confront him. He was always giving art away, to everyone, yet people were stealing his work left and right. That was sad, being generous to people and have them steal from you.

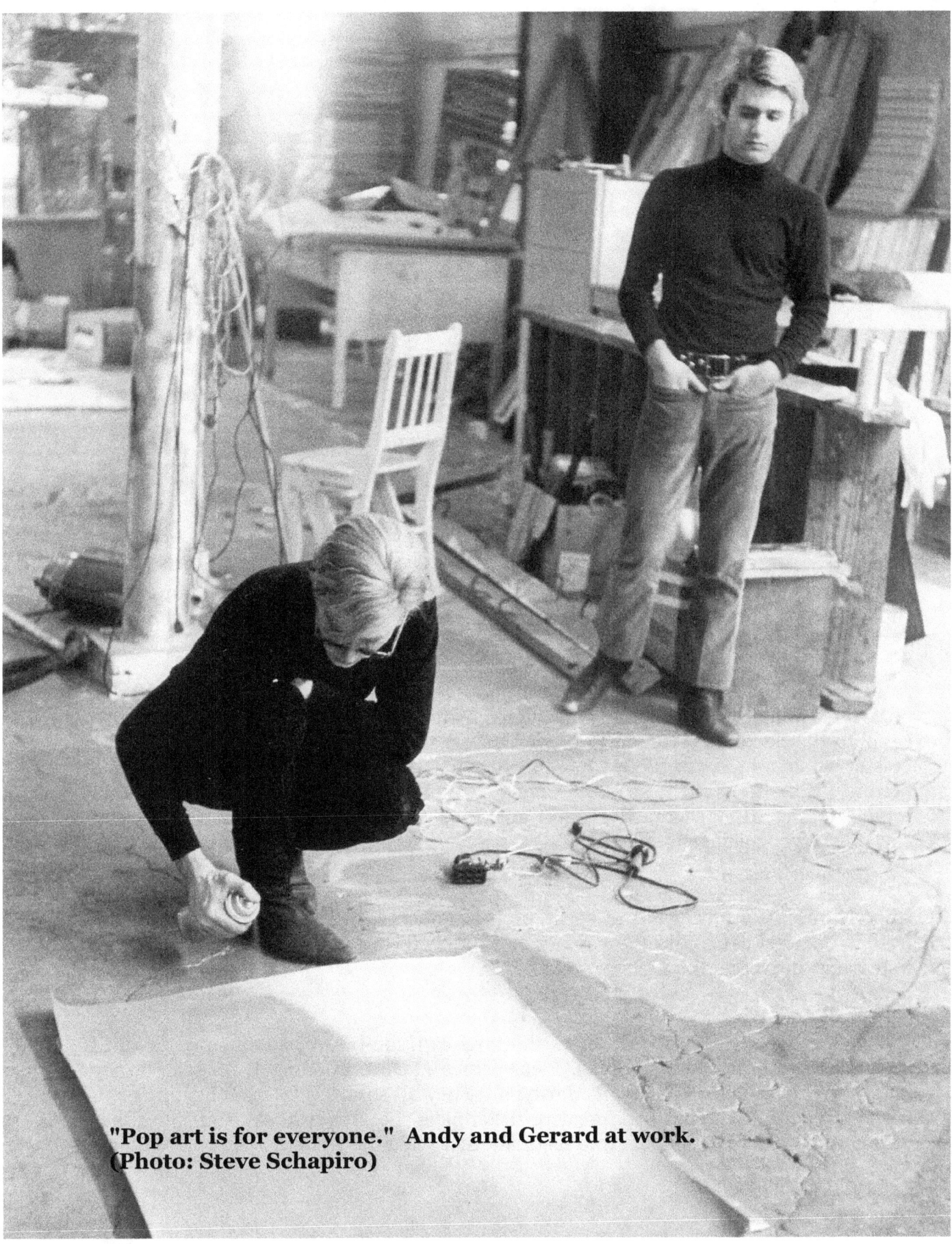

"Pop art is for everyone." Andy and Gerard at work.
(Photo: Steve Schapiro)

OUT OF CONTROL

Everybody should be nice to everybody.
—Andy Warhol

Victor Bockris: The third period, '67, '68, marks the end of the Silver Factory. Things did get out of control. One of the main signs of this is the number of shootings. There were three or four gun incidents before Andy was actually shot.

As early as 1964, Warhol had witnessed a shooting in the Factory. Dorothy Podber, a performance artist and amphetamine-fuelled friend of Factory foreman Billy Name came to the Factory costumed in black leather, sunglasses and a gun snapped to a holster on her hips. According to Billy, Warhol told her he was busy shooting a picture. So, she asked if she could shoot a picture, too. Warhol said he "didn't mind," so she whipped out the pistol and took aim at a Marilyn portrait, one of several stacked against a wall.

Billy Name: Dorothy was the spirit of the Underground from Hell—anarchistic Dada. Dorothy came into the Factory one day with her gun, and actually shot the Marilyn Monroe paintings. . .

When Dorothy shot Marilyn through the forehead, the bullet passed through all of the paintings. Warhol begged Billy, "Please don't let Dorothy come over again." They later became known as the 'Shot Marilyns'. They all sold. . . In a similar incident, Allen Midgette, who had had 'creative differences' before with some of his rather unpredictable female co-stars, told us of another witch he worked with by the name of Orion, one of the A-Head 'Mole' people. (She went by another, similar name, but in the interest of saving us from yet another lawsuit from a lunatic, we will use the name 'Orion'). As a favor to her friend Billy Name, 'Orion' finally accepted Warhol and Morrissey's offer to star in a movie. With Maria Callas singing at top volume, Paul decided Orion and Allen, who were both on LSD, should fight or have sex to liven things up. So Orion picked up a handy machete hanging on the wall (wow!) and smacked the chandelier, scattering glass shards all over Warhol, who simply stood there, white-faced and frozen with fear, as ever. . . Taylor Mead had yet another violent tale from his own Cold Case files, and as long as we ordered him a scotch and water—"to sooth the cords"—he was happy to divulge it.

Taylor Mead: I probably saved his fucking life. I'm there with Nico, Viva and Paul Morrissey, and the gunman came in. They had a big car outside, and they claimed Andy owed them 500 dollars since 1964. And everybody just sat there, stunned, like they were watching a movie, while this guy fired a bullet into the wall! I was bombed enough not to be stunned, so I jumped him. It was like hitting a brick wall—the guy was very powerful. But he insulted Andy. He put a rain hat on him to make him look funny, and I thought, "Who is this bum insulting a genius?" So I jumped him, took that hat and smashed the whole window out! When I'm bombed, I'm accurate.

According to Warhol biographer Victor Bockris, the gunman, called 'Sammy the Italian', played Russian roulette with them, putting the gun to Paul Morrissey's head and pulling the trigger. It didn't go off, which could have considerably changed the pecking order at the Factory. The next shot did go off. The gunmen then made Warhol kneel, and Taylor attacked. Police arrived and snidely said, "Why didn't you film it?" The New York Times refused to report on the incident.

Victor Bockris: The fact that this could start happening was a sign that something is really breaking through the door. The entourage swelled. There were three or four women who were competing for lead place; a lot of women were throwing themselves at him.

Ivy Nicholson: I was always throwing myself at him. Once he asked me to be in a movie called 'Nymphomania'. I thought, "He wants me to break up with my boyfriend, so he must care." We slept together once, and there were fourteen other people in the room, on mattresses. I felt like the bed was on fire, that's how hot it was! Then he got nervous, because I would always try to get closer and closer to him.

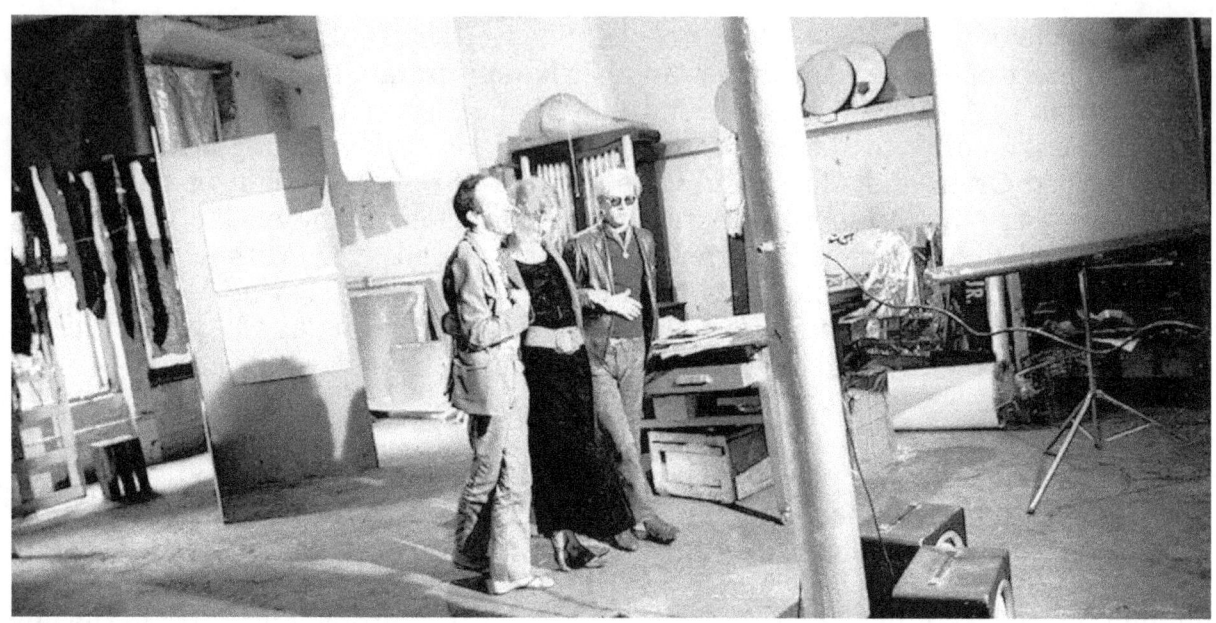

Taylor Mead and Viva join Andy before embarking on their next film adventure. Or they're asking for money for the last one.

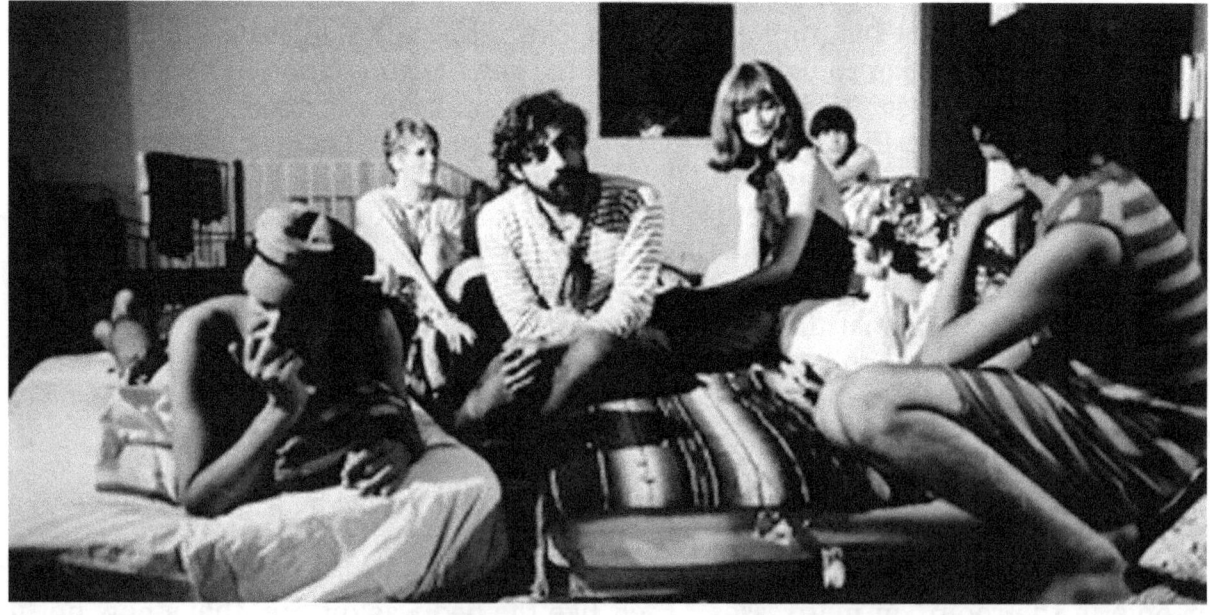

Ivy, center right, bedding down in Ultra Violet's apartment with the banana boys rock group (that's one of the guys on the right) and Susan Pile in B.G. (Photos: Billy Name)

Mary Woronov: Billy threw Ivy out, and the reason why he threw Ivy out, is because she wanted to be close to Andy, and oh, everyone was really bored with her. So she took a *dump* behind the couch so that a part of her would remain with Andy. Well, this infuriated everybody, and so bang, Billy just literally threw her out. Ivy was nuts, nuts, nuts! But anyway, Billy had that kind of power. He could throw someone out. He was the general, you know, the Emperor. But he started cracking, too.

Jonas Mekas: In the Factory, they came from some very confused backgrounds. I think they were helped, really, they were not *destroyed* at the Factory. Those who self-destructed were already too far gone. Nobody could help them anymore.

Danny Fields: Several people were lost to drugs. There were a lot of heroin victims, and amphetamine victims. A junkie's a junkie's a junkie. Andy was not a drug supplier. But Edie was getting into downers. Who knows? One never knows. The dealers—their names, they have no names—they had a lot to do with it. Edie was getting too stoned to do anything. She could barely stand up without tipping over.

Henry Geldzahler: I went to her apartment, which I thought very grim, a couple of times. It was dark, and the talk was always about how hung-over she was, or how high she was yesterday, or how high she would be tomorrow. She was very nervous, very fragile, very thin, very hysterical. You could hear her screaming, even though she wasn't screaming—this sort of supersonic whistling.

Geldzahler had voiced his concern to biographer Victor Bockris, but had felt helpless to intervene. In some of the footage we found of Edie, shot toward the end of '65, the disquiet and tenseness between her and Warhol was becoming evident. Though she was still the 'carefree' young star photographed in magazines, her insecurities—and drug use—were starting to show, and she seemed frailer than in the earlier Warhol museum footage that we used. The following conversation was caught as an aside while Edie was preparing for a film shoot at the Factory. . .

Edie Sedgwick
You're just going to put me down, so I'm not going to say anything.

Andy Warhol
Put you *down*?!

Ultra Violet: Drugs were rampant and people were very ignorant. Tim Leary would say, "You're only using ten percent of your mind, and thanks to this and that you can *expaaand* your mind." When I saw Edie, a few months before she died in California, indeed those drugs had expanded, physically, her skull. She became a monster.

We met the producer of 'Ciao! Manhattan!', David Weisman, a charming man, at our atelier in Paris, and we spoke of using some of Edie's footage in our documentary. But Ultra Violet was right—Edie was not remotely the same person. In the first part of the film, directed by Ivy's then husband John Palmer, Edie dances at the '67 Be-In in Central Park. She is thin, pretty, and totally wrecked. Worried friend Danny Fields was on hand to help, but when Edie burned down her room in the Chelsea Hotel, killing Smoke, her cat, it became painfully obvious she needed more than a friend's intervention. She took off for California, the film unfinished. In 1970, after umpteen drug relapses, hospital stays, and electroshock treatments, Edie was ready to resume filming—even the graphic shock treatments made it into the movie. Edie looked bloated and puffy, her hair grown out dark, her naked breasts swollen with silicone. As she mumbled and stumbled, I became uncomfortable with the feeling she was being exploited. Edie had tried to lead a normal life, even getting married to a man she'd met at the hospital. She died less than a year after filming, suffocating in bed after an overdose of downers. She was twenty-eight years old.

Danny Fields: At the end there, it was very sad. Oh, I loved the girl. I didn't want to lose her to drugs. . . So, the golden era was over, and Paul Morrissey was calling the shots on movie making. The charming involvement of Andy Warhol in movies was over.

'San Diego Surf', filmed in L.A., would be one of the last films Warhol physically made. It was never finished. Aaron Sloan and director Robert Emmet Smith filmed Warhol, Morrissey and their contingent of actors while they 'cavorted' in the crashing surf. A naked Eric Emerson pisses into the ocean, but the beach looks cold and uninviting. Warhol is hunched behind the camera, rubbing his hands to keep warm, while Paul scurries around with equipment. The actors, which include Taylor Mead and Louis Waldon, huddle in jackets against the blustery wind, looking tired and miserable.

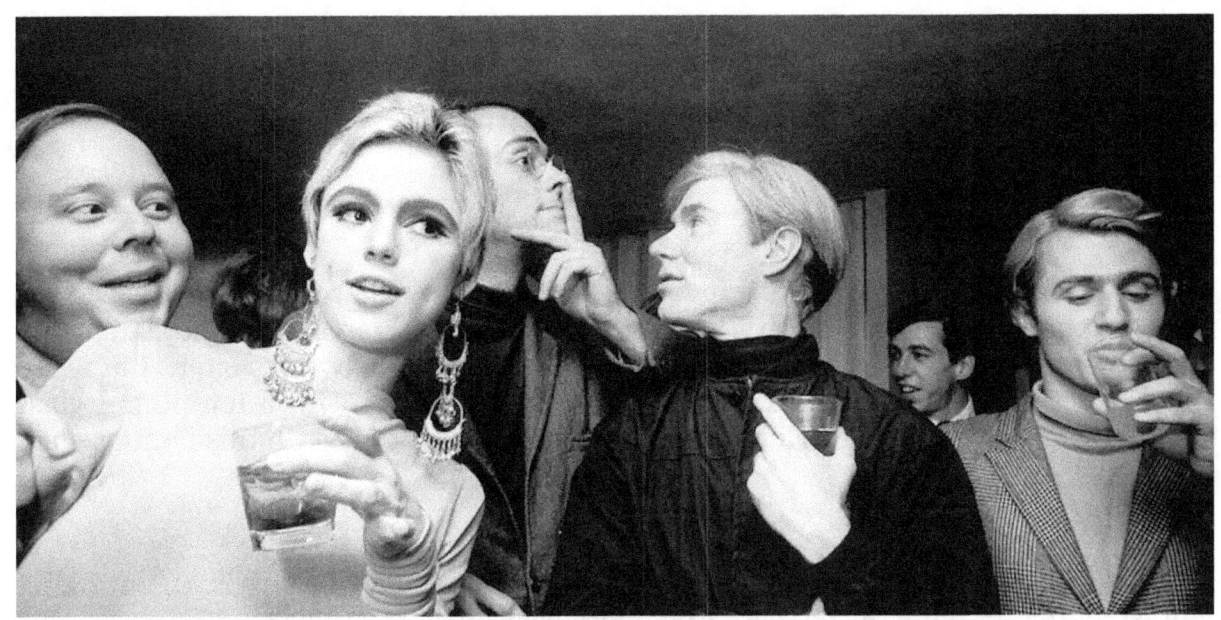

Edie in happier times, with a cherubic Henry Geldzahler on her left, Andy and Gerard at right. (Photo: Steve Schapiro)

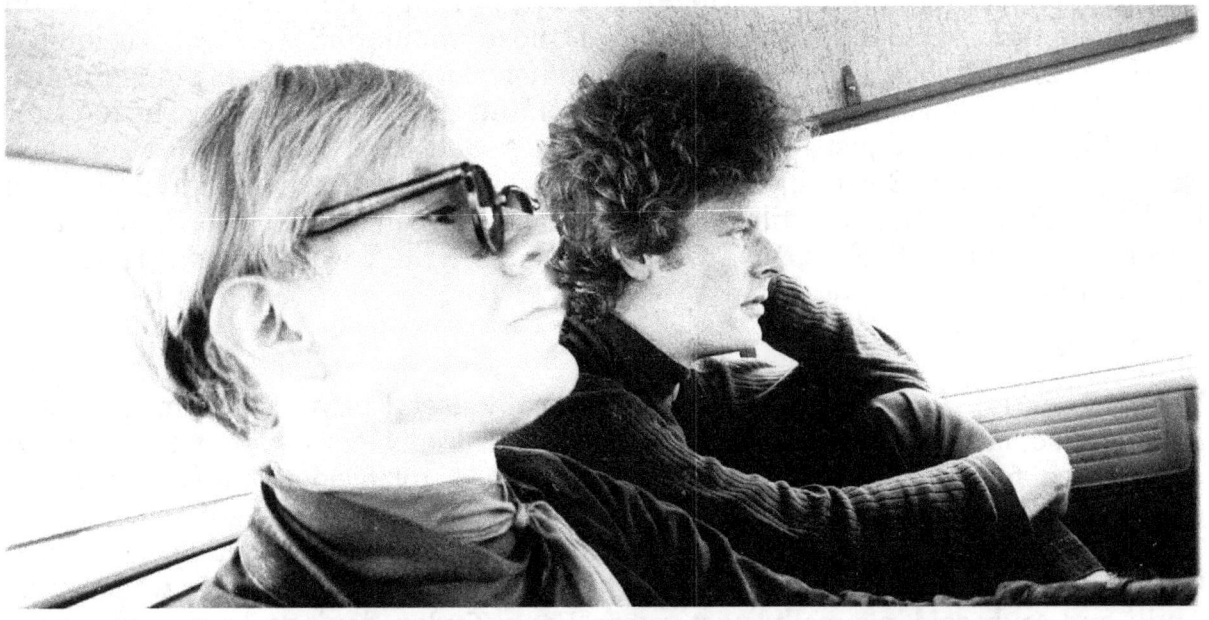

Andy and Paul Morrissey, on the road again. A film location at the home of a wealthy art collector could also clinch a sale, to make more movies. (Photo: Billy Name)

Paul Morrissey *(on location of 'San Diego Surf")*
If you zoom in close to their faces, you can see their faces.

Andy Warhol
Okay. . . We're coming to the end.

Taylor Mead: Paul thinks that he invented Andy, give me a break. Paul makes great films, but he did not invent Andy. I tried to introduce Andy to Paul in the sixties, but Paul did not want to meet Andy then; they came together a few years later. But when I had a terrible fight with Viva, where she tried to kill me with a ten-pound glass ashtray. Paul saved my life. He grabbed her before she hit me with this famous glass ashtray.

Having once thrown a massive glass ashtray with equal fury—he survived, but didn't quit smoking—I empathized with the mercurial Viva (*née* Susan Hoffman), the talented painter, who would become Warhol's most gifted Superstar. Slim and striking, with aquiline features and a mad halo of frizzy hair, she looked ethereal— until she opened her mouth. Her endless verbiage of complaints and sharp retorts quickly made her a Warhol favorite, and her non-stop stream of consciousness made it into every Warhol movie. I n trying to arrange Viva's interview, we often spoke on the phone, for ages. I wish I had taped those wonderfully surreal, disjointed conversations, because I so loved talking with her, but we could never pin her down. Later I heard from Louis Waldon that Viva was "unhappy about the way she looked." So I said, "Viva should just get the fuck out of L.A. and she'll be fine." Sure enough, she's moved to Palm Springs, where one can stay, if not sane, at least well-preserved in the desert air. Her art still sells faster than she can paint it, so there, Andy. According to Victor Bockris, Viva was also a good writer, working on scripts with Paul Morrissey.

Victor Bockris: Paul Morrissey was a technically useful man in the film business. He was, also, in many ways a very intelligent guy. Initially he was very well-liked and appreciated for his good points. But as soon as Andy tried to move out of the directorial position and to replace himself with Paul, the actors got really upset. Taylor Mead went through a tantrum and was walking off the set of 'Lonesome Cowboys' *(mimicking),* "I've had it! I'm not going to take any more!" He walked past Andy, and Andy said in a really quiet voice, "Look, Taylor, don't go," and Taylor went right back and did the scene.

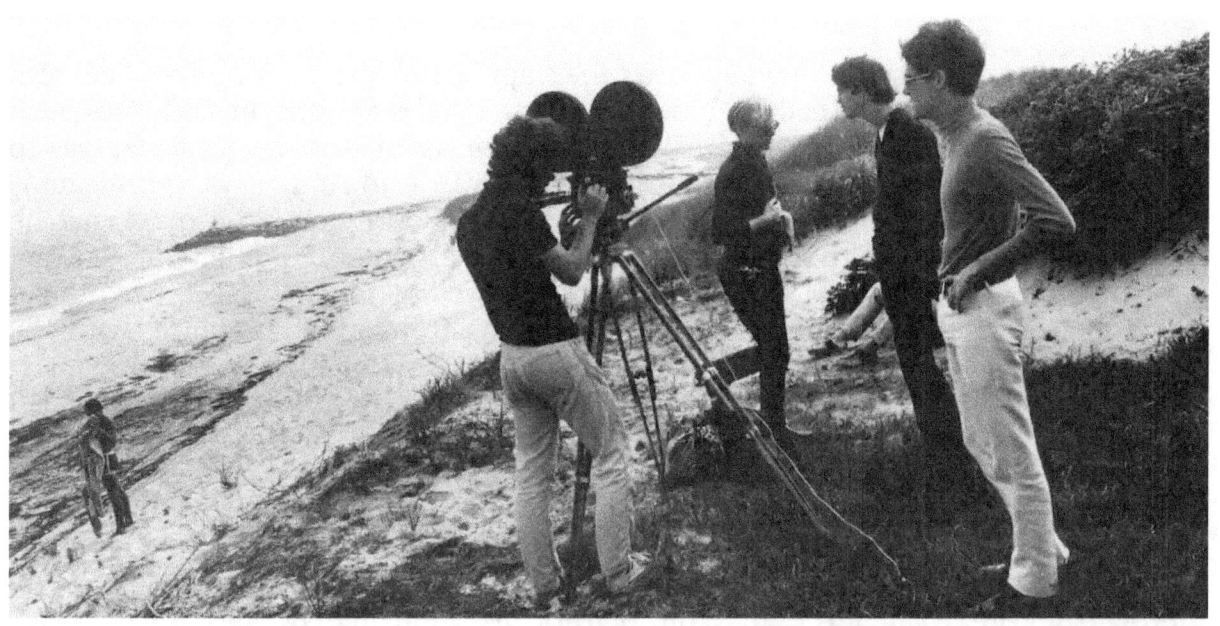

"Zoom in for the money shot. . ." Andy and Paul on film location at the de Menil summer estate, all eight acres of it, in East Hampton, filming Ondine on the private beach.

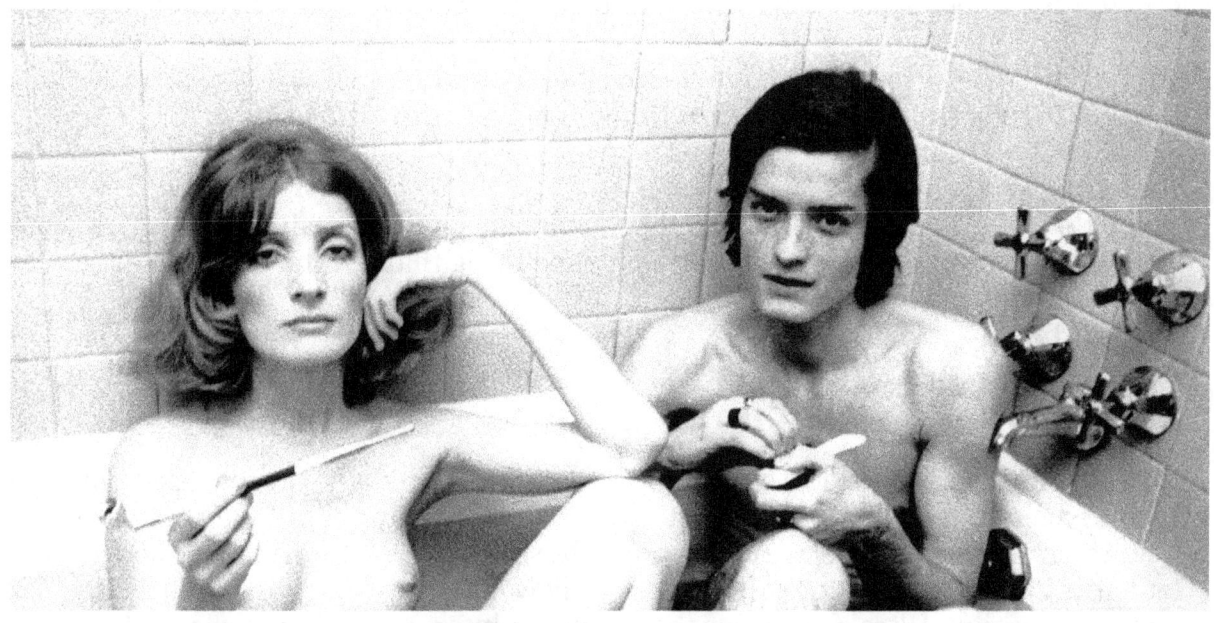

Warhol muse Viva takes a break from filming with Alexis de la Falaise, son of Yves St. Laurent muse Loulou. (Photos: Billy Name)

Taylor Mead: 'Lonesome Cowboys' was the happiest movie set I've ever been on. Working with Andy was really a breeze, always. We're filming in Old Tucson, a reconstructed movie set for Westerns, and I'm inviting these cowboys on horses to come up to the ranch to have a good time with Viva. And Andy says, *(mimicking)* "Taylor, too much plot." This is the way he talks: "Too much plo-o-ot." What he meant was he wanted us to relate, get into a fight or argument. So there are a lot of fights in 'Lonesome Cowboy'. . . And we were followed by the FBI. They tried to get something on Andy. In one scene, I'm out in the front of Viva's place, with the magnificent beauty Joe Dallesandro. And I'm going down on my knees in front of him. If I'd unzipped him, we'd have been arrested. The film would have been confiscated, and Andy could have been put in jail. The FBI was watching us with binoculars. They wanted to nail Andy. In 1968, we were all under surveillance. And Viva's paranoia, I think she'll admit to that. I don't think she ever took drugs; she couldn't handle it. We were all crazy, when we worked on the ranch in Old Tucson.

Victor Bockris: The F.B.I. files on Warhol are amusing, because they are so paranoid. There's these agents flying around the country trying to pin Andy down for transportation of interstate pornography, based on the filming of 'Lonesome Cowboys', where they thought they saw—through binoculars—Viva being raped by Taylor Mead *(laugh)*. The F.B.I. actually spent money asking people to fly down there, so they could arrest Andy. The stupidity—it becomes a Marx Brothers comedy.

Andy Warhol *(in a recorded phone call to Billy Name)*
The F.B.I. man is still calling us. They think Viva was really raped.

Billy Name
It's not the rape thing. He told me that someone had complained that guys were going down on her. That's what upset, that's the thing that got the F.B.I. on us.

Andy Warhol
We don't have that in the movie. Do we?

According to Victor Bockris, who had documented the above conversation, the unplanned simulated 'gang rape' scene surprised Viva, who was being punished by fellow actors as being too temperamental. After the 'rape' she stormed off screaming, "Get Ultra Violet for the part! I quit!" Not only were both women in competition for Warhol's attention, Ultra's lover, macho, mega sculptor John Chamberlain—he of the Provincetown front yard filled with junked auto parts—was also sleeping with Viva.

Allen Midgette: After 'Lonesome Cowboys', I said to Andy, "I have *got* to get out of here. I want to go to Haight Ashbury (San Francisco)." "Well," Andy said, "We'd like to take you to the Cannes Film Festival. We're all going to go." I'm thinking, "I have had movies at the Festival that have won prizes. I do not want to go to Europe, sorry, with these people, and be seen, again, oh yeah, as one of them." So, I'm going to Haight Ashbury. Then he offered me a painting. I said, "Andy, I travel with a bag about this big. I don't have room." They gave me five hundred dollars and off I went.

Allen was not about to get off that easily. As the sixties slid into disarray, the disfranchised hippies sought refuge in San Francisco, where Allen Ginsberg and Timothy Leary were "gathering the tribes" for the Summer of Love. With rather interesting timing, Warhol's nihilistic 'Chelsea Girls' was scheduled to premiere in San Francisco. He brought along a slew of Superstars, including Ultra Violet and Ondine—but did not invite Gerard who, deeply hurt, went off to Italy in a huff. . .

Gerard Malanga: Yeah, the Bergamo Film Festival, just about an hour outside of Milano. I was on the program with Jean Luc Godard, who was showing 'Two Or Three Things I know About Her'. I go to Milano, met Eugenio Montale, the Italian poet *(and Nobel Prize winner, 1975)*. We became close. I was poor; he would take me to lunch. Then I took a train to Rome. I felt like I was in an Antonioni movie.

An actor who actually *did* work with Michelangelo Antonioni, Allen Midgette thought he was reliving a film of another sort, perhaps 'Batmen/Dracula, Revisited', when Warhol and his underground Family swooped in to San Francisco. . .

Allen Midgette: Andy arrives with Nico and Ondine, and says, "Do you think we can make a movie here?" I said to my friends, "This guy I know from New York wants to make a little home movie if it's okay." They of course said, "Yeah," and continued to do business the way they always did: Get up, eat, go to Golden Gate Park and hang out. Andy was used to people responding to his being Warhol. He couldn't get any reaction from somebody who doesn't know who Andy Warhol is. So they didn't make the movie. Instead they had lunch with Gypsy Rose Lee and asked me to go. I was barefoot, with this fur coat that was deteriorating before your very eyes. The restaurant wouldn't allow me in. Ondine starts screaming, "Don't you know who he is? He's a star!" So I ran back to my friends in the Haight. End of story once again.

OUT OF MONEY

A lot of those people in the sixties were like bottomless pits
as far as money was concerned.
—Victor Bockris

Louis Waldon: When you go to talk business with Andy, he really didn't want to talk about it. He would say *(mimicking),* "I can give you some money, but not very much. I can only give you maybe a hundred dollars." I said, "Great!" I thought that was perfect. You did a movie in two hours; at that time that was good pay. But the actors, especially Brigid and Viva, said, "Don't accept anything from Andy except money, because money really gets to him, money really makes him nervous."

Brigid Berlin: Oh I know, People like Viva *(mimicking),* "He owes me money," and everybody else, "Oh he never paid me! I mean, I made him famous, it was, you know, all *me.*"

We licensed video footage of Brigid where she simply sits and talks or complains to the camera, much like Viva, which is why they became such friends. During these gossipy tirades, Warhol would be an occasional presence in the room, entreating Brigid to, "Just say whatever you feel like." But Brigid felt more comfortable without Warhol in the room. While smoking endless cigarettes, eating chocolates, or sucking down a canister of Reddi Whip, she would confide to a featureless camera. Is this frankly any better than the eye-rolling reality shows of today? Well, no. But Warhol did it first. . .

Brigid Berlin: So I made this fantastic tape for Andy, and he said, *(mimicking)* "Well, we just don't have any money just now." *How* could he not have any money? I mean really. . .

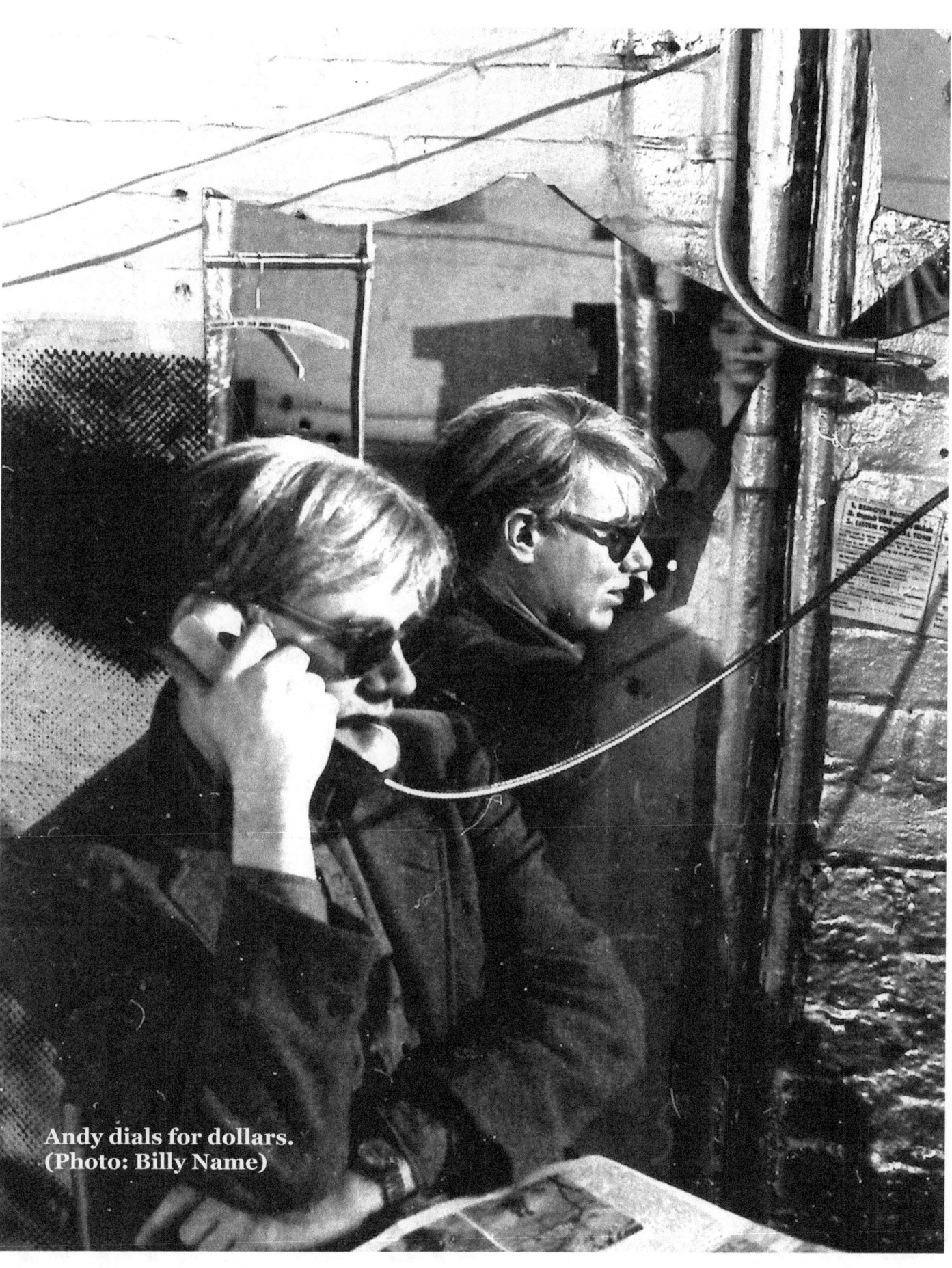

Andy dials for dollars.
(Photo: Billy Name)

Taylor Mead: I was determined to get cash from Andy. I lost. In fact, the son of a bitch— Well, I shouldn't put down his mother; his family are darling. But Andy was as cold as ice. It was sort of a brilliant act. He was a cheap, cheap genius. When he owed me fifty bucks and I'm in the street starving to death, he wouldn't send the money. . . My father was cheap and rich, and I find that is one of the basic ABCs of the world. If you're rich and cheap, like the United States, my father, Andy, If you are cheap. . . "Moooon River."

Taylor had once again broken into song with 'Moon River'. I'm guessing he wanted to say "Kiss my ass, you cheap filmmakers." It was time to get Mr. Mead, former Beat and unredeemed downtown reprobate, another drink.

Billy Name: Taylor Mead was already an established underground film star, but when he started working with Andy he would be a little snippy sometimes, like, "Gee, where's all the money?" or "Warhol is so cheap and tight."

David Croland: He wasn't stingy at all. Andy was always giving money to everyone, left and right. He gave everyone money, every one of the Superstars, their girlfriends and their boyfriends. Thirty people a day. I think I could name fifteen off the top of my head I think he gave money to, including Susan (Bottomly) and myself.

Jonas Mekas: Andy was a very, very, kind person. And everybody felt very, very good in his presence. I disagree with all those accusations that are sometimes thrown at Andy. There were misunderstandings like, "Oh, he just went up to, he sucked up to the rich people." No, they came to him. He did not go after them. They all came. I know, I'd been around then. They just flocked to him, searched him out. They did because of that openness, because Andy did not reject anybody.

Nat Finkelstein: It was all a facade. I think the key point here, and bringing it up in a very nice way, is to say that Andy created this place to work, and as a social environment it could do more for him. In doing that, he incited a lot of people to get excited about working with him, and be part of it. You can always manipulate somebody by lying. But shaking hands on a deal and turning your back on it is something else. I suggested and wrote the outline for 'The Andy Warhol Index'. He and I came to a handshake agreement about a 50-50 split. I did the proposals. Black Star my agent put him under contract, and I sold the book to Chris Cerf up at Random House. All of a sudden Andy appears with a whole bunch of high-powered lawyers behind him. So, as far as the free living, blah blah—that was crap, man. >

. . . That was Andy manipulating an aura for himself. It was all about promotion, and Andy would sell himself to just about anything. Once he drove around in this truck— on the side of it was 'Dannon Yogurt'. He sold himself for a year's supply of yogurt.

Vincent Fremont: He really revolutionized and turned the 'cultural' world upside down. He is synonymous with American and International culture. With the help of the press, he built a myth, because they believed everything he said. They neglected to understand his sense of irony, his sense of humor. They took everything verbatim. So he played them. It got him in trouble sometimes. He said, at one point, 68ish, that Brigid Berlin did all his paintings—which was very clearly not true. But people got freaked out when they heard that. They (journalists) started reading each other's articles and pretty soon that myth starts up, based on no fact.

Of all the myths that sprung up around Warhol like magical beanstalks, perhaps the most enduring and egregious was his perception as a demonic 'Pied Piper' for rudderless children, and the furor was to reach fever pitch. As members of his disenchanted troupe began to drop by the wayside, Greenwich Village elders, far less benevolent than their sage-smudging West coast counterparts, were readying the acetylene torches. As Mary Woronov would say, "Enough already with Warhol."

Mary Woronov: I never went anywhere with Warhol—we just kind of formed a line and followed him. When they started setting things up for me, like in a bedroom with this fat man, "Okay Mary, get on the bed with him." I said, "No." I would not be pushed around like that or set up. But Ronnie Tavel wrote plays for me, so even Warhol sensed that I was actress to be used. But what happened to me is that I had a fight with Paul Morrissey. He wanted me to sign a release. I said, "I don't have to sign unless you want to pay me. And I know you don't, so I'm not signing." Warhol was very, very angry and I stopped going to the Factory. My mom got on the phone. "My daughter didn't sign the release. Would you like to go to court or would you like to settle it?" So he settled and gave me money. Hey, I'm not going to be squashed like that. So, enough already with Warhol. I'd done enough with him. It was a good thing to leave him. I mean you can't stay there forever.

Victor Bockris: Mary's mother sued Andy after she appeared in 'Chelsea Girls', because she was underage. Not for that, but to get paid for her role. She got a thousand dollars, which is all she was looking for, and Andy subsequently had to pay everybody who acted in the movie a thousand dollars, so *(laugh)* he wasn't too happy.

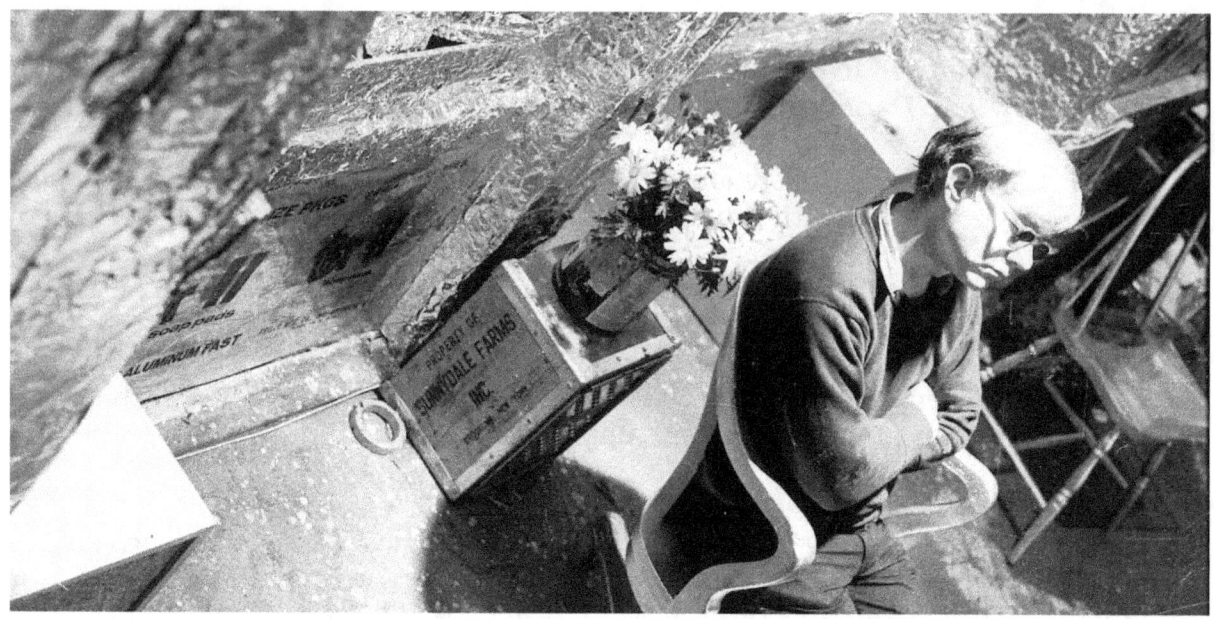

Andy enjoys a rare moment of solitude. (Photo: Billy Name)

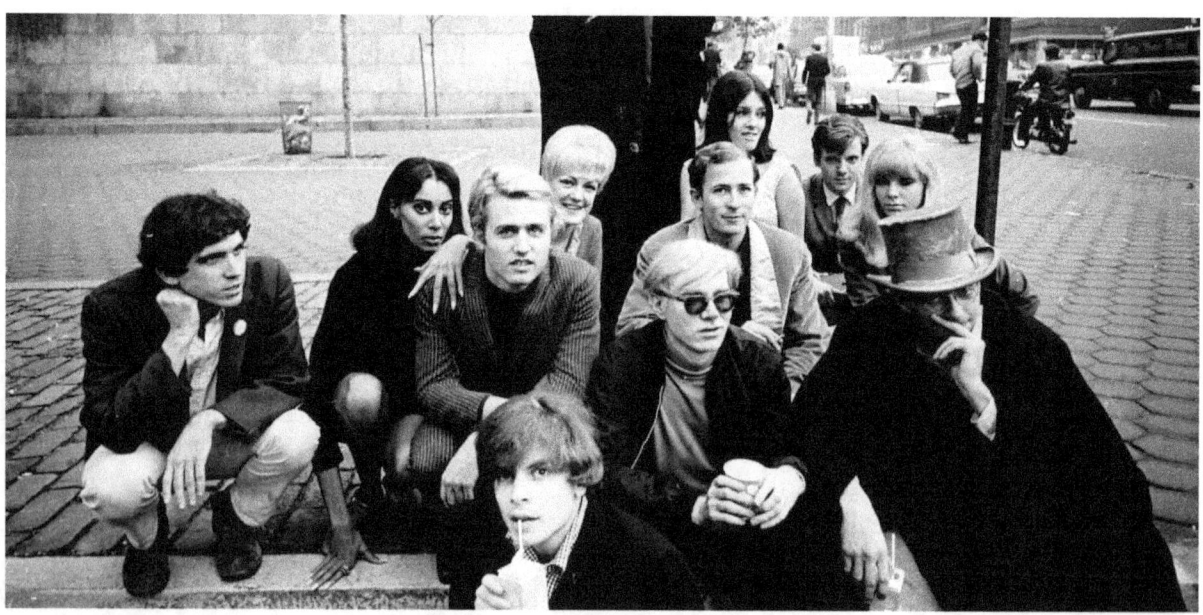

Andy and Family, including Gerard with model Donyale Luna and Ingrid Superstar, Danny Williams, Cathy Starfucker, Paul Morrissey. Handsome Kip 'Bima' Stagg (foreground) starred with Edie Sedgwick in 'Beauty 1', then married my cousin Deirdre. (Photo: Nat Finkelstein)

Jonas Mekas: Paul Morrissey became very, very powerful. So it was a combination after 'Chelsea Girls', not just pure Andy. Like some movie companies, a certain production style is imposed upon the films—this is MGM, this is Warner Brothers. So that was the end of Andy's cinema, in a way, because at that point Paul Morrissey wanted complete control, and he used a lot of the same stars. Later Morrissey went on his own, and those films, 'Trash', 'Heat', 'Flesh' cannot be called Andy Warhol films. One could say they were produced by Warhol, but those were Paul Morrissey films and they have his stamp on them.

Paul Morrissey: I don't remember ever saying anything to Andy where he didn't say it was a good idea. He was so glad to have any ideas, because Andy was not the kind of person, who had ideas. He never directed anybody, he didn't interfere with anybody, because he didn't know what to interfere *with*!

Ivy Nicholson: I can't stand Paul. He was doing really bad business. He would always say, "Oh, Andy's gay." Which of course he wasn't—Andy was bi-sexual. He'd promised people if the movie 'I, A Man' was a success they'd all get paid much better money. Andy got the idea from a Swedish movie called 'I, A Woman'. And 'I, A Man' was about a man who goes out with a lot of women and has affairs with all them, all totally different. The movie had a more evolved script than usual. The photography was better, the sound was better. So 'I, A Man' was a huge success. And we are not getting any more money. Why not? If ever I get money I am going to sue him.

Billy Name: It's the same old story. If you were not there to do the work, and the groundwork to make and build something you have no idea what it costs to produce what happens. So people came in and said, "Oh wow, Warhol can make me! And he is supposed to pay me isn't he?"

Louis Waldon: Right. What they didn't understand is, Andy had a big Factory. He paid the rent on it. You could go there and hang out all day if you were liked. And hang out while he was working. They had like a little club. They had a lot of fun. Andy would produce the movies. They cost $1500 to $2000 at that time to produce an hour, two hour film in color, with sound. So, he paid for all that. I went because of the immediate publicity. The notoriety was great. Here you were on the cover of magazines and newspapers. Your name is mentioned all the time. It was a good move for an actor like me, who was working with off-Broadway, which was a hundred years behind the times.

Kip 'Bima' Stagg: I was instantly part of Andy's inner circle, the 'pretty boy'. It was fun being part of the hottest scene in NYC. But it was soon clear that apart from >

Andy's paintings, there was no creativity going on except for acting 'fabulous' and 'outrageous'. There was as much substance to Andy's 'Superstars' as all those shiny silver mylar balloons floating on the ceiling.

As wiser heads left the scene, a fresh crop of street kids arrived, thrilled to be part of the Warhol sideshow. As before, some came from wealth and ennui, others were runaways, eager for adventure. Among those replenishing Warhol's disgruntled, dwindling troupe were Geraldine Smith and her vivacious friends Patti D'Arbanville and Andrea Feldman, future Warhol stars, of which more about in the upcoming chapter devoted to Max's Kansas City, which would become the Factory commissary.

Geraldine Smith: When I ran away. I was about fourteen, running down the street in the Village. I had on these skin-tight clothes and hair down to there, all this black eye make-up. A couple of guys invited me to a party, and I went with them to the Warwick Hotel. It was for the Beatles, and we hung out with them all night, smoked pot, and ate steaks at Max's Kansas City. That's where I met Andy. I went in with my friend Andrea. She wrapped a towel around her head like a turban and went up to Andy and said, "I'm Mrs. Warhola." And that was it. Everybody was there, and we kept going back every night because it was one great party. Paul was doing 'Flesh' and asked me to be in it. I'd say yes to anything. I'm on an adventure.

Allen Midgette: Max's Kansas City, I go in there that night, I see Paul Morrissey. He's sitting in a booth. And he says, "Oh, would you like to have a drink?" Well, Paul never asks me to have a drink, okay? (*mimicking*) "Would you like to go to Rochester in the morning and pretend to be Andy?" So, now I'm going to do a college lecture for Andy for free? That's what I expect, I mean that's what I had learned to expect. So, he said,"Well, you get six hundred dollars." "Oh, that's fine. When do we leave?"

The luckless Allen Midgette, always the brunt of the hip Factory's hippie prejudice, had recently returned from San Francisco. He tended to leave New York for calming Zen periods, only to come back for yet another surrealistic filming experience with the Warhol Family. After a while, fed up with their "aggressive amphetamine-fed histrionics," Allen would take off again. While he worked on the films, Allen often bunked in with his good friend and fellow mellow actor Louis Waldon, who lived in the Meat Market district. Whenever he arrived in New York, Allen, like all the others, was usually broke. And there was Warhol, waiting with open arms, with offers of imminent stardom, but don't expect SAG minimum. At least Paul paid him.

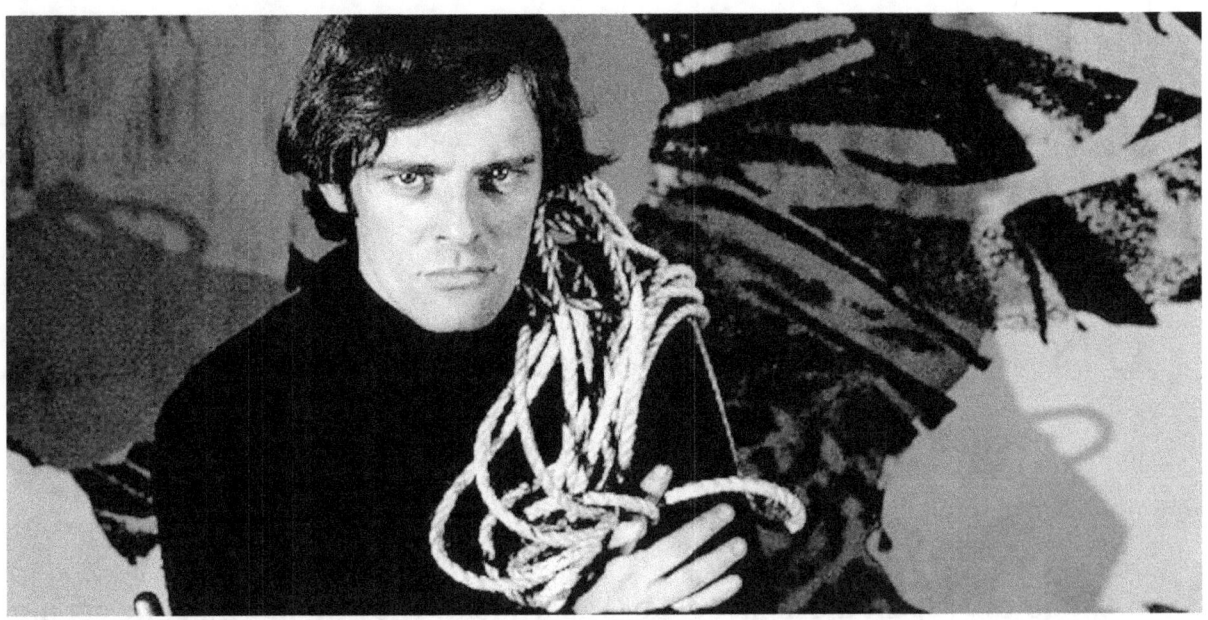

According to those who worked on Warhol films, Paul Morrissey really taught Andy the ropes. (Photo: Nat Finkelstein)

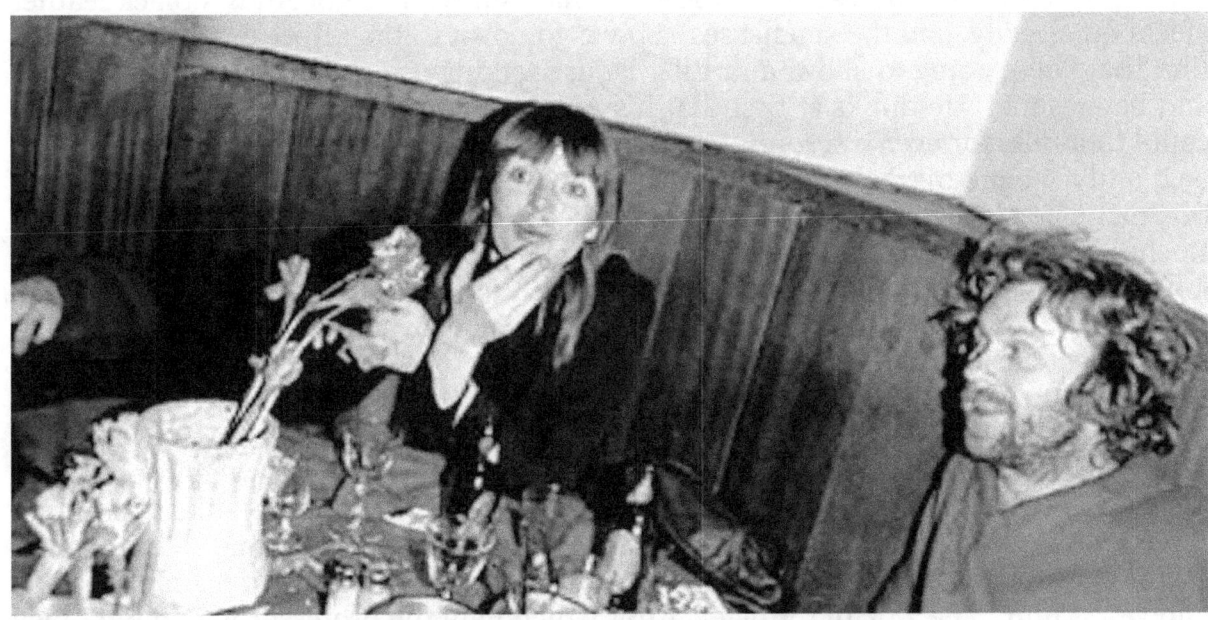

"Like a little club." Louis Waldon, Nico, and some sad flowers share a few beers at Max's Kansas City, the favored Factory hangout. (Photo: Billy Name)

ON IMITATING ANDY WARHOL

Well, they liked him better than they would have me.
—Andy Warhol

Allen Midgette: I spent the night at Paul's apartment. The next morning, we get into a taxi. Nothing's been planned, you have to understand. So I said, "You'd better stop at a pharmacy, and I'll get some makeup." I buy the lightest shade of Erase, Max Factor, and just smear it on until it's so thick it's almost dripping. . . Then I have talcum powder, and hairspray. I spray my hair silver, in the cab, in this tiny mirror. And I put the talcum powder over the silver hair spray. I've got Andy's black leather jacket on already, and the sunglasses. So we go down to the Silver Factory to get the film that we're going to show, and Billy is just waking up, and comes from the back and he *sees* me. He thinks at first that it's Andy. That was great for me, because if I could fool Billy for even a *second*!. . . When we got to the airport, I bought a Pan Am bag, and a Vogue magazine that had Jackie O on the cover. I was thinking, "God, if this plane crashes, no one will know that I died!" Well, it didn't crash. We arrive in Rochester, and it's one of those clear, autumnal days. We're walking down the street, a little early for the lecture. I'm checking myself out in the store window. And I'm thinking, "This doesn't look so bad." Suddenly, Paul turns to me and says, "Andy." Then he catches himself.

Allen Midgette really did look enough like the ephemeral Warhol when he dressed the part. He was better than a look-alike, because he even sounded like Warhol. . . But why was Warhol sending Allen around to pose as him? According to biographer Victor Bockris, "The typical Warhol road show included segments of his most boring and worst film, 'The 24 Hour Movie'. After which Paul the professor would put down art films and hippies, and Viva would rant, "We make these movies because it's fun, especially the dirty parts." Warhol, togged out in leather jacket would remain >

totally passive, saying nothing. The audience would respond appropriately by becoming hostile, hissing and booing. They hated them, but were especially disgusted with the non-communicative Andy. . . Accommodating actor Allen Midgette, in his capacity as Warhol's stand-in, never worked harder at Improv.

Allen Midgette: We get into this basketball gymnasium and students are coming in. I had never seen this film before. So first, I have to watch it, because they're going to ask me questions about this damn movie. And the movie was basically somebody asking, "Have you ever smoked or taken drugs?" And people saying, "Yeah, I smoke it all the time." Nothing too clever, to be honest. . . So the movie's over and I come up to the podium, and the first question is, "Mr. Warhol, why do you have so much makeup on?" Then, "Mr. Warhol, are you homosexual?" And I thought, well, if I were speaking for myself it would be one thing. But I'm not Andy Warhol either. So I said, without hesitating, "No." And you could hear a pin drop. It was like, "Why would you look like that if you're not completely *gay* and out of your mind?!" Suddenly, there's this revolutionary type, beard, long black hair, dark glasses. And he sits in the front, lotus position, and says, "When I saw this movie I thought it was a piece of shit, but after hearing you talk about it, it's really interesting." Now I'm thinking, "Oh my God, what am I getting into here? I'm convincing people who don't like something, that it's actually quite good!" Then this TV crew comes in, and they want an interview. Oh my God, maybe I'm committing some kind of *crime*! Finally, we get out of there, and Paul says, "We have to go to a cocktail party." And I'm, "Now wait, Paul." To boot, I'm going to the house of one of the art professors who's met Andy before, and he's going to present me with a drawing he did of Andy. I get to the house, he presents me with this drawing, which looks exactly like Andy. And he still doesn't know! It shows you how the mind works—nobody knows anybody. By now I am saying, "Paul! Get me out of here!" Then the students arrive. One brought me this poster, a guy kissing a girl, the scene from the movie of me and Susan Bottomly, which had become a famous photograph. And he said, "My girlfriend thinks this is you and her." So, as Andy, I signed it. That was the Rochester trip. I don't know if you want me to do another. . .

Oh my God, please no! By this time we were too stoned from Allen's casual toking to even continue filming. I seem to remember room service making frequent snack and fizzy drink deliveries. Fun! The Chelsea Hotel was still its charming and eccentric self, but, sadly, the scaffolding had gone up and the writing was literally on the wall. We took our leave. A few days later, we headed for California, where Louis Waldon had his own Allen Midgette story. . .

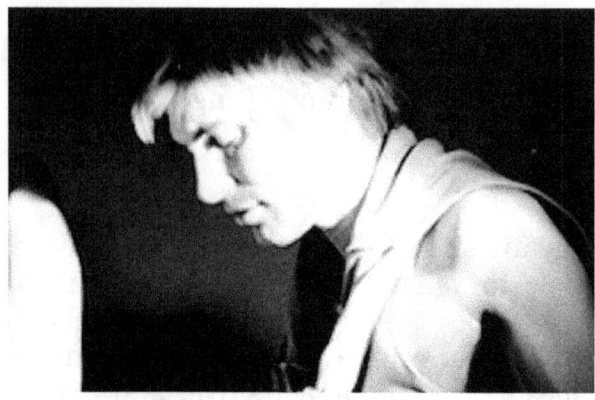 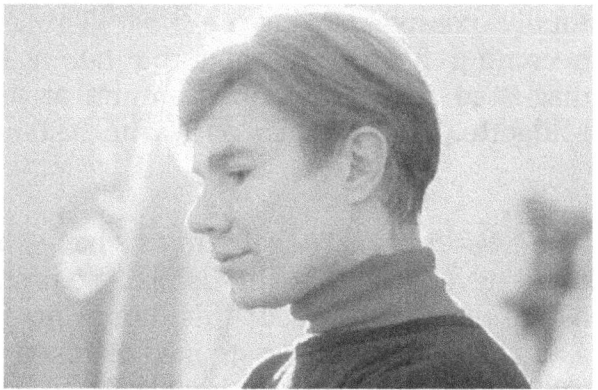

Allen channels Andy. The actor even mimicked Warhol's distinctive voice perfectly, fooling quite a number of university folk, who were understandibly outraged (and embarrassed) when the revelation came out in Time and Newsweek, (Photo: Billy Name)

To deflect possible threats of lawsuits for fraud, or repay them, Andy was obliged to go back to all those schools and bravely face a firing squad of disgruntled students and professors. Luckily, he had little patience for authority figures. As Mickey Ruskin of Max's would say, "Oh, fuck 'en if they can't take a joke." (Photo: Nat Finkelstein)

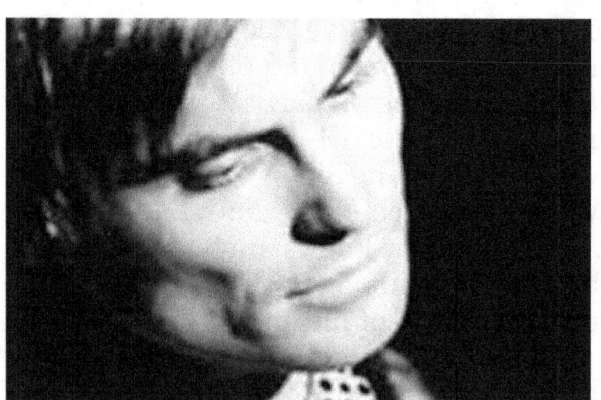 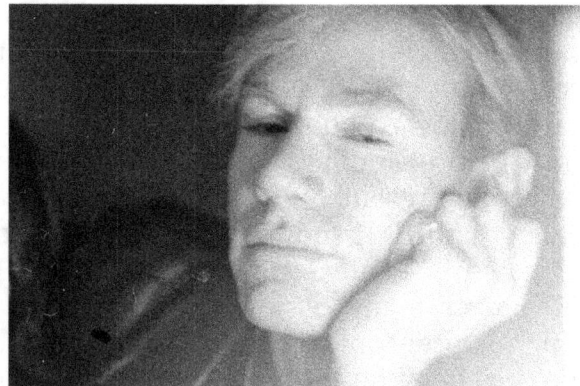

Allen as an actor, starring in ****, also known as 'Four Stars', also known as 'The Twenty-Four Hour Movie'. (1966/67) (Photo: Billy Name)

Andy, starring as himself. Although he was reluctant to appear in front of the camera, Louis Waldon contends that Andy "really wanted to be a famous personality." (Photo: Billy Name)

Louis Waldon: 'Andy' *(Allen Midgette)* was traveling around doing universities at that time. While we were down in Santa Barbara filming 'Surf's Up', 'Andy' would be talking and showing his movies. Viva would talk, and Allen would play Andy. They caught up with him in Oregon. Allen was out there with someone who had known Andy. He saw Allen up close and said, "You're not Andy Warhol." Started yelling really loud in the audience, "That's not Andy Warhol—that's a fake!" Allen just backed off and kept quiet. . . But Allen could *talk*. He could *imitate*. He's an actor, a good actor. He could imitate Andy really well. He looked like him, but much better looking. He made Andy look really good. In fact, I'd love for him to come out if I did a show. I'd love for him to come out and play Andy at the show.

Interviewer Aaron Sloan
Andy, how many college tours do you do a year?

Andy Warhol
Oh, we did about fifty this year.

According to Louis Waldon, when Allen Midgette was finally outed in the press, Warhol told the New York Post, "Well, they liked him better than they would have me." We interviewed Louis on his ramshackle rented sailboat, docked in Marina Del Rey, California, the 'Old Man and the Sea' sort of, though I'm not sure if it ever moved out of the harbor. He was living the bachelor life (we noted the dishes piled in the sink), rocking serenely on the water, a dream he'd had since shooting 'San Diego Surf ' with Warhol in 1968. . . Louis became an increasingly important person to Warhol in the late sixties, interceding for frustrated Family members, and basically being a heterosexual bar-hopping buddy for Warhol, who was still nervous about his homosexuality. Louis was charming, funny, very frank, and happy to share with us the secret of his post-Warhol success: making silk screen copies of Warhol's most famous art works, using the original silk screens from the Factory. . . Louis' choice of career did seem ironic, in light of the fact that he—like most of the other Factory members—had always refused Warhol's art as payment for their work, since, as he said, "Warhol's own work at that time wasn't selling for more than two or three hundred dollars a painting." On another ironic note, Warhol convinced one of his secretaries to accept a self-portrait in lieu of payment. She kept it in her closet for decades, and then recently auctioned it for over $6 million. So Louis' philosophy no doubt harked back to Marshall Mcluhan, who once wrote, "Art is anything you can get away with."

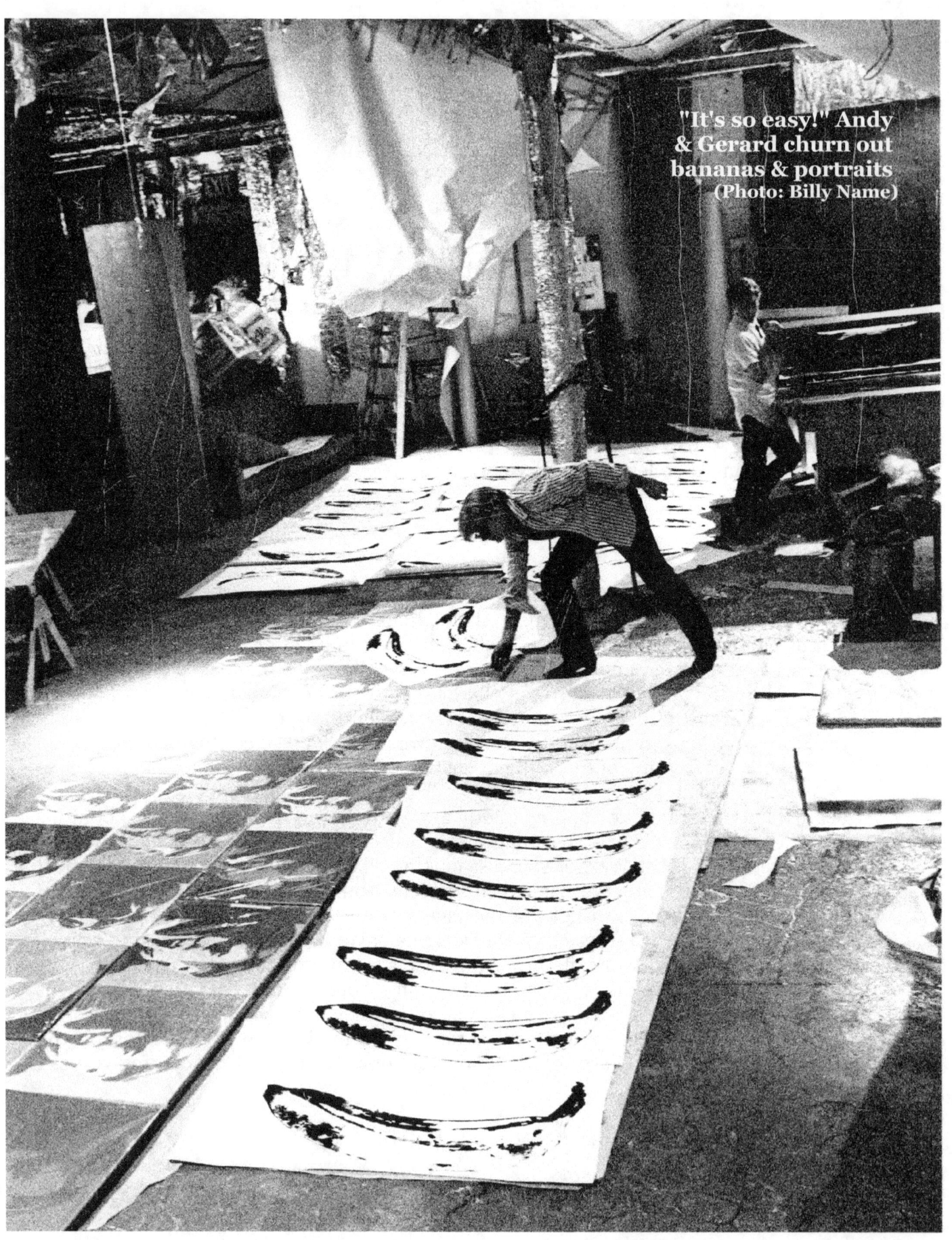

"It's so easy!" Andy & Gerard churn out bananas & portraits (Photo: Billy Name)

ON IMITATING
ANDY WARHOL'S ART

*My idea of a good picture is one that's in focus
and of a famous person.*
—Andy Warhol

Louis Waldon: Andy's legacy, Andy's fame is getting bigger. It's not dying down. I know, because I've been making his paintings for the last twenty years, so I know how the market goes. One day I couldn't sell a painting. The next day I get five phone calls, so I know how it's building. I was happy to be a part of the Factory, because I was in the most significant part of it. Now I'm keeping his art out there. People can purchase the paintings; they can own them. That's what he really wanted. That's what he told me many, many times. He was reading the paper one day, and he says, "Oh no, no, I don't understand it, Louis. Why are they buying these fake Dali's? My God, there's something like 20,000 of them out there. They're buying them up at these prices!" I said, "You don't like it.". . . "Oh no, I like it! That's a compliment when somebody makes someone else's art." He had written in his books the way to make his silk-screen art, step-by-step. That's all I did. A little thief came to me with three of the screens he said he got from the Factory. That's how I first got started. I can't remember his name. He'd been at the Factory. He died of AIDS. So that's how I got started, but I've learned a lot more since then. Because the ones I make are better than the ones Andy made. Andy's are overlapping and there are little pieces missing. I know, because when I'm using the screen it happens to me. . .

Of Warhol and his silk-screened Marilyns, The New Yorker art critic Peter Schjeldahl wrote: "That the works don't seem like disembodied layouts but are true paintings—raw handmade objects—registers as a tonic shock when they are viewed in person and in glorious variety. . . The semaphoric image of those eyes, those lips and that hair seems fated to be the most lasting icon of the past hundred years." *Bien sur*—in Paris, a chic shop in the Marais offers, right in the window, a plush living room chair where one can sit on a silk-screen of poor Marilyn's face. And, you can even make your own. . .

Louis Waldon: Here is how you do it: You get the photograph, of the subject, if it's Marilyn or whatever, and you take it in and have a copy made on a negative. Then you take the reverse negative and you have it put on a silk screen. Then burn it in and you've got it. You drop any color and you have the image—the ink is the image—the eyes, the eyebrows, the hair. That's the image. You make a round oval place like that and then you paint it flesh color, then you paint the eyes, the lips. Then the background. Then you screen over it. And you've got it. It's a print. Anybody can do it. But if they catch you, they make you stop, because if you start making them and selling them. . . I sign them and stamp them with *my* name on them. I've had one go for almost a million dollars. These people had a Brando that I made and they sold it to this Swiss German, who was a big collector for an Arab who had one of the biggest estates in Switzerland. They sold it for $1,000,000 to this Arab. They wanted to get the Brando with some history behind it, so he was making an Andy Warhol catalogue book and put it in there so it would be an authentic Warhol. . . But the guy who thought up the whole thing died of AIDS, so . . . the painting is still sitting in that Arab's library. It's an absolute tribute to Andy.

Louis reminisced from the merry, messy claustrophobic galley of his boat. If he has made any serious money from selling Warholish art, it must be treasure deeply buried in an offshore account. He seemed content with his life, unlike other frustrated Factory survivors who have long outlived their ersatz 'celebrity' fame, with nary a new reality show on the horizon. Though he had a long, satisfying acting career, Louis never achieved real movie stardom either, but in Marina Del Rey, California, he appeared to have found his 'Waldon' Pond. . .

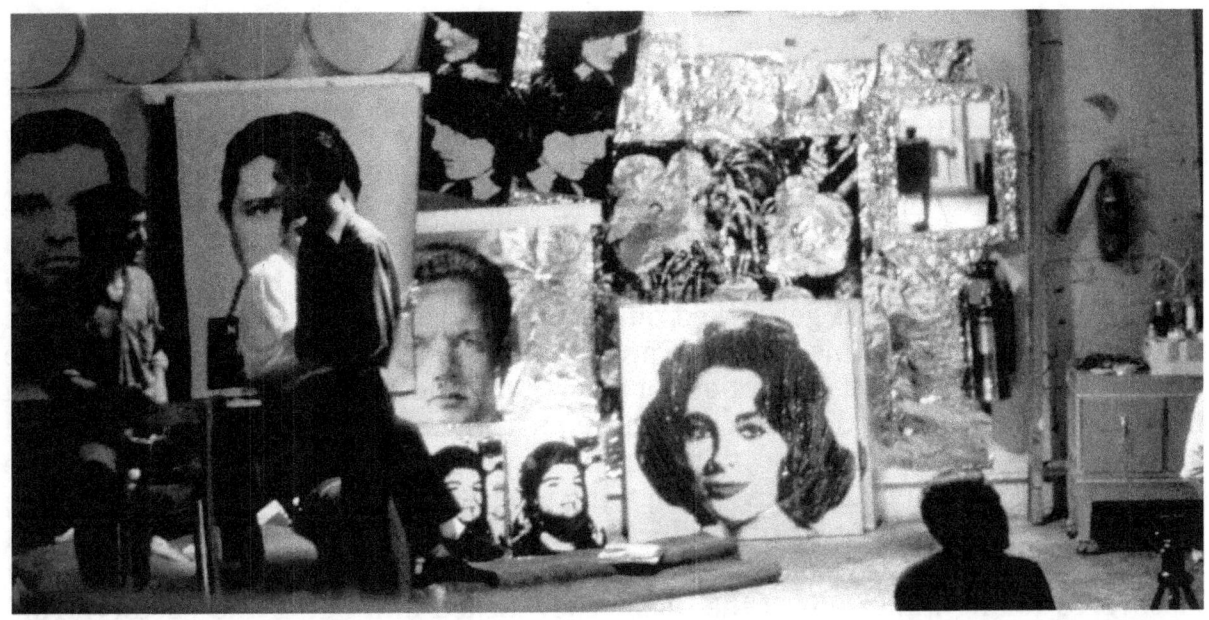

In the Silver Factory during a filming session, a tempting sampler of Warhol art goes ignored.

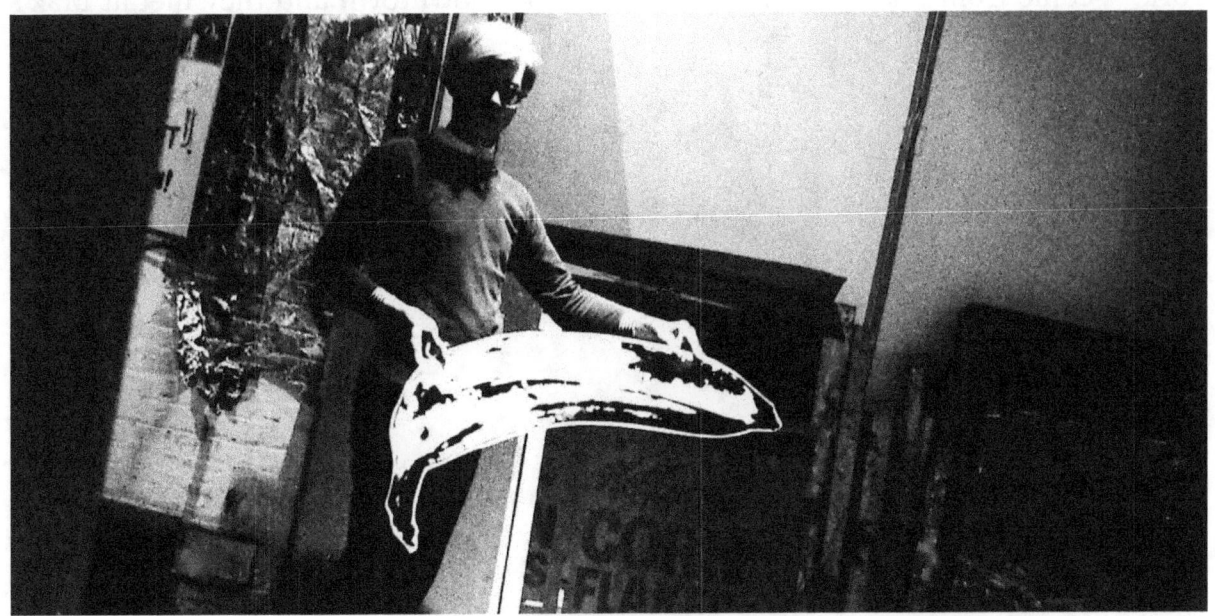

Money needed for more movies . . . means making more bananas. (Photos: Billy Name)

Louis Waldon: I do the screens because I'm not really an artist. I can't draw or anything like that. But I've got a good eye for color and for printing, and this is what it's all about—printing. All you need is a photograph. I've got this girl now who's my assistant; she does it all. You get the Liz Taylor photograph, or Marilyn, or Brando. You can buy those anywhere they have those Hollywood things. They're the same ones Andy used. Gerard Malanga came up with this idea. He never did explain it to me. But I know what happened, because it's a fever—it's so easy to do and you make so many of them. Gerard got kicked out of the factory, and I really liked him. He went to Italy and made this 'Che Guevara', and they closed it down the night before the show opened. Gerard just got out of town and came right back. So Gerard was a little nervous, and Andy didn't want to have anything to do with him. Gerard came and talked to me one day, and said that he would really like to come back to the Factory. I said, "I'll talk to Andy." The thing was, Gerard was doing this typed page of interviews, which turned into 'Interview Magazine'. He and this other guy got together and they were coming to the Factory and typing.   But then, he got discovered taking things out of the files. They kicked him out of the Factory. And this time I couldn't get him back in. Andy said, "No way. Please, don't even talk about it." Everybody who started with Andy, except Billy Name, thought they were going to be just as important as Andy. There was this tremendous assertion going on, because everything was changing. The whole anti-war thing was changing New York. People from Madison Avenue were coming downtown and they met at Max's Kansas City. . .

WELCOME TO
MAX'S KANSAS CITY

We were Superstars, and got a lot of attention at Max's.
—Holly Woodlawn

We all loved Max's, and you didn't have to be a Superstar to have fun—you just had to feel like one. Owner Mickey Ruskin, a Village impresario, had moved uptown, barely, to Union Square. His new place quickly became a magnet for the pioneer artists who had first settled there. The downtown crowd followed. The neighborhood was still industrial, at night a wasteland. Then, a glow from a storefront window, and a peek into a Hieronymus Bosch painting come to life. To describe Max's heady atmosphere as hedonistic would be akin to calling Caligula's Rome a bit decadent. Instead of grapes one nibbled hard chickpeas guaranteed to crack a dental crown. Mickey's favorite line—"Fuck 'em if they can't take a joke"—I used liberally throughout my Hollywood career as a film editor. Artists, musicians, and demigods held court in the front room, while in the back Warhol's legions held on to their king's round table, blithely signing his name to dinner tabs. Here in Mickey's latest foray, the fringe art scene was made as welcome as the art establishment, though an unspoken hierarchy ruled. A rite of passage for the vainglorious: The ceremonial ejection, a prone or flailing body (depending on the drug) being carried outside by a contingent of henchmen. Mickey's policy: Moochers and mongrels sniffing about for fame or freebies were tolerated only if they could be entertaining.

'Leee' Black Childers: Max's had a very strict door policy, believe it or not. There were people who couldn't get *into* Max's, but these stoned-out drag queens wearing garbage were welcomed! Max's was a big mixture, but the mainstay of the back room were the Warhol people—Andy and Ultra, Ingrid Superstar, Ondine, Gerard. In the front part of the bar were the artists. John Chamberlain gets millions of dollars for pieces of foam rubber. I should have gone into art. So, the artists were in the front room and the crazy people were in the back room. I ended up quite naturally with the crazy people, because in those days Andy was very open. And Mickey was so fabulous. He let us do anything we wanted to. Andrea would get up and take her clothes off while Geraldine Smith poured salad dressing all over her. . .

Andy takes Billy Name's picture, while Viva and
Ondine enjoy the notorious back room at Max's .

Geraldine's friend Andrea Feldman starred in the film 'Heat' in which she portrayed, all too realistically, a psychotic mother who drugged her baby with sleeping pills. Andrea would sometimes self-harm and put cigarettes out on her face, leaving sores.

Geraldine Smith: It was one great party! We'd go there every night at midnight and stay out till six or seven in the morning. Andrea used to do her Showtime, and that was really a lot of fun, because she would dance on the tables, singing "Everything's coming up roses." At the end Mickey and the other guys would carry her out. This went on almost every night. It was great fun. Andrea was living at her uncle's house on lower 5th Avenue, and she kept saying, "Let's jump out the window and make a splash hit! Wouldn't it be great, it would be the best Showtime." But no one took her seriously. And one day she just jumped out the window with a bible and a crucifix. Nude. She landed there on 5th Avenue in rush hour traffic.

Gerard Malanga: Andrea 'Whips Warhola'. Very tragic. I didn't realize that she was that troubled. I mean, I know she was a nut case, but what an extreme to go to, you know? Very sweet. I got along great with Andrea.

Andrea killed herself in 1972 at the age of twenty-four, just before the opening of 'Heat', after a violent verbal assault on a fearful Warhol. As before, according to biographer Victor Bockris, no one called Warhol "a fag and an asshole" and was still welcome in the Factory. We licensed footage of her dancing, lips painted bright blue to match her mini, from Anton Perich, whom we had interviewed in Paris. Earlier, he had sent us his fabulous fly-on-the-wall photographs and video films of everybody at Max's, including Ondine, Mary Woronov, and Eric Emerson. Andrea's dancing partner, Eric, would die in 1974, of an alleged heroin overdose. He was then apparently run over by a truck in front of Max's. Eric was last interviewed while filming Warhol's 'San Diego Surf' in California.

Interviewer Aaron Sloan: How do you become associated as a Superstar with Andy?

Eric Emerson: I'm not a Superstar. I don't want to be a Superstar like everyone else. I just come to add my two cents. I was in 'Chelsea Girls' and the cowboy movie ('Lonesome Cowboy'). I don't know where it is. I don't even know the name of it. Now I don't know where I'm at.

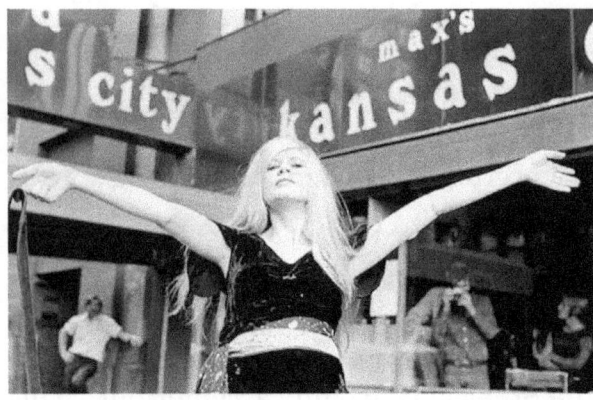

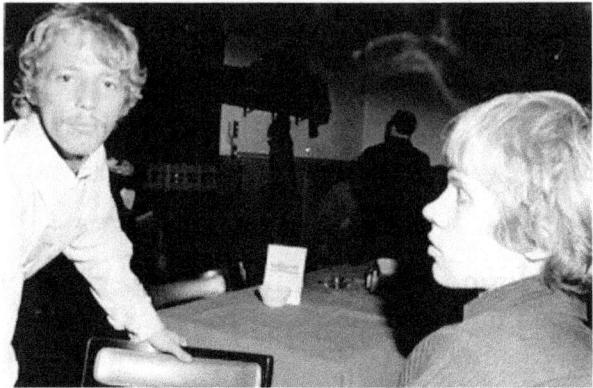

Andrea 'Whips' Feldman, tragic dancing queen of Max's Kansas City, was known by the Warhol crowd as "Crazy Andy."

(Photo: Anton Perich)

Eric Emerson and young friend enjoy a busy night at Max's.

(Photo: Billy Name)

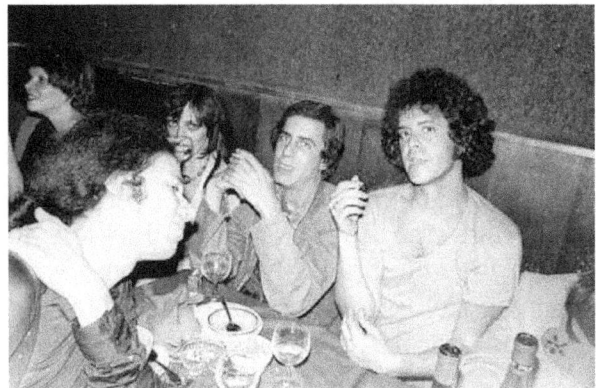

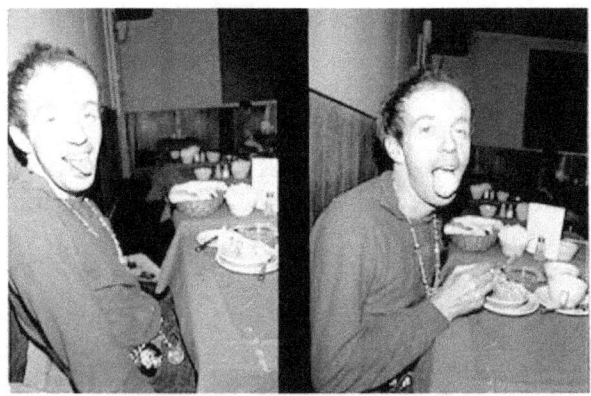

Nico, Steve Paul ('The Scene') and Lou Reed in a booth at Max's. . . The Velvet Underground often performed upstairs at Max's to a packed room.

(Photo: Anton Perich))

Taylor Mead clowns around in his favorite bar, the place where. according to Andy, "Pop art meets pop life."

(Photo: Billy Name)

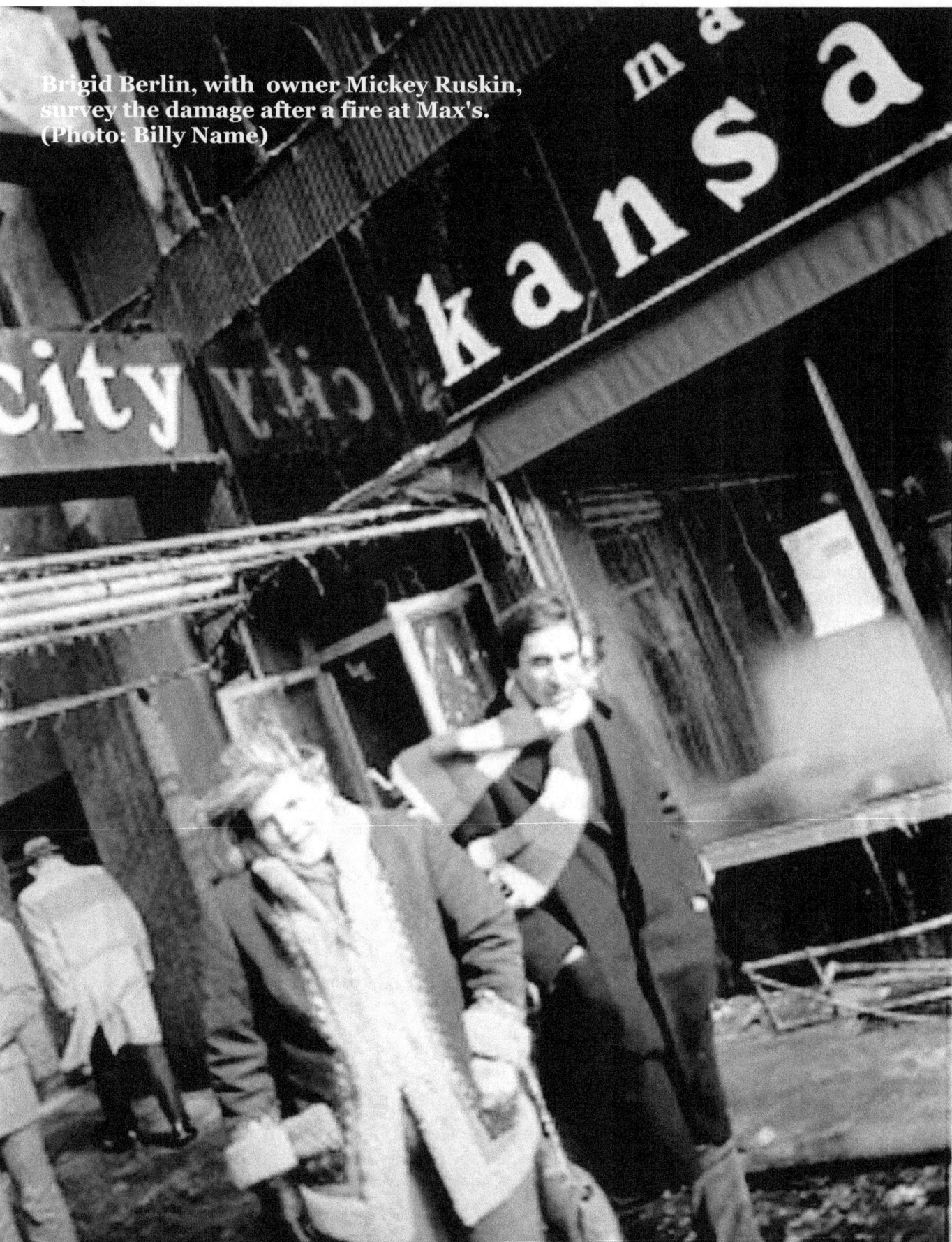

Brigid Berlin, with owner Mickey Ruskin, survey the damage after a fire at Max's. (Photo: Billy Name)

Anton Perich: I spent years in Paris as a poet and a painter. Then I came to New York, and the first night, I went to Max's. I thought I came to La Dolce Vita, a Fellini movie. I could not believe what was going on. I died and came to purgatory *(laugh)*. Taylor Mead, Eric Emerson, Andrea Feldman, Cyrindre Fox. Candy Darling, Jackie Curtis, Holly Woodlawn, Viva, Ondine—they were my favorite subjects. Because I would be taking so many pictures of the same people every night, they didn't believe I had film in the camera. But I didn't speak English when I came to New York, so the camera became an object of communicating. They were all very narcissistic, so it was like holding a mirror to them. To me, Taylor Mead was like Mastroianni, an old-fashioned movie star. He'd lived in Paris and spoke French, so I could talk with him.

Taylor Mead: Mickey Ruskin, who runs Max's Kansas City, one of the great seminal cafés of New York, said, "Taylor I have this new café, you'd fit right in." And I came back (from Paris) to Max's, the most important café since the Moulin Rouge!

Anton Perich: After a while, Andy asked me to do pictures for Interview Magazine. So Andy was really nice to give me a job *(laugh)*. Max's back room was like a studio, I could just sit there and shoot. These people had a kind of radiance about them. I didn't have to use a flash; they would just light up the picture. It's rare, that quality of radiance. I didn't find it with celebrities or movie stars. I found it in the Max's regulars.

Along with other special people in Warhol's orbit, Anton Perich and his brother deserve their own documentary. They have always been superstars in their native country, I forget which one, but it holds nice film festivals for them. We used Anton's home movies of Taylor Mead in Max's with drag queens Jackie Curtis and Candy Darling, dancing, blowing smoke rings and a whole lot more. We juxtaposed that footage with archive film of the old Moulin Rouge and its can-can high kickers, and realized why Taylor felt at home in both places. Max's fulfilled all one's fantasies.

Taylor Mead: I remember sitting there (at Max's) with Nico in the back corner, under a Dan Flavin, a beautiful simple pink neon tube sculpture. . . A lot of people got their careers going in there, artists who were then really challenging everything.

Like Taylor, a number of Warhol people moved easily between Max's front booths and the busy back room, and were considered creative artists in their own right— Billy Name, Gerard, Ondine, Mary Woronov, Nico, Viva and Brigid Berlin among >

them. Brigid had fashioned an enormous 'Cock Book' which she brought with her nightly, cajoling male patrons to draw and decorate their penises. It reads like a Who's Who of celebrities, including Dennis Hopper, Leonard Cohen (who wrote a polite, poetic Zen abstention) and former husband of Brigitte Bardot and Jane Fonda, French film director Rogar Vadim.

Gerard Malanga: In those days, it was the frontier. At night that neighborhood was *dead*, not a soul on the street. When you entered Max's, you went from this quiet space outside into this party that was going on for the next five hours. If we went to eat, it went on Andy's tab, which he would then pay for at the end of the month.

Mary Woronov: At Max's, Ondine would get in these situations that were bad, and he would not be careful. He would laugh and make it worse. He was very scary. He was talking to this person who was getting more and more nervous. Ondine ordered salad and started mixing the salad with his hands and laughing, and the person is panicking and sweating. Then, all of a sudden, Ondine takes the salad bowl and puts it on his head! In most places you would laugh. This guy was shrieking in terror.

Ivy Nicholson: Sometimes there was a food fight in Max's Kansas City. We'd get angry and pick up the food, and it would go flying across the room.   If that happened today they would throw people out, but they didn't. The owner must have been 'lacsadaisical' *(sic)* or something. Anything could happen and nobody cared. We were just having fun.

Ivy's violent food flinging would have Warhol running for the door and into a taxi for the safety of home, though once he got there, he feared she might be already there waiting for him. According to Ivy, she'd needed money to go to Mexico and get a divorce from her present husband, so she could come back and marry the elusive man of her dreams. Ivy chose not to notice Warhol shyly holding hands under the table with any number of cute young boyfriends.

Danny Fields: What was nice about Max's was not that you could fuck anyone, but that there was no one you could *not* fuck if you tried hard enough. It didn't matter in what anatomical way, or what sex you were. It was sexual contact. It originated on a level other than teenaged hard-ons and dripping pussies. You'd have to pretend it was much more profound than that, and then you got your fuck, okay? So, that's about sex at Max's.

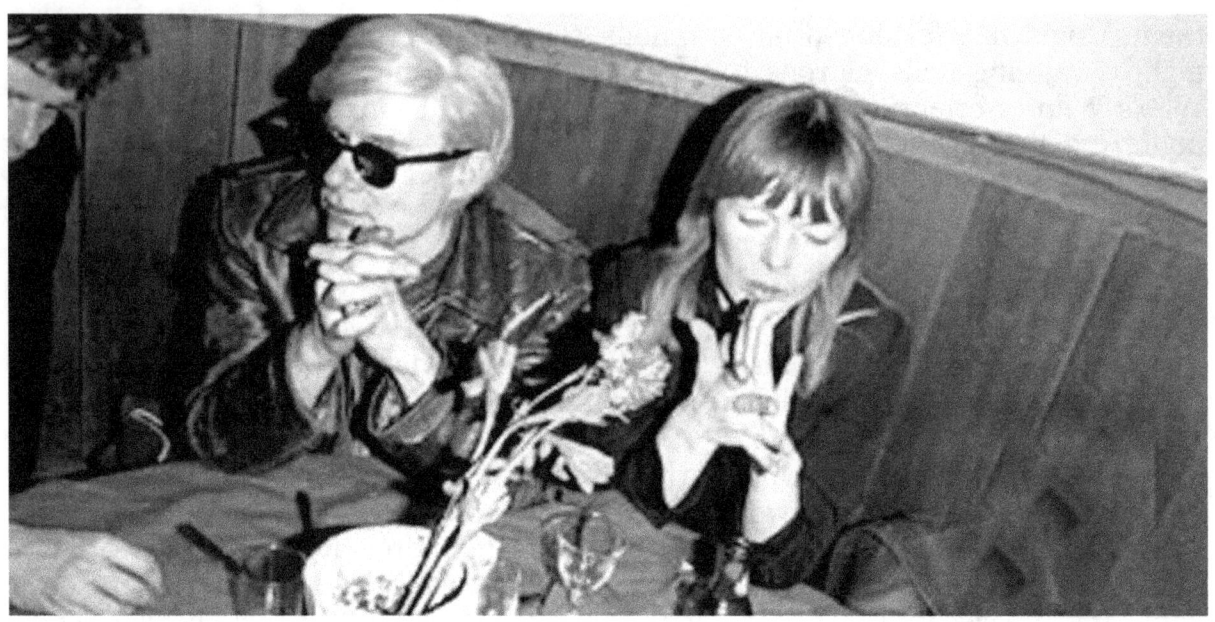

Paul Morrissey, Andy and Nico in the back room of Max's.

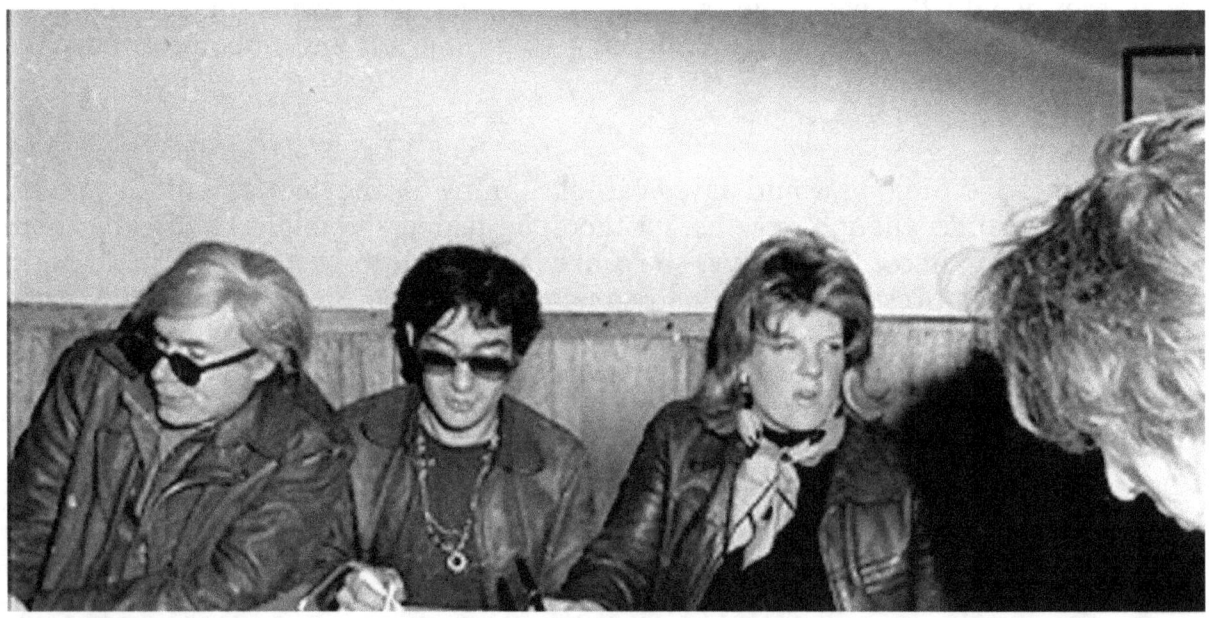

**Andy, with Ondine, Brigid and Rene Ricard, picks up the tab for another night at Max's.
(Photos: Billy Name)**

Warhol was a regular at Max's, arriving almost every night with his Factory Family, which by '67 could often be in flux. The backroom's round tables evolved into a nightly game of Musical Chairs. Or Chess. . . Ivy Nicholson thought of it as "the King and his knights and princesses." Viva preferred "the Queen and his pawns." Her acerbic wit could also easily dispatch the unwanted pest at the party. One night, according to Victor Bockris, Warhol noticed Valerie Solanas—his future assassin— huddled at a nearby table, and encouraged Viva to go chat her up. She obliged. Signs of future unhingement were not yet noticeably evident.

Victor Bockris: Viva marched right up to Valerie. "You dyke! You're disgusting!" Valerie immediately told Viva her life story, how her father had gone down on her when she was eight. "No wonder you're a lesbian," Viva responded. "No man could be better than your father."

Louis Waldon: I took Candy (Darling) to Max's Kansas City to meet Andy. She stopped me at the door and said, "I can't go in there. It's against the law for a man dressed as a woman to go into a New York bar, because of the Blue Law." I said, 'Well, baby, this ain't old New York, this is the *new* New York. Nobody is going to arrest you. In fact you're going to feel right at home." Sure enough, she went in, and all my Italian buddies were coming up and hitting on her. They were hitting on her! I said, "Later you guys, what the hell is wrong with you?" They were like flies!

Holly Woodlawn: So, we went back to Max's, and Jackie devised this plan: "Why don't we just go there and sign Andy Warhol's name, and eat dinner, and order steak and lobster and wine?" And Andy got all the bills.

Leee Black Childers: I remember Holly Woodlawn once saying, "No one will ever believe all these people were in the same room, on the same night." And that was night after night after night. The back room was lit entirely in red lights. It makes anyone look beautiful. And as soon as you heard *(sings Patsy Cline),* "Sometimes it's hard to be a woman," he'd go *click,* and the whole room would glow white, and honey, those platform shoes were heading for the door as fast as they could get out of there. . .

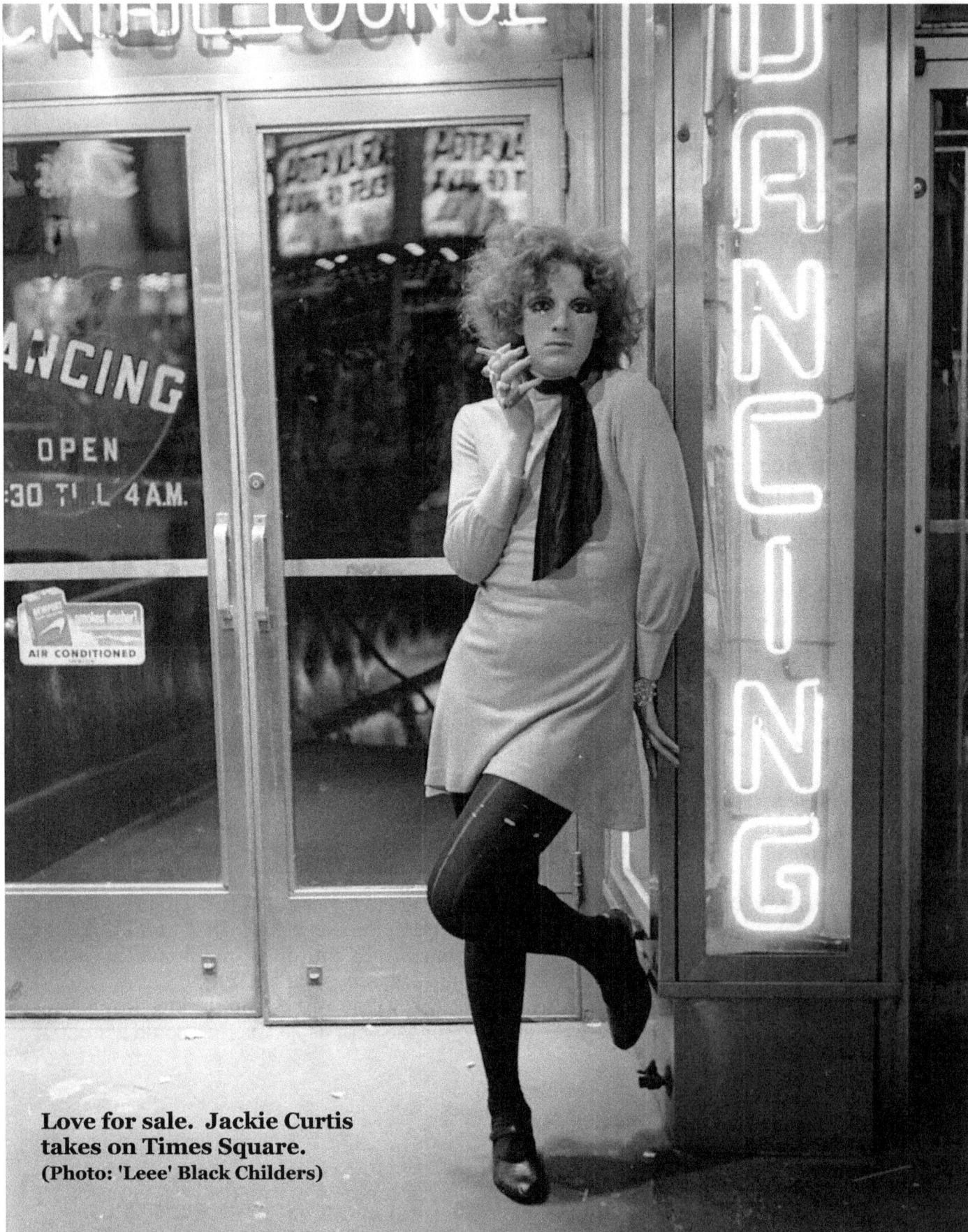

Love for sale. Jackie Curtis
takes on Times Square.
(Photo: 'Leee' Black Childers)

QUEENS & SUPERSTARS

*Warhol films were about sexual disappointment
and frustration, the way Andy sees the world.*

—Viva

Billy Name: At one point, we went out to Columbia Studios to explore making a Hollywood movie with these hetero studio heads. And we get there late, with all the faggots and flaming people, wanting to do a grand scale art movie. I mean, it stopped right there. They could not comprehend what this Warhol guy was doing. It certainly was not like a Hollywood studio where, "We select you. Come in and get paid to do your stuff." No, here is the Roman arena. You come in as the gladiator or the siren and conquer the whole thing if you can. Fine with us, if you want to be *the* Superstar.

Andy Warhol: I still think it's nice to care about people. And Hollywood movies are uncaring. . . They're not-real people trying to say something. We're real people trying to say nothing.

Viva: Andy believes in winging it. . . The feeling that we were on to something good led us to approach this seemingly random method with contagious enthusiasm, and a deadly seriousness that we tried to hide.

Victor Bockris: The Superstars began to compete with each other. They started putting each other down. Now Viva was unlike the previous female superstars, in that she had a very biting tongue. Andy said that the thing he really loved the most were good *talkers*. His favorite thing of all was for a beautiful woman to talk to him in detail about her sex life, so he could experience it vicariously. His form of homosexuality was that he really would have been happier to be a girl. So Andy >

certainly had an interest in trading places, or becoming a woman through the woman's openness to him. That's a relationship that could work on all sorts of channels. That would not involve *sex* necessarily of the physical kind, but could be an emotional sexual relationship of a kind. I think he had very close relationships with some of these people and certainly with Viva. Viva wanted to *marry* him. Viva was an intelligent woman, she was no idiot, she was no crazed person. She fell in love with him. Andy was very lovable. A lot of women fell in love with him.

Viva: Do you know what my opinion is of Andy? I think he's the Queen of Pop art. *(maniacal laughter)*. . . and Queen of the Underground.

Mary Woronov: If you hear Viva talk, she mentions everybody's name, phone number, serial number— "Oh, remember when we went off to France, and we slept in the blah blah, and the whole blah blah, and we went on so and so's plane." So, obviously, I just didn't handle it right *(laughs)*.

We licensed footage from 'Andy Makes A Movie', which documents the unfinished film 'San Diego Surf'. In it, Viva makes a star appearance, along with Taylor Mead, Louis Waldon, Eric Emerson, Ingrid Superstar, and a contingent of hippies picked up along the way—probably from the notorious L.A. 'Castle' in Los Feliz. Coming in from the beach, the cast wander aimlessly, waiting for something to happen, chain-smoking and draping damp bodies over furniture. The beach house Warhol and Morrissey filmed in belonged to the actor Cliff Robertson, who probably had not been aware of the goings on, like many formerly proud homeowners who had been foolish enough to give their property over to filmmakers. You'd think Cliff would have known better, being in the business. . . Anyway, interviewer Aaron Sloan doggedly follows Viva around as she prepares for a beach scene, begging for a juicy tidbit on her relationship with her equally elusive director. He had his work cut out for him. . .

Interviewer Aaron Sloan *(to Viva)*
This kind of acting is sort of impromptu. Do you find there is probably more satisfaction, say, in working with a strong director who knows where the acting is going to go?

Viva
I have no idea, because I've never worked with any other director. . . *(to Warhol)* "I guess I'll have to wear a bathing suit, right?"

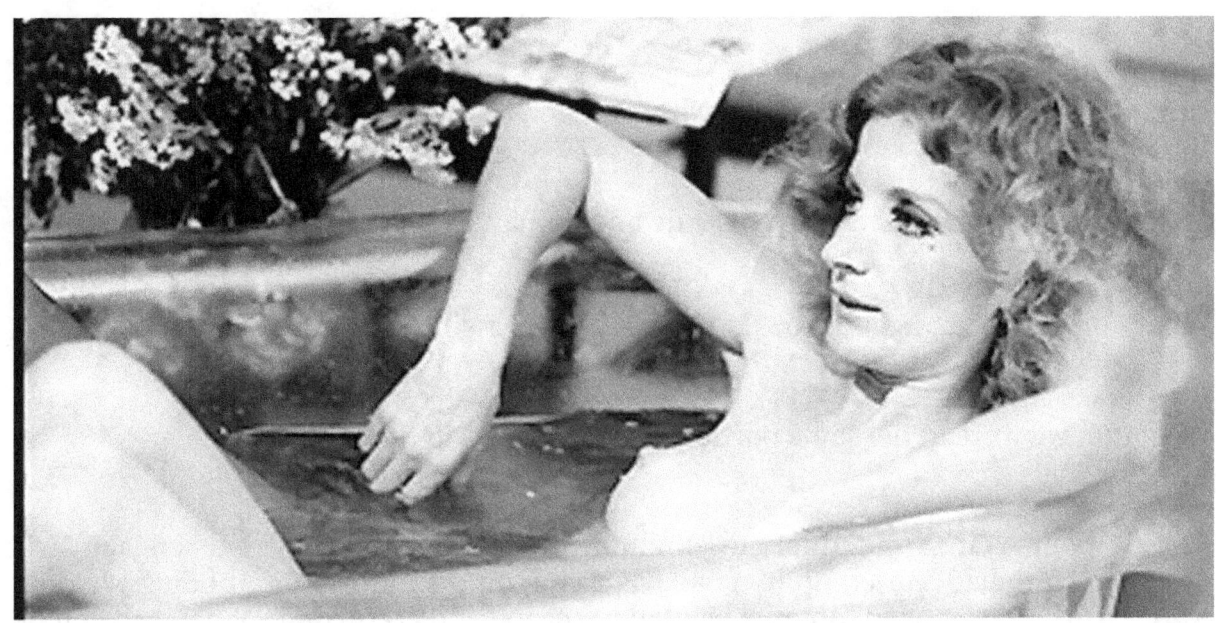

Viva soaking in 'Tub Girls', also starring Abigail Rosen, Alexis de la Falaise, Brigid Berlin, and Taylor Mead.

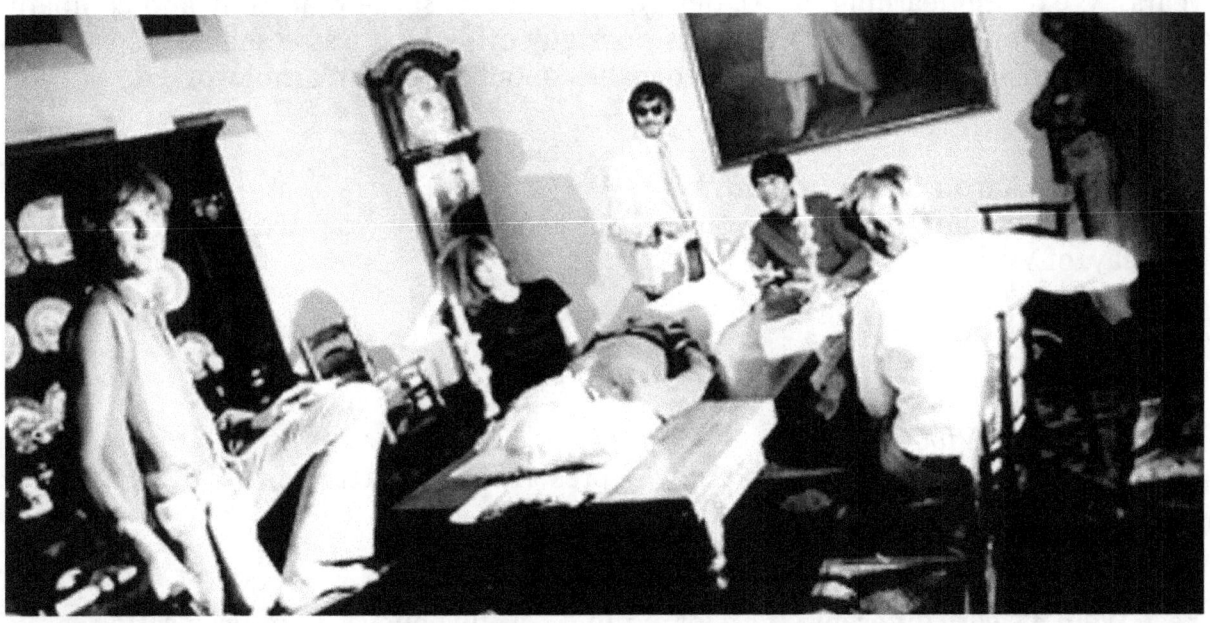

Filming of 'Katrina Dead'. Katrina Tollem starred with Ivy Nicholson, Kit Carson, and Rodney Kitzmiller. (Photos: Billy Name)

Aaron Sloan *(to Viva)*
How did you first become affiliated with Andy?

Viva
After I saw 'I, A Man', I went up to Andy and demanded to be in the next movie.

Interviewer
What do you mean, demanded? Is Andy easily accessible in New York?

Viva
Well, um, we were at the same parties. . . I have to go to the john.

At this point Aaron the Interviewer almost gave up. He'd tried to engage Eric Emerson, who had' curled up in a ball, rambling on disjointedly, and Louis Waldon, who was friendly enough, but just wanted to escape and go surfing. When asked if he had "ever done improvisational performing," Waldon replied, "Every single day of my life." Paul Morrissey scurried about, motioning silence for a take, which did not seem to appeal to anyone, so Sloan once again went after Warhol, who was his vague, inscrutable self: "Well, we're still just learning to use the camera. It's only been four years. We're still learning." Yes, one got the distinct sense that Andy and company were all languidly trying to brush this poor guy off, which was a shame, because he was so enthusiastic, if not too knowledgeable, about the way Warhol worked.

Interviewer Aaron Sloan *(to Warhol)*
I want to know how you select your cast in general, how you decide, with a screen test, say, of Viva.

Andy Warhol
Huh?

Interviewer *(to Viva)*
Do you find that working with Andy represents a departure from the otherwise established trends in cinema today?

Viva
Yes. Well, it's very different. It's a lot of fun. . . Andy believes in improvisation.

Interviewer
How specifically, say in 'Nude Restaurant', do you figure that your approach works?

Andy Warhol
Uh, well, 'Nude Restaurant' was just part of the 'Twenty-Five Hour Movie'. I mean nothing very much, aaahhh . . . happens.

Yup, nothing much sure does happen, and plenty of it, but it's so zenly hilarious that it just doesn't matter. In the footage of 'Nude Restaurant' that we licensed from the Warhol Museum, Viva, as a topless waitress, rambles on in her aristocratic drawl, exposing life with her dysfunctional family and sounding like a demented Katherine Hepburn. Seated next to her, nodding out on Quaaludes, Taylor Mead agrees with everything, occasionally picking his nose and yawning. Later, Viva tries to get the amorous attention of Allen Midgette, who just wants a sandwich, extra mayo, hold the sarcasm. . .

Viva *(to Allen)*
"I don't have all day."

Allen Midgette: The first 'Nude Restaurant' actually happened. But, it wasn't the way I had envisioned it of course, which I expected from Andy. At that point I was living with Robert Thurman, who had just gotten out of a Tibetan monastery. And he said, "Don't worry about it Allen, just be a calm center." So that movie went down, and then after that, they redid the film, and gave the lead to *Viva*. I don't mind; I'll just take some more LSD and watch what's going on here. . .

Andy Warhol: Well, we were trying to make an anti-war movie, and made it into a 'nudie' so more people would be able see it.

Taylor Mead: Paul said 'Nude Restaurant' was no good. "Taylor was on drugs and being very slow" and all this, but it was a beautiful film. Then we made 'Imitation of Christ' which in my opinion was the excavation of Taylor Mead. See, Paul wasn't involved in 'Nude Restaurant', but in 'Imitation of Christ' he was, and they were two wonderful films but never shown. I am buried alive, you know.

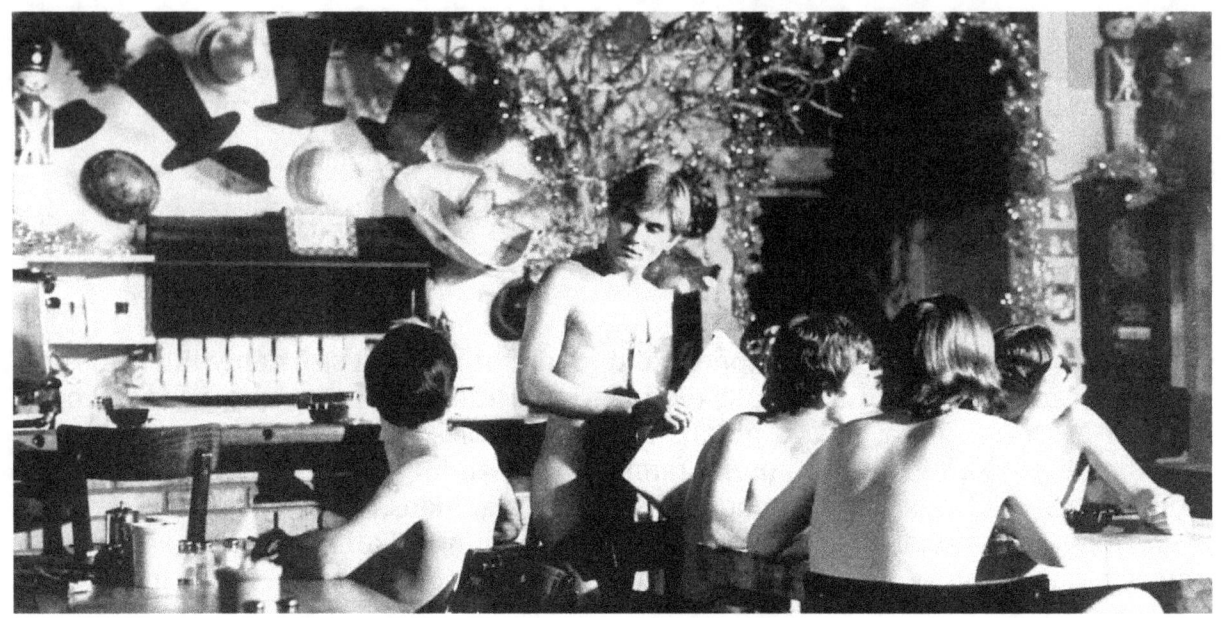

Allen Midgette, center, takes orders (hold the pickle) in the first 'Nude Restaurant'.

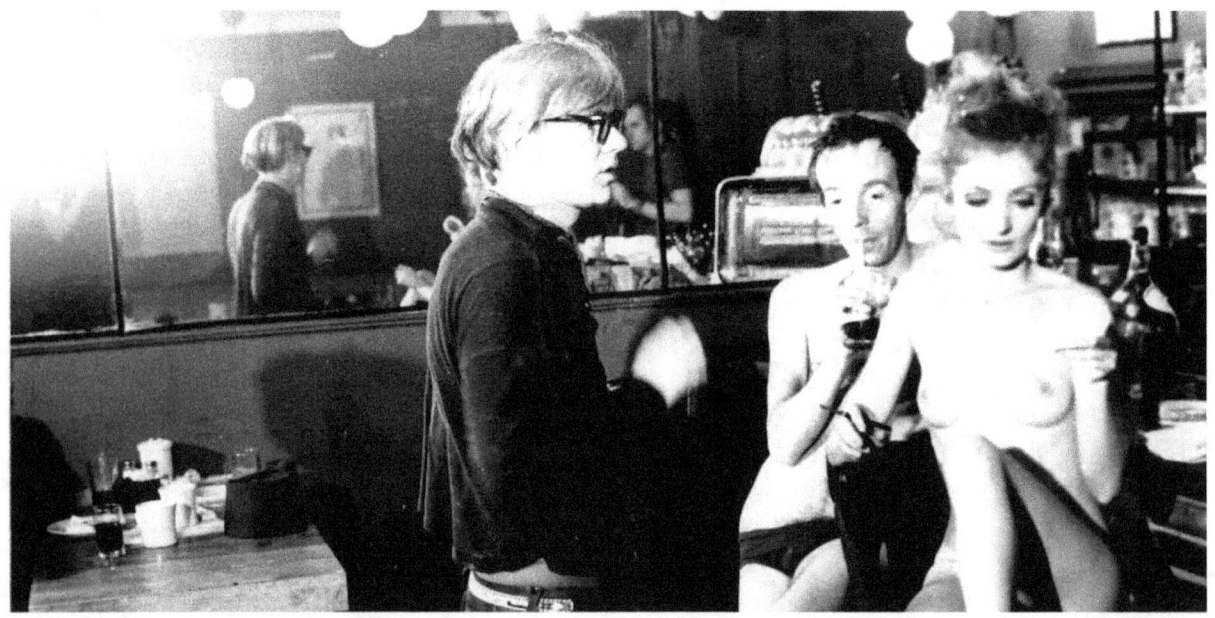

Andy directs co-stars Taylor and Viva in the revised 'Nude Restaurant'. (Photos: Billy Name)

Taylor had a point. 'Imitation of Christ', which also starred Ondine and Brigid Berlin as a couple whose son wanted to wear a dress to school, was pulled by Warhol after only one screening—even though Jonas Mekas had just proclaimed him "the Victor Hugo of cinema." A month later, Warhol did the same with 'The 24 Hour Movie'. The actors were outraged. A year's work buried, and with it the promise of stardom. Or 'stardoom', according to Allen Midgette...

Allen Midgette: There were other movies made from the first 'Nude Restaurant'. I got put in jail. *(entitled 'Allen in Jail', filmed in 1966, not to be confused with 'Jail', which featured Allen and Ondine and Ingrid Superstar, not to be confused with— oh, never mind)* They used what is now Jonas Mekas' Film Anthology. They had been given the property, but it was still a prison. I was in a cell and Ondine came in, telling me that he was my lawyer. And I said that I don't need a lawyer. And he said, "Don't you want to get out of here?" I said, "No." Let's face it, you could be in a little box and be free. Or you could be supposedly free and be a prisoner, it doesn't really matter. There was a window with bars, and I put my feet in it and hung there. I would also stand on my head naked, which would scare the shit out of Andy.

'Leee' Black Childers: In those days, when things were much safer, you would just walk into the Factory, and there would be people taking pills in various states of undress. At the same time there would be a serious art critic from Germany there to look at Andy's silk screens. There was this big mixture of total trash off the streets— Holly Woodlawn, wearing an old curtain she found in a garbage can, just wrapped around her, and of course Brigid Berlin, only we didn't know she was rich. Then there would be people like Jackie (Curtis) who didn't have a pot to pee in.

Toward the end of the Silver Factory period, Warhol began to introduce more transvestites into the combustible mix of actors, superstars, singers, socialites, con artists and bottom feeders. The over-the-top 'damsels' and their dramas brought a welcome touch of levity to what was increasingly becoming a fractious and bickering Family. Warhol's and Morrissey's new triumvirate of Superstars, Jackie, Holly, and Candy, simply wanted to dress up, have fun, and maybe get famous along the way. But in truth, life was a lot harsher for 'Les Girls', whose major way of making ends meet entailed giving blow jobs in the aptly named Meatpacking District, or 'Meat Market'. The residual whiff of rotting beef must have given some male clients indelible olfactory memories for the rest of their days.

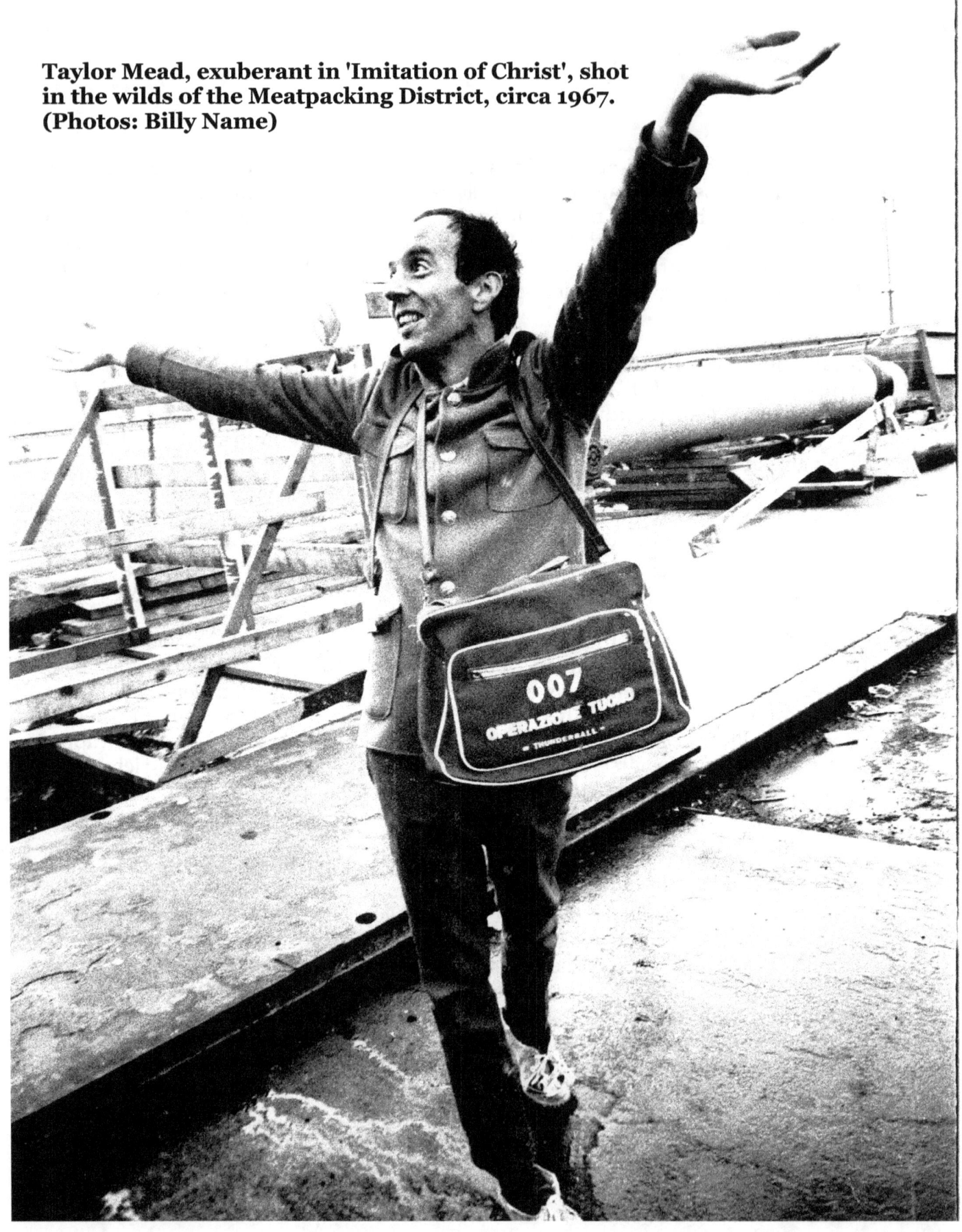

Taylor Mead, exuberant in 'Imitation of Christ', shot in the wilds of the Meatpacking District, circa 1967. (Photos: Billy Name)

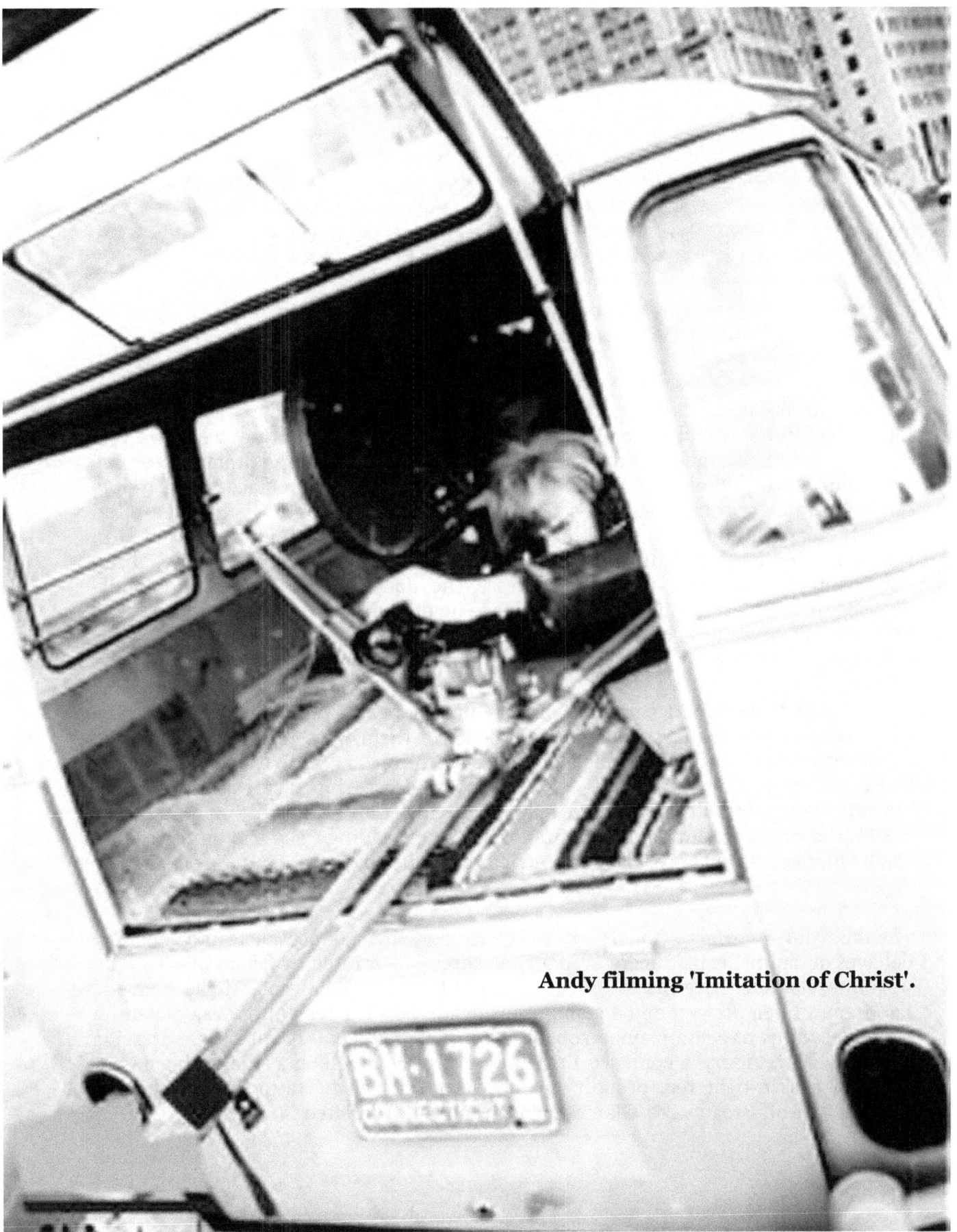

Andy filming 'Imitation of Christ'.

BN·1726

ALL THE LOVELY LADIES

I was born beautiful, and I will die beautiful!
—Jackie Curtis (1947-1985)

As *une habituée* of Max's back in the day, I was thrilled to befriend extravagent Holly (Harold Ajzenberg) and sweet Candy (James Slattery). To me they were the real Superstars, because they had to work so hard at being women. As drama queen Ivy Nicholson readily admitted: "When I left, Andy said he had to replace me with drag queens." True, Warhol felt much safer with them—Mario Montez had been around since the early filming days—and they were often the only company one wanted to spend time with at four in the morning. In 2004, Craig Heilberger made a delightful documentary, 'Superstar in a Housedress, The Jackie Curtis Story'. He kindly licensed us some of the divine archive footage he dug up. 'Leee' Black Childers, who roomed with virtually all of them, also shared his revealing photographs. . .

Leee Black Childers: I started taking pictures here in the Village, mostly of the drag queens and the outrageous people. Some of them were just—well, you could never call Jackie Curtis a drag queen, because she never looked like a woman. There is a knock on my door and there's Jackie in ripped dress, ripped stockings, worn out old lady shoes, and a little cardboard suitcase, saying "Can I live with you for a day or two?" She was there a month. The first of her fake weddings, she had on the roof of some building around here, and she married the maitre d' from Max's Kansas City.

The multi-talented Jackie Curtis, *née* Curtis Holder, sings, dances, acts and generally behaves outlandishly in 'Superstar in a Housedress'. Narrated by friend Lily Tomlin, with interviews by Leee Black Childers, Harvey Fierstein, columnist Michael Musto, La Mama's Ellen Stewart and a glamourous candy box assortment of drag queens, a portrait evolves of a complex personality who switched genders with ease, dressing coquettishly to 'marry' a confused Eric Emerson, or channelling a smoldering James Dean in a skin-tight tee, proudly flexing the crude 'Andy' tattoo on his biceps. Jackie's way-off Broadway's 'Glamour, Glory and Gold' debuted in 1967. . .

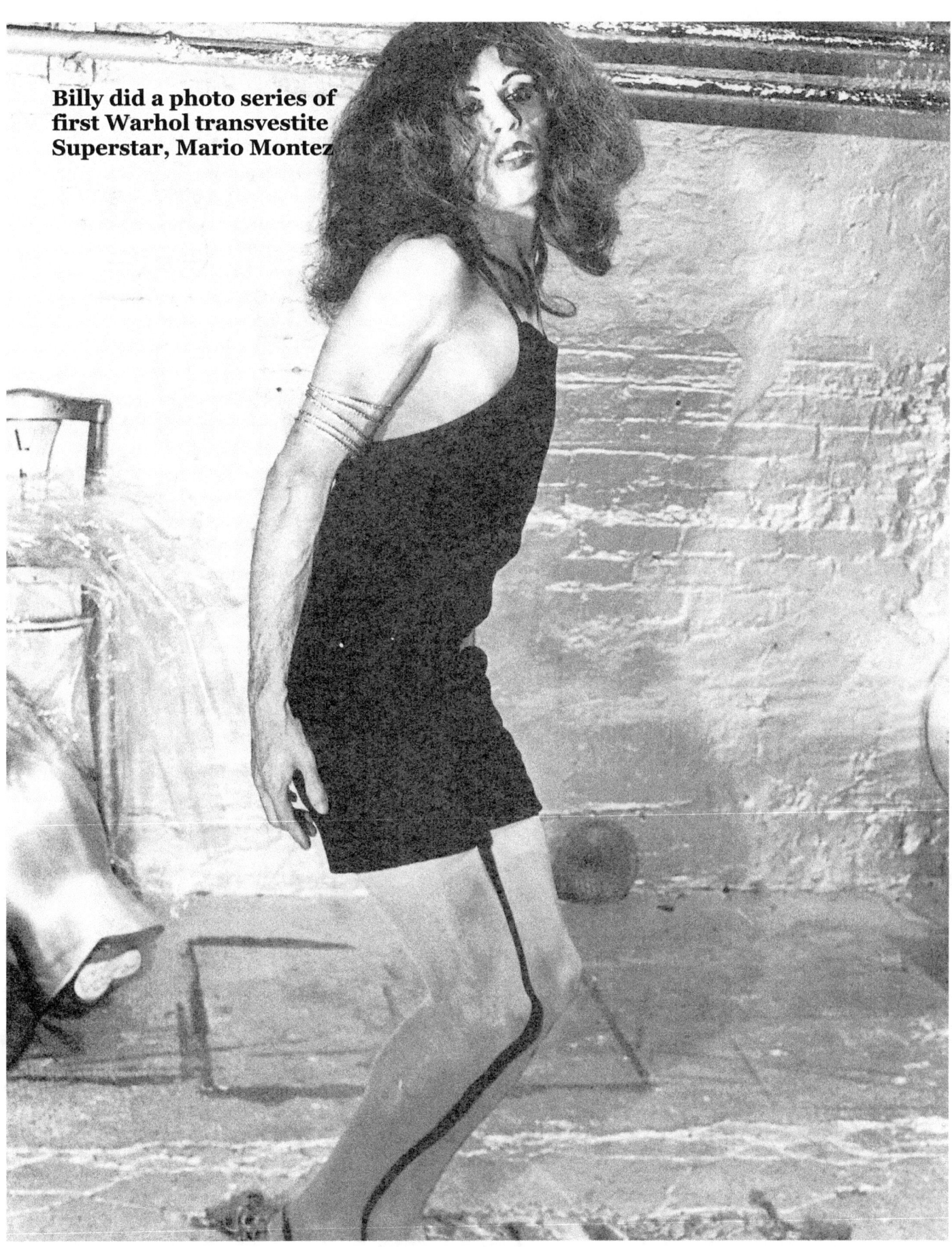

Billy did a photo series of first Warhol transvestite Superstar, Mario Montez

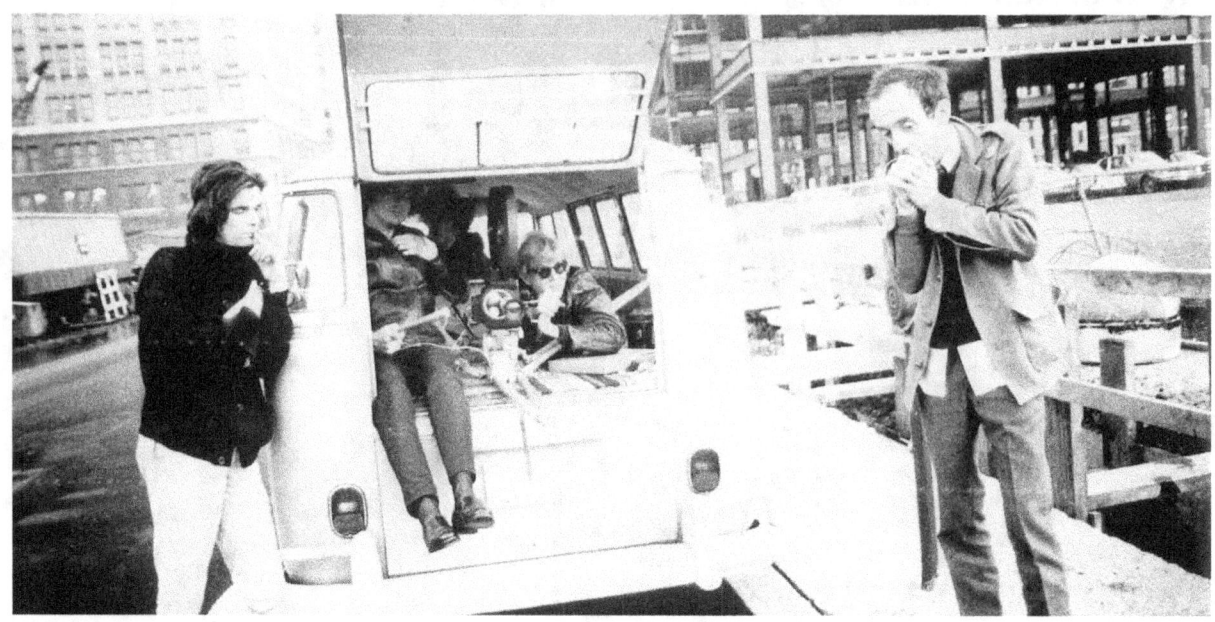

**Wrapping up 'Imitation of Christ', Paul, Andy and star Taylor Mead try to keep warm.
(Photo: Billy Name)**

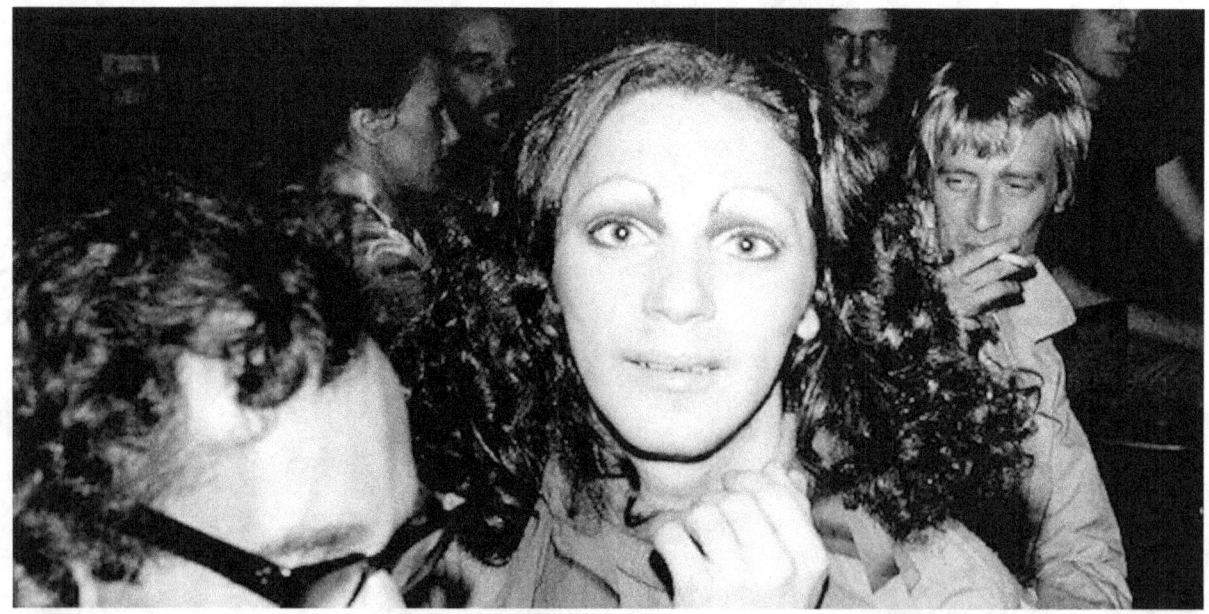

**'Imitation of a girl': From Meatpacking District to Max's. The glorious Holly Woodlawn.
(Photo: Leee Black Childer)**

. . .'Glamour, Glory and Gold' featured a first-time Robert De Niro. Twenty years later, when I was trying to sell him the house on Mulholland Drive, for peanuts, I mentioned that I had been in the audience. He didn't buy it (the house). Too bad, Bobby—it resold for five million. . . 'Vain Victory' was an 'homage' to Hollywood and its Betty Davis movies, especially the frightful delightful later ones, cult films in themselves. An early classic, a tear-jerker called 'Dark Victory', met up with 'Who's Afraid of Baby Jane' in the fertile mind of Jackie Curtis. . .

Paul Ambrose (*as Joan Crawford*)
You wouldn't be talking to me like this if I weren't in a wheelchair.

Douglas Fisher (*as Betty Davis*)
But ya'are, Blanche, ya'are.

Jackie Curtis also wrote the entrancing song for this segment our film, which went: "Who are yooooou, where did you come from?. . ." Though originally crooned to Candy, I don't think Jackie would mind that we paired the song with footage of best friend Holly Woodlawn. In 'Broken Goddess', she swans by Bethesda Fountain in Central Park, draped in Grecian goddess evening gown. She did have a lovely figure.

Holly Woodlawn: I was a mess! I was in jail for thirty days, so Larrry* took us to Bloomingdales and said, "Girls, go shopping" And we did. I bought faaaabulous dresses, and Jackie bought a faaaabulous—housedress. What does she do? She *rips* the shit out of it! I said, "Jackie what are you doing?" She said, "It's a *look* isn't it?"

Holly Woodlawn (*'Women in Revolt'*)
They're gonna think we're lesbians!

Jackie Curtis
No, they're not gonna think we're lesbians, Holly. A schoolteacher and a model? Those are lesbians?

---

*The "Larry" that Holly Woodlawn mentions is the late artist Larry Rivers, a beloved maverick with a mile-a-minute mouth who could be counted on to get a girl out of trouble, especially if she was a transvestite. Their families didn't want to know. The incident Holly refers to happened in the early 'White Factory' period. . . >

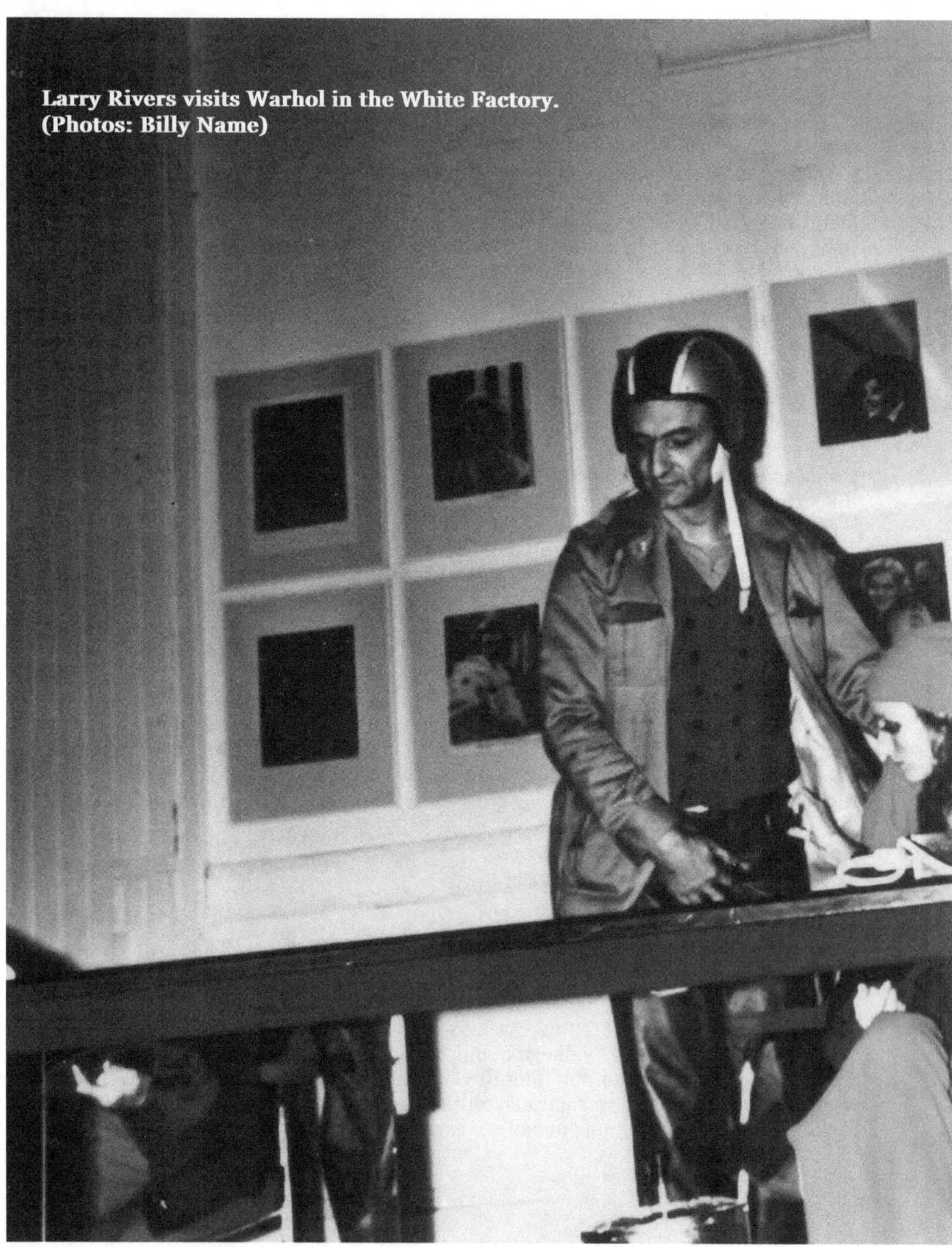

Larry Rivers visits Warhol in the White Factory.
(Photos: Billy Name)

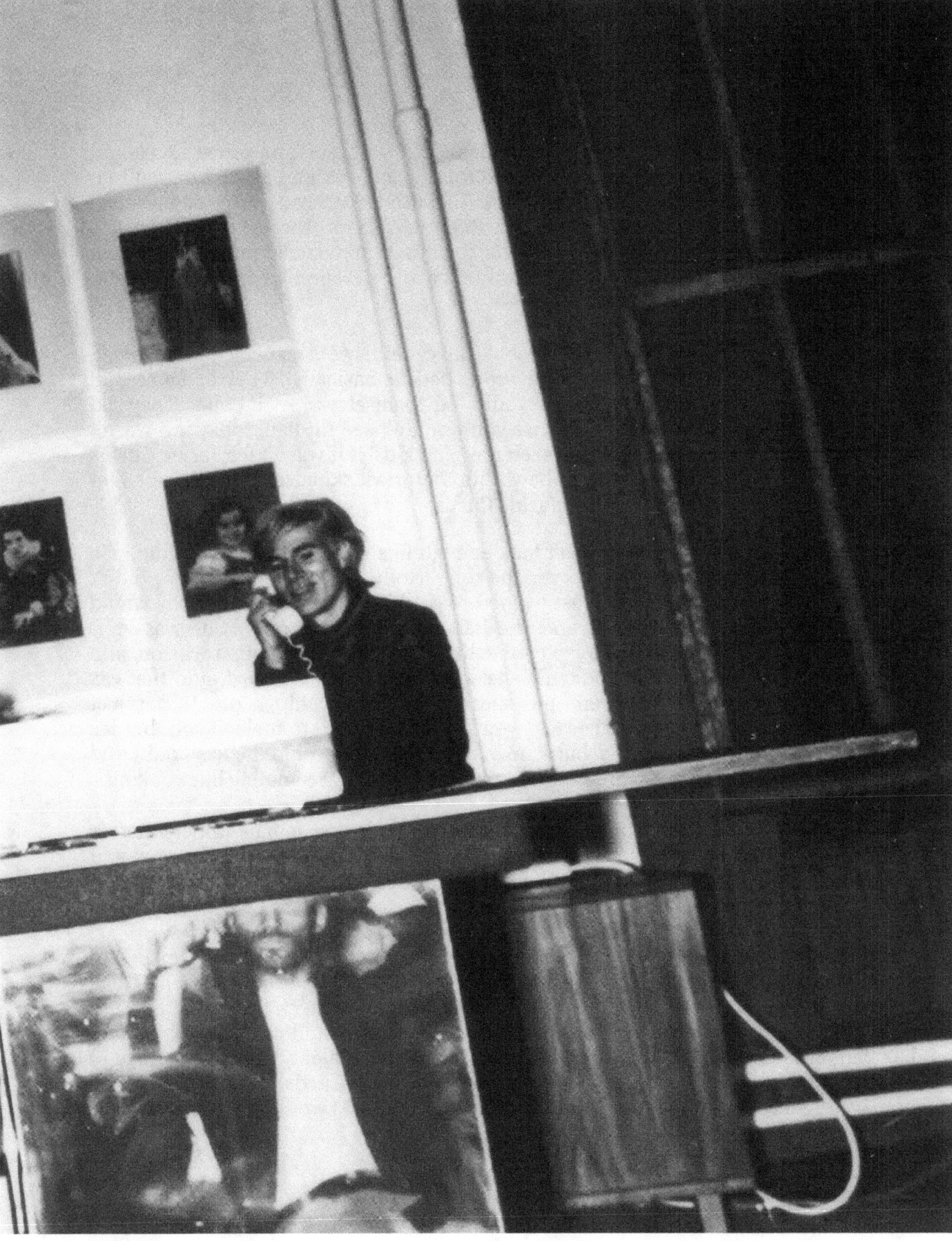

. . . When 'Trash' opened in 1972, Holly got herself into a bit of jam, something about posing as the French Ambassador's wife and forging a check and getting tossed into jail. The headline in Variety read 'Trash Star Found in Trashcan'. . . Holly, Candy, and Jackie would be immortalized in Lou Reed's 'Walk on the Wild Side' (1972), which touched on previously taboo subjects such as transsexuals, hustlers, oral sex and, of course, drugs. For the queasy U.S. market, all references to oral sex were cut.

Nat Finkelstein: These transsexual people in general were usually pretty sweet, pretty fucked up. They were cast in the wrong bodies, basically. They had a certain form of bravery in what they were; they allowed themselves to step out. They did have an ongoing affect on society because you wouldn't see Ru Paul today if it wasn't for Jackie Curtis, nor would you have seen the 'club kids' if it wasn't for Jackie Curtis. These are people who are satisfied to be within their own skins, and they can be that way only because of forerunners like Jackie Curtis.

Leee Black Childers: Women didn't look enough like women, in Andy's mind. He wanted men who were *completely* over the top! Holly Woodlawn said, "We didn't think we looked like women. We just wanted to get high and get laid." Holly would use Zip wax on her facial beard, and she had quite a strong one. She was half-Spanish and half-Jewish, so she wasn't some little wisp. She'd glob that wax on, and of course, she'd be stoned, so suddenly she'd be listening to a record, and the wax had completely hardened by then, and she was having to chip it off. It was just everywhere, mostly on the stove because you had to heat it up to make it soft, but it's impossible to remove once it's hardened. The kitchen would be covered. And nothing *ever* got cleaned. Fortunately, we never did anything remotely like cooking.

Paul Morrissey (directed 'Women in Revolt'): These pioneer female impersonators were so gifted and so funny, and had such a hard time making very little money, if they made any at all. They led very difficult lives.

The drag queens would also call Paul Morrissey if they got into trouble. According to Allen Midgette, who had spent an eventful night at Morrissey's apartment, "The narcotics police came to the door at five in the morning to check for drugs, because Paul had been bailing the drag queens out of jail." They would call Warhol in vain, but Paul always came through. He was right about their talent. Archive footage of Candy Darling, in a theatrical piece written by Jackie Curtis, is an off-the-wall homage to 'The Honeymooners'. The other Jackie (Gleason) would have just loved it.

Candy Darling *(as Alice, long-suffering wife of Jackie Gleason's Ralph Kramden)*
This is Disneyland, Ralph. See those dishes in the sink over there? Fantasyland. See this furniture, Ralph? Frontierland. And your friend Norton upstairs? Fairyland.

Geraldine Smith: I *lived* with Candy! We all went out to this restaurant in the Village and it was about four or five o'clock in the morning. When the check came nobody had any money. Holly said, "Wait a minute, I'll be right back." And she went down the street and she did a couple of blow jobs or something, and came back with like fifty dollars. That's how we paid the bill.

Leee Black Childers: In those days in New York, nobody had any money. But money was not really expected of you. Our rent for a one-bedroom apartment between 1st and Avenue A was seventy dollars a month, and in it lived me, Jackie Curtis, Holly Woodlawn, occasionally Candy Darling, Rita Red, Rio Grand, all in a one bedroom apartment. It's not like we interfered with each other's sleeping arrangements, since no one slept. Everyone was just on speed all the time. Jackie would get up and you'd see her putting the speed in the coffee and she'd say *(mimicking),* "I don't really take drugs. I just put a little something in my coffee in the morning—just to get me going!" Of course, morning was usually the afternoon.

The professional life of a "glam tranny" was anything but glamorous. She worked the Meat Market, which happened to be the real thing, a smelly, spooky, scary area that by day bustled with trucks, butchers, dead pigs and cows. By night, the flesh for sale transformed into a vivid assortment of trawling transvestites working out of trailers. We came for excitement and the after-hour clubs, getting a taste of the danger that for these 'girls' was all too real. Today it's one of the hippest, noisiest, most expensive neighborhoods in New York, but sometimes I can still hear their ghostly stilettos clicking across those cobblestones. . . Geraldine Smith, who acted in Warhol films with Holly, ('Flesh', 'Trash'), hung out with them as a street kid, and found lifetime friendships. Geraldine was, and still is, a Garboesque sort of beauty, but even she sometimes got jealous of her spectacular-looking roommate, the glamorous Candy Darling. who on a good night could remind one of '60s screen siren Kim Novak.

Geraldine Smith: I dyed her hair, but I put Nair hair remover in the bottle instead of dye, and a lot of her hair came out and she was freaking out. I thought, "Well I realy got her this time." I don't know if was on purpose, but that's how I got back at her.

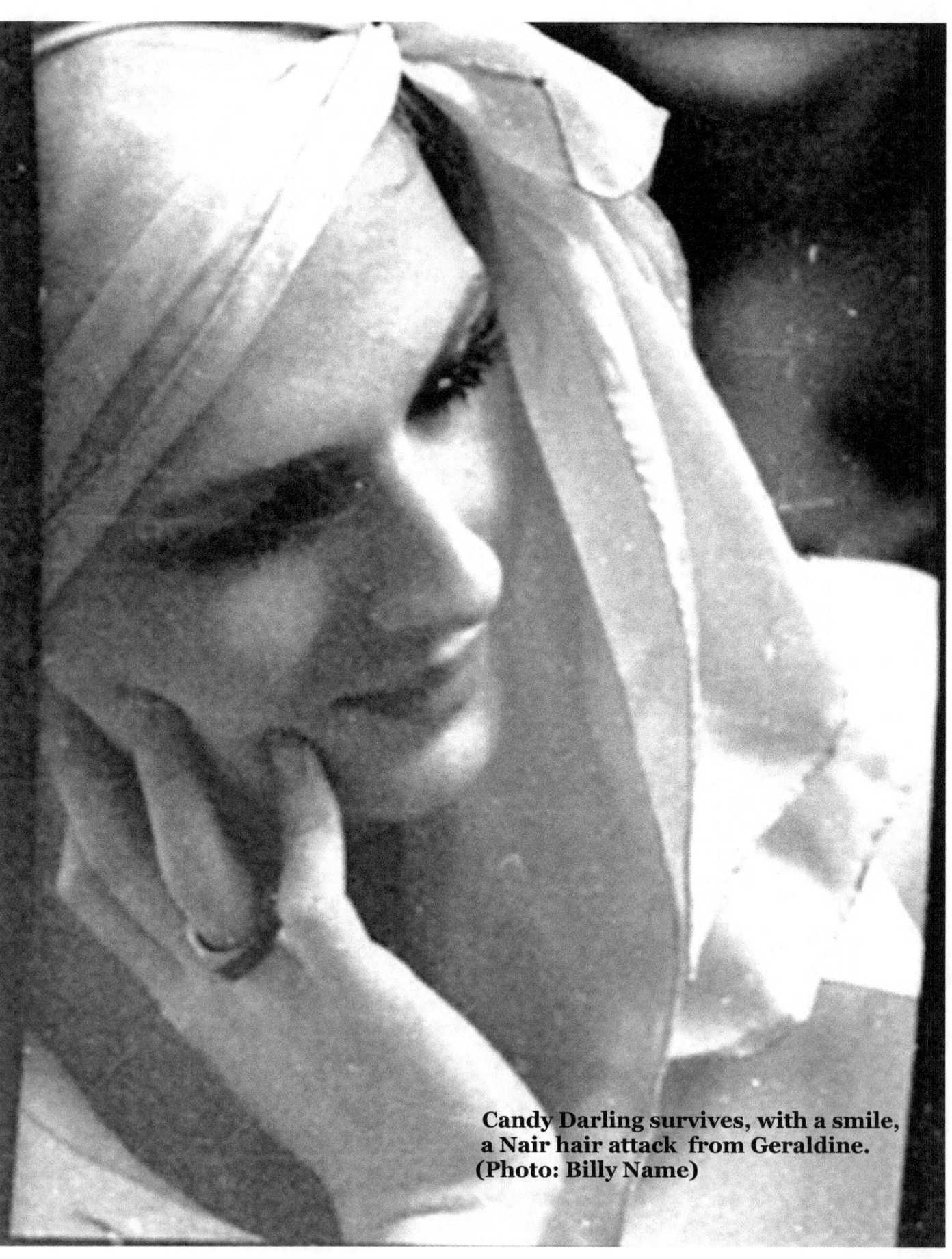

Candy Darling survives, with a smile,
a Nair hair attack from Geraldine.
(Photo: Billy Name)

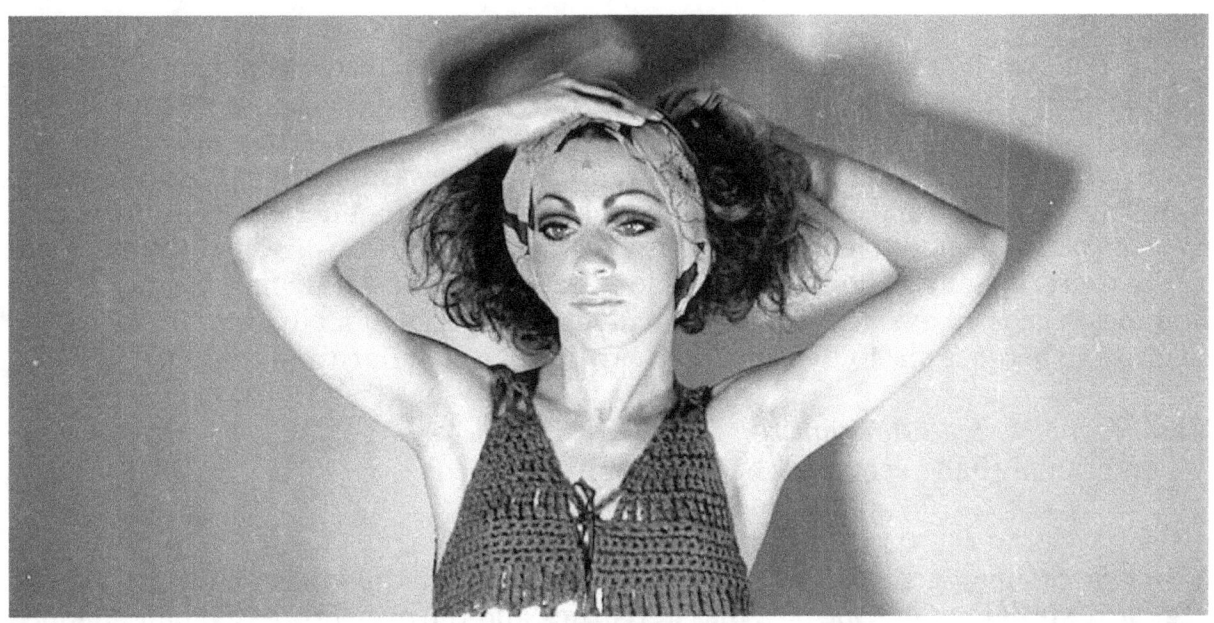

Don't forget the armpits. Holly proudly shows off the results of her Zip waxing to roomate Leee Black Childers, her photographer friend.

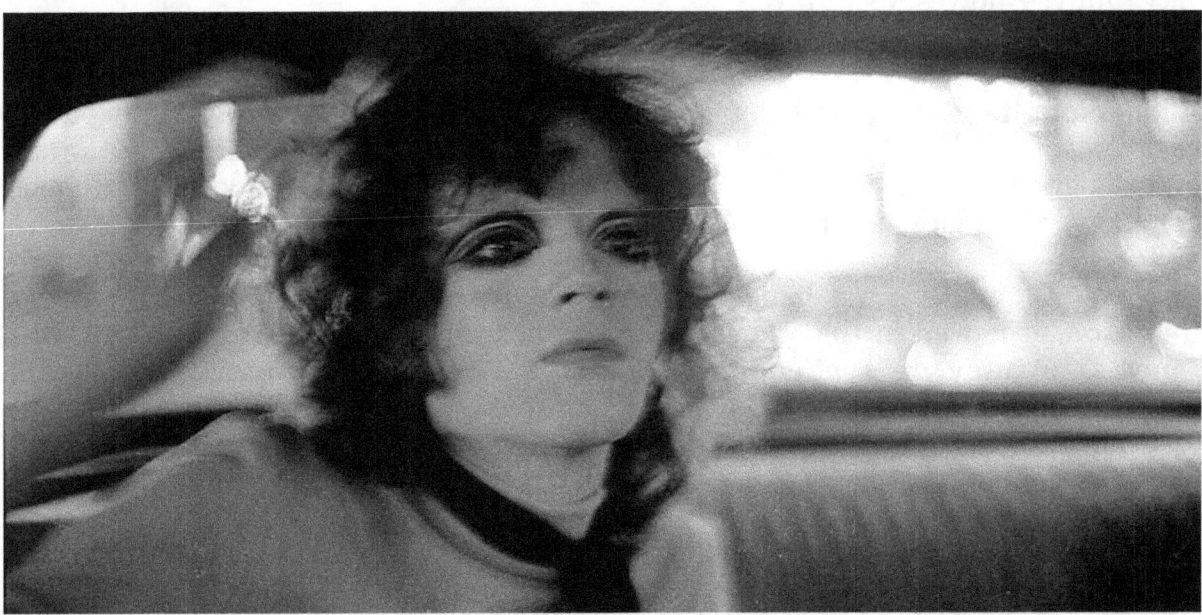

Taxi tranny: The 'Glam, Glorious, and Golden' life of Jackie Curtis, actor, singer playwright and Warhol Superstar, documented by the late Leee Black Childers.

Louis Waldon: Candy Darling looked like a slut. She looked like a whore. She did her make-up and everything, and she didn't have one good tooth in her mouth. They were all rotten. She'd smile and she would look like this real street kid. Then, she got together with Andy and it worked out, because she was quite good. . . But at that time I also knew Viva, then called Susan Hoffman. I had met her before. She wanted to be an actress, and I told her what classes I was taking. She was very attractive, but really weird-looking. She sat that whole time talking and scratching her head. She had these scabs all over her head. She had just gotten out of an institution. She'll get mad at me because she told me never to say this. I said it once and that's it.

Viva *(from 'Nude Restaurant')*
When I ran my hand across my head, it felt like burned grass.

Viva's modelling agency didn't think much of her wild kinky hair, and insisted she regularly straighten it. One day, disaster struck and the over-processed hair snapped off, leaving only stubble. Viva quite naturally freaked out. Erstwhile boyfriend, the mellow Louis Waldon, told us he had really loved Viva, but eventually knew "they could never make it together." In 'Nude Restaurant', Warhol just lets her run on about herself and her dysfunctional family. The whole film is very revealing, and very funny. And yes, very brave.

Allen Midgette: I told Viva to let her hair frizz out, because she'd say, "Oh, I gotta go to the beauty parlor and get my hair straightened." And I said, "What for? Your hair is really great that way, you should go with that." The next thing I know her hair is out all over the place, natural. And she's looking very good.

Louis Waldon: Viva was hanging out with artists, too. She was a painter at that time, so she moved in the scene. Then she got invited up to do this movie with Andy. Right away, we went and did 'Lonesome Cowboys'. Flew out to Arizona and stayed in a camp where city slickers go, a dude ranch. The University of Arizona had just inherited it, in mint condition. . . Navaho rugs on the floor, little drawings on the walls. We took everything. When we left, everybody dumped their clothes and took the rugs in the bags. Well, we were pursued from the first day. On the set, the first thing I said to Viva was, "What the fuck are you doing here? You know women aren't allowed in this town!" It was old Tucson, John Wayne's town. They had tours coming through. When the tours heard us New Yorkers saying all this shit, they immediately got us kicked out. We had shot the entrance and a couple of scenes, then it started raining. It was horrible. We shot the rest at the dude ranch. The sheriff >

would come on the hill and spy on us with field glasses to see if we were raping women. But that's what the scene was! I was supposed to screw Viva. In the movie, nobody screwed her. Everybody got up and left. We'd be in a romantic scene and she's seducing me, "Come on, come on," and I'd say, "Excuse me, I have to go feed the chickens."

Taylor Mead: After 'Lonesome Cowboys', we got to Phoenix airport, Andy and Viva and I, and they would not serve Viva at the bar at the airport. She was like thirty years old or so, and she started raging and raving and all Andy would say was "Oh Viva, oh Viva." But Andy loved it when Viva went crazy and he wished he would have been filming it.

Actually, it seemed Viva's behaviour was beginning to worry Warhol, even though the outspoken and unconventional beauty was still his 'adored sidekick'. She'd been considering him marriage material—Yikes! Another Ivy Nicholson—and actually proposed, but Warhol had turned her down. Soon, she would be going through the same hurtful experience Edie Sedgwick had, without the drugs to fall back on. Louis Waldon remembered Warhol begging him to "Please do something about Viva. I just can't take it anymore!"

Louis Waldon: Nobody wanted to screw her. Andy wanted this so bad—but nobody would touch her. Though we did knock her off her horse and throw her on the ground.

Viva (*to writer Barbara Goldsmith, in 1968*): Andy has a certain mystique that makes you want to do things for him. He's completely mastered the art of being egoless. But I love it when they talk about 'Viva and Andy'.

Victor Bockris: One day Andy went to the Factory and it's raining heavily and Viva is outside hammering on the door. "Why does so and so have a key and I don't? It's because I am a woman, and you're all faggots!" No one in the Factory ever said anything like that to Andy. It's like spitting in the face of Louis the Fourteenth. You're dead! Viva was probably the most intelligent, the most self-aware of those people, but when she threw her handbag at him and hit him, Andy was very, very upset. I once tried to take his arm and drag him to a limousine—in fun one night— and he got really angry with me, so I know whereof I speak. So when Viva did that, it changed his attitude toward her. And he never felt the same about her again.

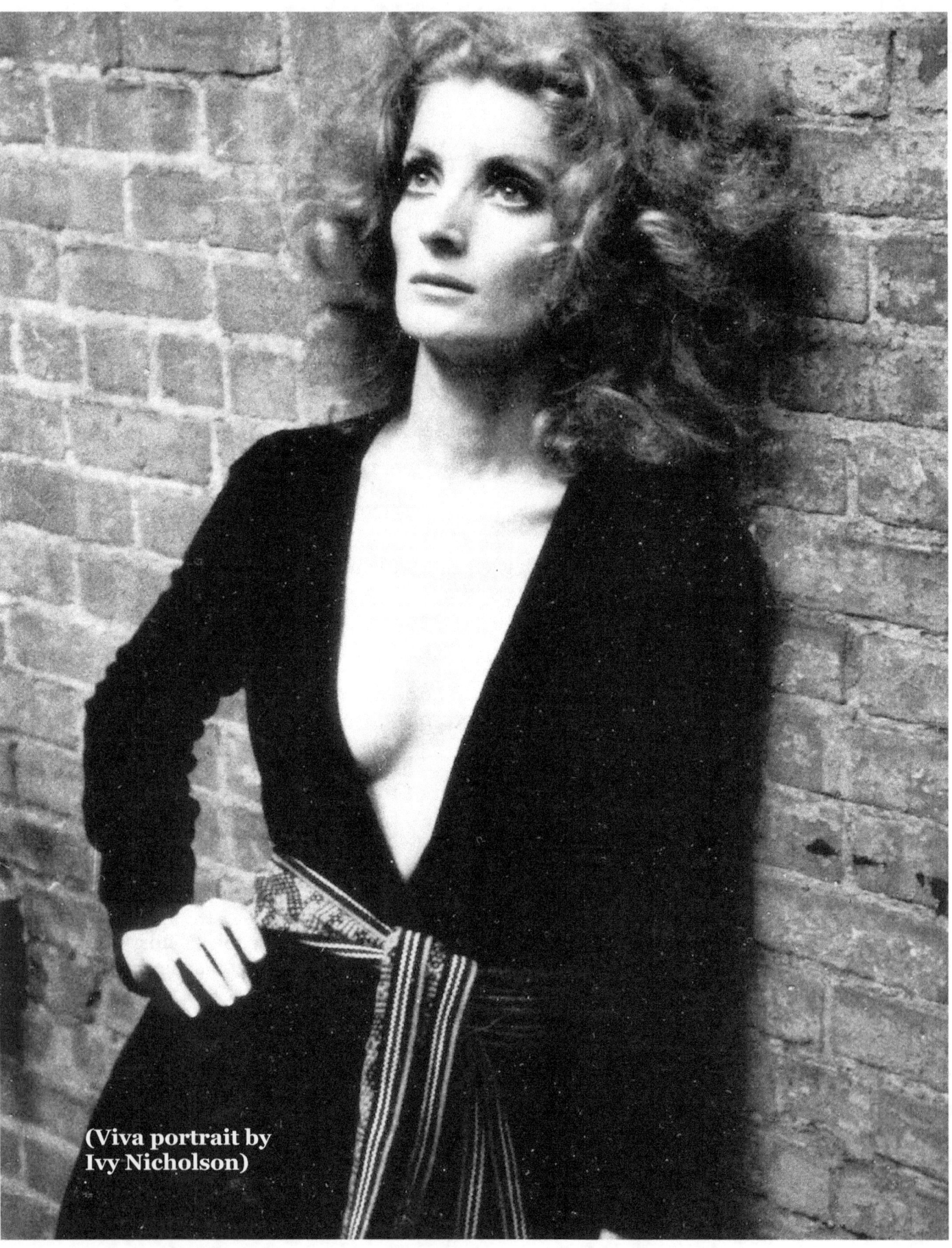

(Viva portrait by
Ivy Nicholson)

Viva's sudden violence seemed a natural segue into the archival 'News Break' we'd made an essential part of each segment, to give a sense of what was going on outside those Factory walls: Real violence, and the reality of Vietnam. According to our somber News Announcer from 1967: "Wanting peace, Americans are still poised for war." So much for the unbiased dispatches of the day. Was Fox News around then? All the Americans I knew of were not remotely "poised for war," but rather for protesting it, and for following that mantra to "Make Love Not War," . . . because 1967 also marked the year of the happy 'Human Be-In'. The Summer of Love embraced San Francisco, but not to be outdone, we in New York threw our own version of the 'Be-In' in Central Park, which was surprisingly mellow, since many of the local losers and stoned sleaze bags had trundled off to the West Coast looking for better pickings. We all dropped acid and danced merrily with a bi-coastal Allen Ginsberg. Edie Sedgwick was still floating around, falling apart, filming in the park her last effort, that abysmal, amateurish but strangely riveting 'Ciao! Manhattan!'. . .

Edie Sedgwick: Warhol really fucked up a great many young people's lives. I was a good target. I bloomed into a healthy young drug addict.

Viva: Sometimes when I think about Andy, I think he's Satan. He just gets you and you can't get away. I used to go everywhere, by myself. Now I can't seem to go anywhere or make the simplest decision without Andy. He has such a hold on us all.

Viva also mentioned when interviewed by Victor Bockris that she had been ready to leave Warhol. "I always come in at the end of things, and put the kibosh on it." So what put the kibosh on our 'Summer of Love', our jingling tambourines and tinkling bells? We sensed it, the creepy discordant undertone—time to stop doing 'La Dolce Vita' in Bethesda Fountain. Others would not be so lucky, becoming prey for the burgeoning horde of hardcore drug hustlers. Malaise set in, even with the Vietnam War (drugs anyone?), while riots surged with the killing of Martin Luther King. . . Nat Finkelstein, quite a bit older than us, seemed to have another handle on it.

Nat Finkelstein: At the time, I was documenting the changes going on in America, working with SNIC (Student Nonviolent Coordiating Committee) in Mississippi, with Civil Rights. I was covering the anti-war demonstrations in Washington. . . And I was also working with Warhol. You could see the social changes going on, especially when I went on the road with him. I was documenting American society.

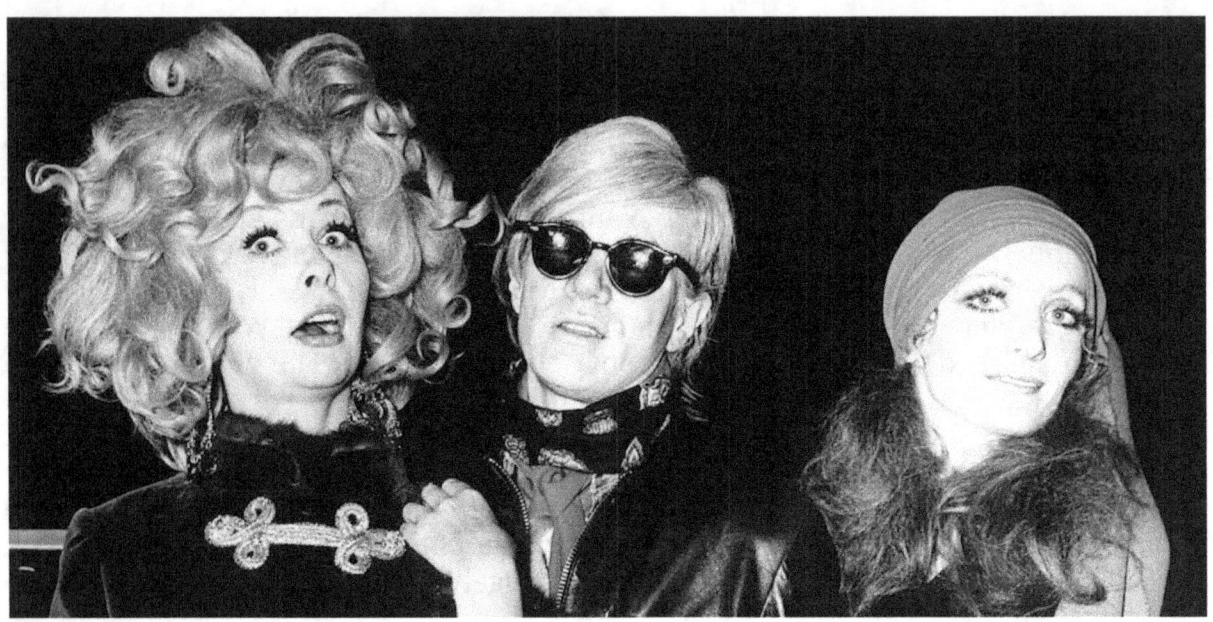

All dressed up and ready for the 'Summer of Love'. Ultra, Andy, and Viva, all with hair issues. (Photo: Corbis)

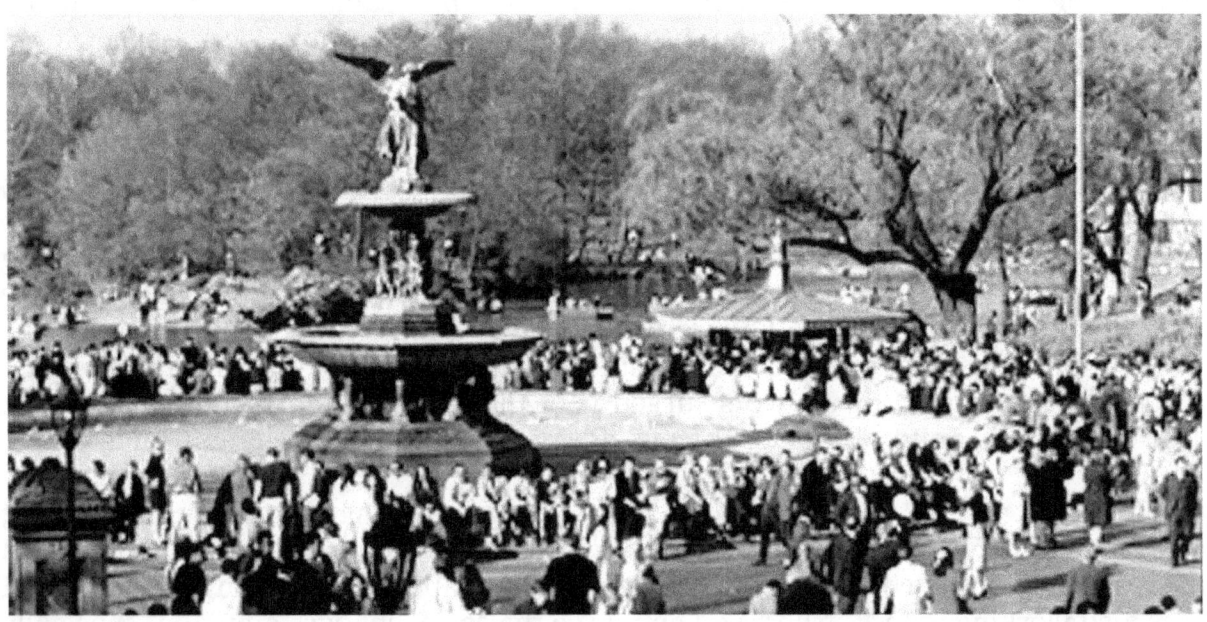

The Central Park 'Be-In', Bethesda Fountain, 1967. Edie Sedgwick might be seen dancing in the background. (Photo: Billy Name)

Sifting through all the depressing archival footage of unnecessary wars, financial plunder and ruin, we found only *déjà vu*. . . But what the hell, we'd paid for it, so we paired those ferocious city riots with the events in Union Square, just after Warhol was shot. The chaos was caught by cameramen as Warhol was carried out and rushed to Columbus Hospital. The suspense and tension is still palpable in those vivid images. Warhol was declared officially dead for one and a half minutes. The June 4, 1968 news headline read: 'Pop Artist Andy Warhol Gunned Down In His Studio'. On hearing the news, his friend Henry Geldzahler, then Assistant Curator of the Metropolitan Museum of Art, was quoted as saying, "Do you know what that does to the value of the paintings?" He quickly chastised himself. Though they'd had their differences over the years, according to Victor Bockris, Geldzahler knew the real Warhol, and loved him,

---

Henry Geldzahler: He was very much a night creature, and literally afraid to go to sleep at night. Night is fearsome. If you fall asleep at night, you're not quite sure of waking up again. f you fall asleep in the daylight, it's kind of a comfort, knowing the sun is out there. . . It's very primitive, kind of an inverted sun worship, because Andy actually detested real sunlight.

Geldzahler also told biographer Bockris that Warhol preferred taking daily naps at home or on his desk at the Factory to avoid going to bed at night, but his longtime habit could not have protected him from that painful fate waiting for him in plain sight, in broad daylight. . .

WEATHER
Tonight:
Clear, 55-60.

Tomorrow:
Mostly sunny,
80-85.
SUNSET: 8:22 PM
SUNRISE
TOMORROW: 5:26 AM

New York Post

© 1968 New York Post Corporation

Vol. 167
No. 169

NEW YORK, TUESDAY, JUNE 4, 1968

10 Cents
15c Beyond 50-mile Zone

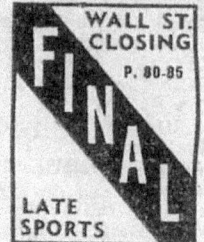

WALL ST. CLOSING
P. 80-85
FINAL
LATE SPORTS

ANDY WARHOL FIGHTS FOR LIFE

Voting In Calif.

LOS ANGELES (AP)— California Democrats were making their choice today in the Presidential primary match between Eugene J. McCarthy and Robert F. Kennedy.

This was the big one for both contestants, with the victor virtually certain to emerge as the final challenger to Vice President Humphrey for the Democratic Presidential nomination.

Generally sunny election day skies were forecast across the nation's most populous state and a vast turnout was expected.

State officials predicted a turnout as high as 67 per cent of the registered voters.

The early turnout of voters was spotty, lighter in Los

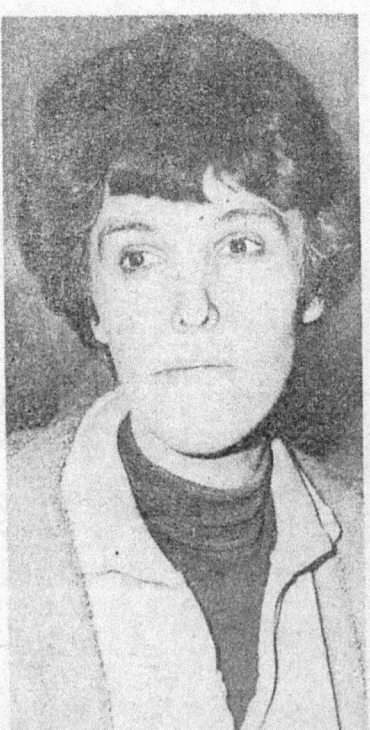

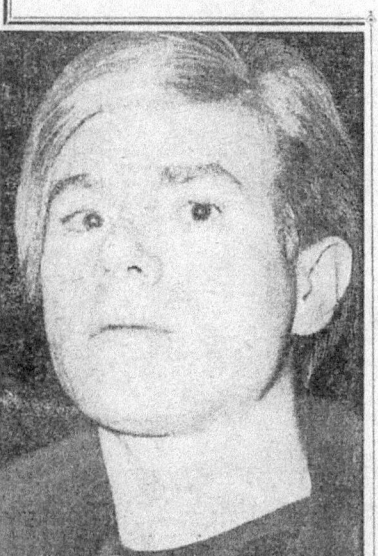

Post Photos by Boxer and Enge

Pop artist film maker Andy Warhol shown right at a recent Long Island party

Marcus' Downfall —The Gov't Story

By MARVIN SMILON and NANCY SEELY

Stock market losses led former Water Commissioner James L. Marcus to raise money by agreeing to "engage in deals" on city contracts, Asst. U. S. Atty. Robert G. Morvillo charged today.

The prosecutor devoted most of the government's opening statement in U. S. District Court to Marcus, 37, who will be the star witness against the four men indicted with him on charges of bribery conspiracy.

Morvillo disclosed for the first time that Marcus, who was getting $30,000 a year, not only was in on the alleged kickback but tried to double-cross his associates by negotiating with another company "for a bigger payoff."

Marcus yesterday changed

I SHOT ANDY WARHOL

I wrote a critique of the movie 'I Shot Andy Warhol'.
I titled my article, 'I would have shot Andy Warhol'.
—Taylor Mead

Taylor Mead was convinced that, "the more destroyed you were, the more likely he was to use you. Andy made promises like crazy, but it was all bullshit." Warhol had been handed a film script by unbalanced 'radical' feminist Valerie Solanas, and it seemed he could never say no, though most submissions wound up in the 'slush pile' or—more likely—lost. So, Warhol offered Valerie a part in his next movie, 'I, A Man'. We licensed footage of Valerie in the film, and found her ingenuous and quite funny, trading gibes with Tom Baker, dressed like a street urchin in a little newsboy cap and pants. We also licensed archive news footage of her arrest and arraignment, and the personality change is profound. What happened?

Billy Name: I was in the dark room when I heard a bang, a strange type of bang. I could not recognise the noise, but I was developing prints, and I said, "Fred (Hughes) and Paul (Morrissey) are up there. They will take care of it until I can get out." So, as soon as I had my prints in the trays, I went up to the front section. And there was Andy, lying in a pool of blood on the floor. I went over to him, and picked him up in my arms. I was holding him and crying, and he came to and looked at me and said, "Billy, please don't make me laugh, it hurts too much." And I said, "Andy, I am not laughing. I am crying." Then he passed out again.

Billy looked at us with a bleakness that spoke of memory still painful. The photos he had been developing that day were of the last formal gathering of the Factory family as they attended the wedding of Velvet Underground musician John Cale to fashion designer Betsey Johnson at City Hall in April of 1968. John wears a suit designed by Betsey, Nico wears black, Warhol is in his brown leather jacket, carrying his tape recorder, Viva is carrying flowers, and a grinning Lou Reed and Paul Morrissey are in English mod. Everyone looks happy, but two months later, all would change when Warhol was shot.

Taylor Mead: Valerie comes in, just a few days after we came back from 'San Diego Surf'. I loved that movie. Paul Morrissey did a great editing job. We had just come back, and I should have been at the Factory (*pause*). She came in and shot him. Well, Andy did make promises. He'd build up people's egos. He promised me that next year I'd be Number One. Two days later he's shot.

Ivy Nicholson: When Andy got shot, Paul asked if he could do the movies. Which were pretty good, but not as artistic as Andy's. Isn't that a bit distasteful? When someone is dying in the hospital and you go in and say, "Oh, why don't you let me do the movies?" Because that's one of the reasons Andy got shot. You have to make everything clear in business. Like with Valerie. They kept leading her on instead of saying, "Look babe, we are never gonna do your movie, so just go elsewhere."

Nat Finkelstein: Well, you know how Valerie Solanas got there, right?. . . This ex-girlfriend of mine named Ellen Marcus was in the loony bin with Richie Berlin, Brigid's sister, and Valerie. Ellen calls me up one day and says, "My friend Valerie has a script and she was wondering if you would direct a movie for her?" I said, "Okay, I'll take a look at the script." Valerie called me, and you could hear the duck quack kind of tone, you know this is a far out schizophrenic. I said, "What's this all about?" She said, "This is called SCUM, the Society to Cut Up Men. We are going to destroy all of the men in the world, and everybody's going to be either a homosexual or a woman." I said, "Why don't you try Andy?" And she said, "I call up the Factory and people laugh at me." At this point, my job at the Factory was finished, and the back-stabbing had started. I wanted to sting it to Andy, because of what happened with 'The Andy Warhol Index'. We had just finished having it out. I said, "I will call Andy and tell him that you have an interesting script for him." Which is what I did, and that's how Valerie got there. I had no idea she was going to be that loony.

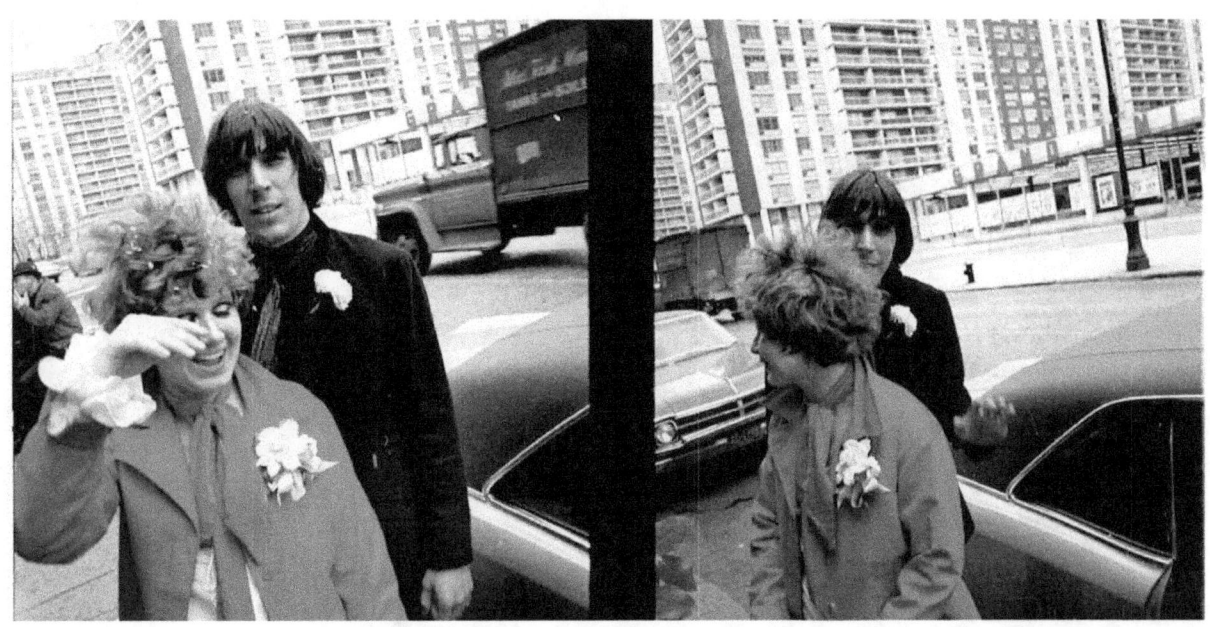

Pop designer Betsey Johnson marries John Cale, April, 1968, at New York's City Hall. By the end of that summer , Cale would leave the Velvet Underground.

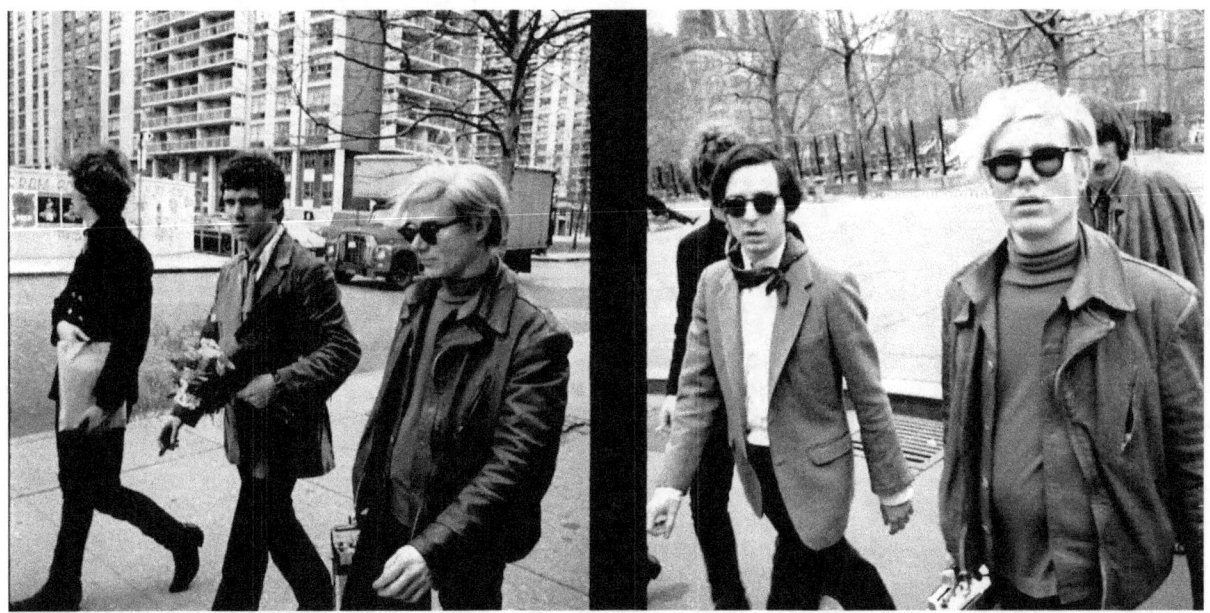

Andy and entourage somberly attend the funeral, whoops, the wedding of the star-crossed lovers. (Photos: Billy Name)

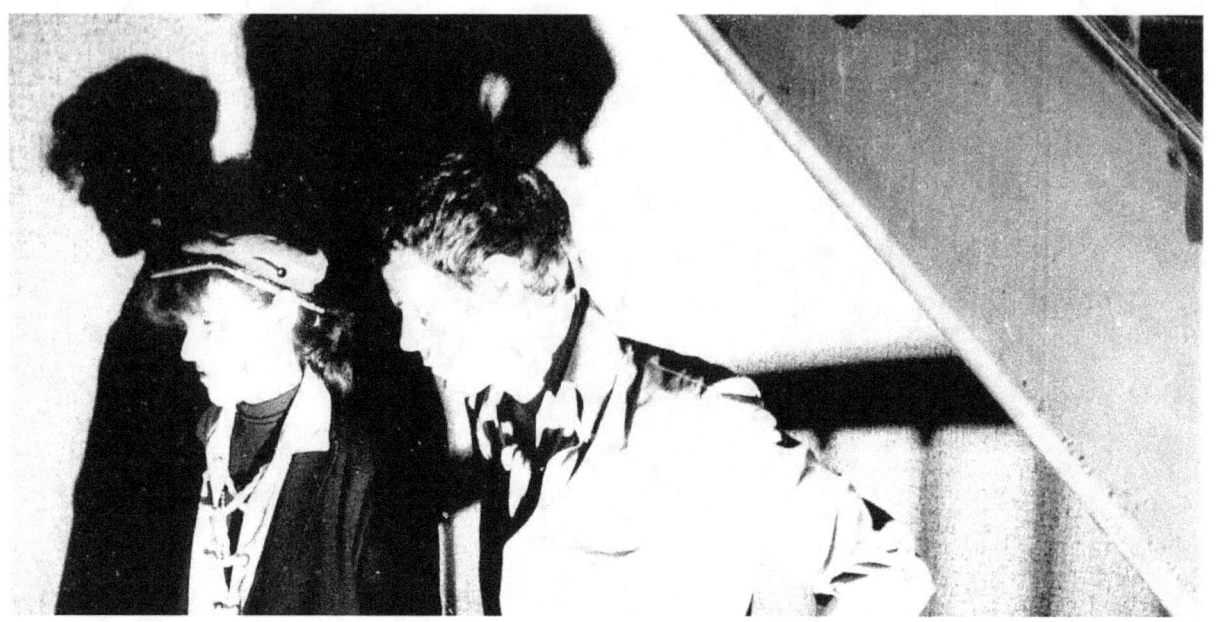

Valerie Solanas and Tom Baker exchange mild pleasantries in 'I A Man'.

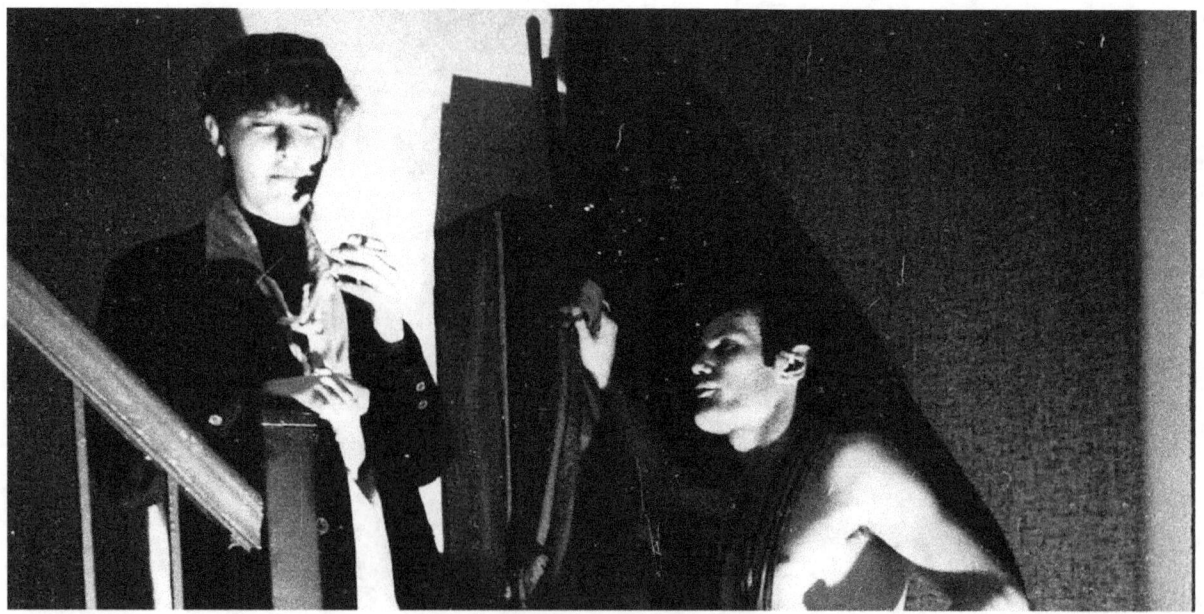

Filming of Valerie's big scene took place in the Factory stairwell. (Photos: Billy Name)

Ultra Violet: Valerie's an interesting character, demented of course. When I first met her on the set of 'I, A Man', I was very intrigued about her philosophy. And SCUM, her 'Society For Cutting Up Men'. . . It's a bit radical I suppose, but she had a point there. She had written that play *(pause),* 'Up Your Ass', and had given a copy to Warhol. Then she wanted it back and Andy could not find it, of course. They finally found it in the trunk of Billy Name, twenty years later.

Billy Name: The bullet went through every organ in his torso except the heart. It went to the lungs, the liver, the stomach, and just ricocheted off the ribs and went around and around.

We licensed newsreel footage of the press interview with the Chief of Surgery at Columbus Hospital, who seemed overwhelmed with the slew of reporters and the huge, hysterical Warhol entourage. It didn't help that he had a very heavy Italian accent.

Chief of Surgery
There is a team upstairs who is operating.

Reporter
How many?

Surgeon
A four-man team.

Reporter
How long will it continue?

Surgeon *(distracted by other reporters)*
Fifty-fifty at this stage.

Andy Warhol
I always wish I had died, and I still wish that, because I could have gotten the whole thing over with. . .

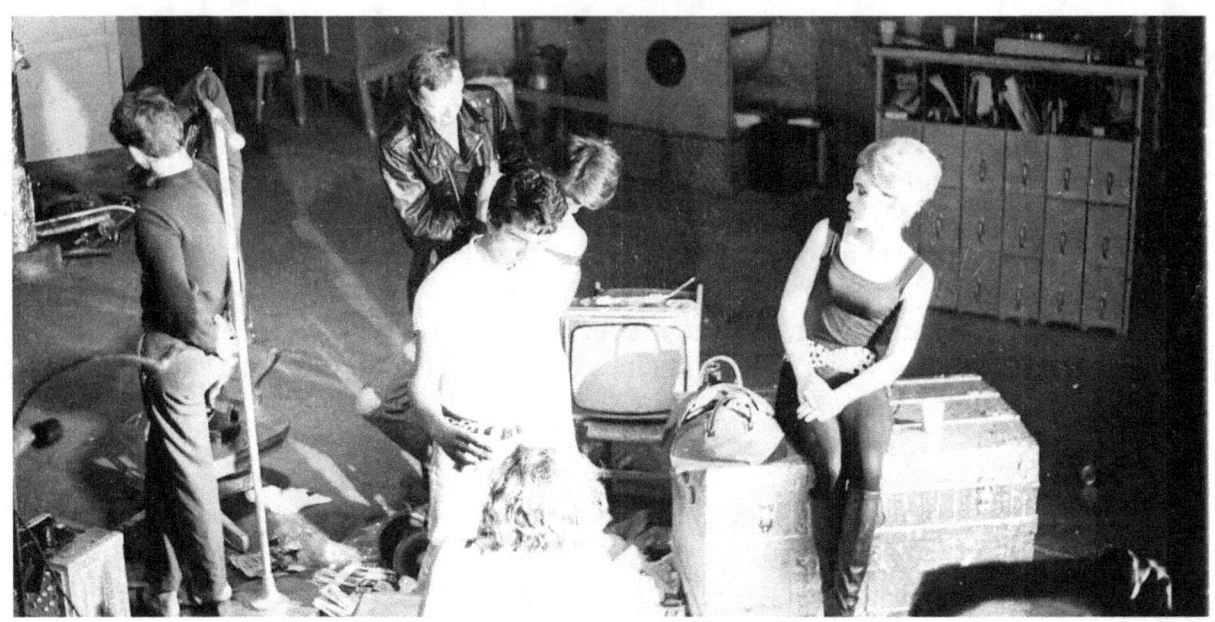

Billy's silver trunk got a starring role under Edie Sedgwick in 'Vinyl', 1965.

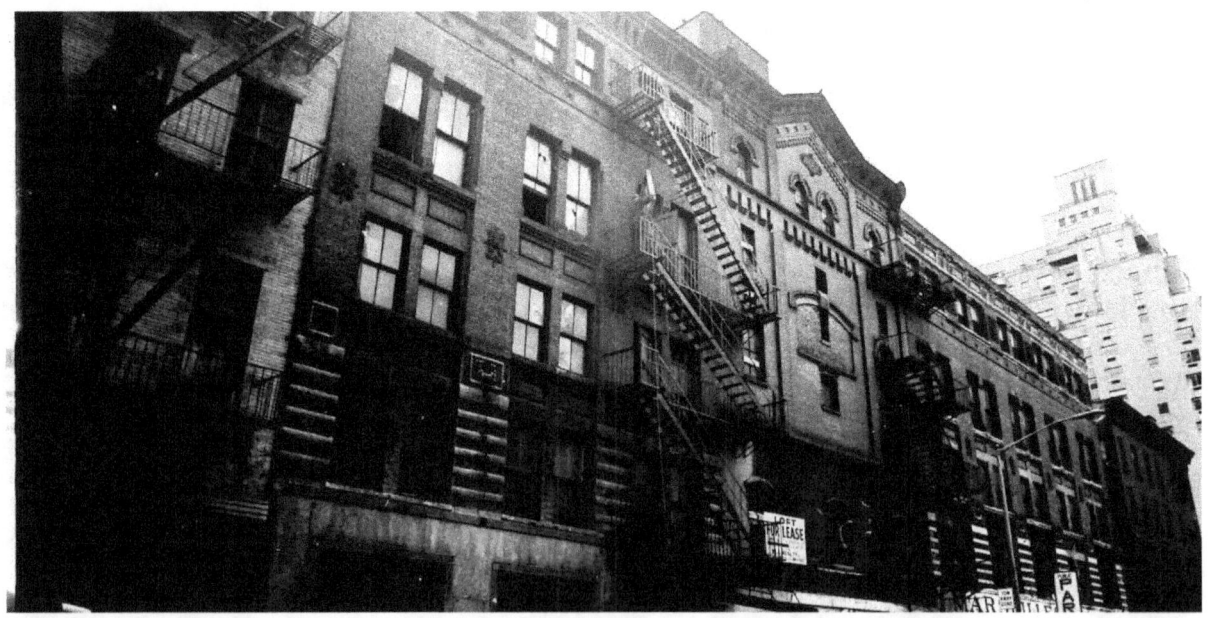

The end of the Silver Factory—1967. The building would become an underground parking lot. (Photos: Billy Name)

Billy Name: The week before he actually died, he still was bleeding from those wounds—he wore a bandage type thing. That's how intensely traumatic it was to his physical being, and how painful it was all those years.

Louis Waldon: His wig was hanging off the side of his head. I wanted to put it back on, because I didn't want anyone to take a photo of Andy without his wig. Everyone was in shock. We all went to the hospital, and we were all sitting around there. . . You should have seen the creeps who came drifting in. There was one who said if Andy didn't die, she was going to finish it. And Ivy was gonna *jump* the moment Andy died, and I was supposed to watch her. I wanted to screw her but. . .

Ivy Nicholson: . . . But Andy would have married me if that bitch— No! 'Bitch' is too kind for her. That thing, that diabolical thing shot him! She could have done something else. She could have told me, and I would have said to Andy, "Hey, give her anything she wants." I would have told him that, because I loved him. I thought she was a bit sickening. I didn't go near her, no, no. And for him to let her get *off*! He let her go. Why? She shot him six times! Oh, I wanted him to live. I did magic. It's not Voodoo; I'm afraid of Voodoo. I was with (son) Sean that day, and I said, "We're going to get dressed up in happy clothing, and we are going to the hospital, and I want you to dance and laugh and be joyous." I knew they would all be in navy blue and black. So I yelled at them, "You're being sad. You are pushing him towards death!" I have been all around the world and I was once posing on a statue that says, in Italian, "*On pensari vole.*" That means: "Each thought flies." This is from the twelfth century. There is power in thought. So we're dancing around, really happy. I think I put his mother in shock. She didn't know I was doing magic. I started yelling, "You know Andy's going to live. We should be rejoicing, because he is going to live." And he did live! Isn't it a miracle? Six shots and he lived? I think my love just went up there, he got the vibes and the thoughts. *On pensari vole!*

Geraldine Smith: When Andy got shot, I was in the hospital, and someone brought me the paper. And there's a picture of Andy and my girlfriend Liz on the cover, and it said 'Actress Shoots Warhol'. I'm thinking maybe *she* shot him. Well, everyone was really upset, it was devastating. Especially for Viva, who was by his bedside a lot, and Paul. Andy and Paul always seemed to get along when I was around. That's when Paul started doing 'Flesh', right after that.

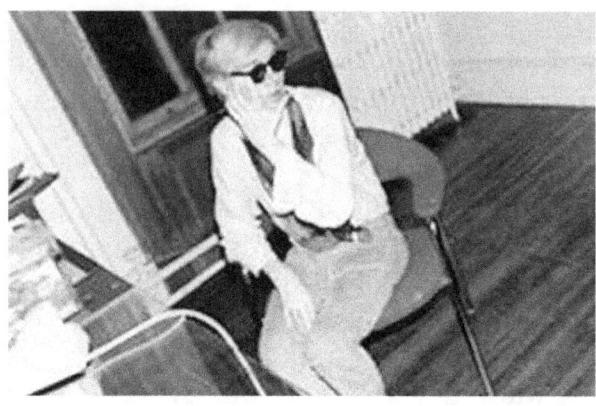

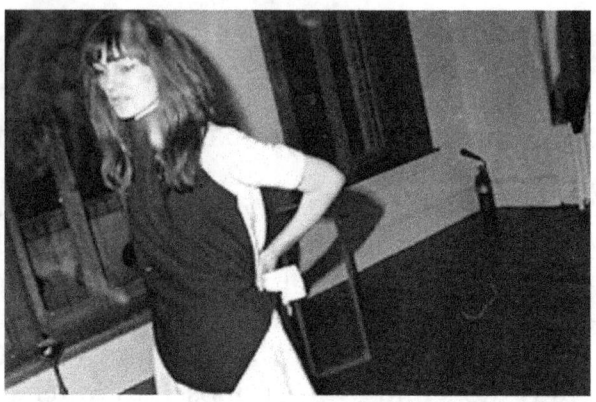

Andy settles into his sterile new White Factory. (Photos: Billy Name)

Ivy works her voodoo on the new White Factory, and Warhol.

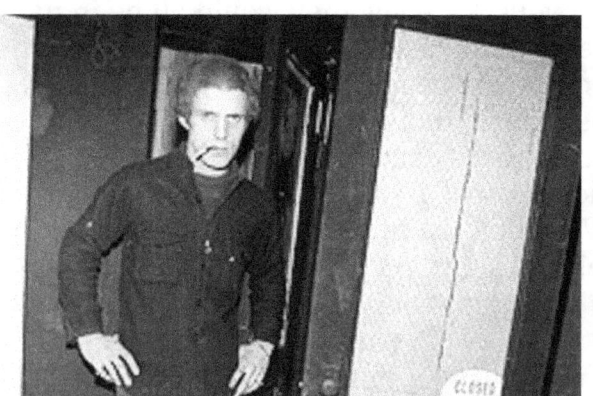

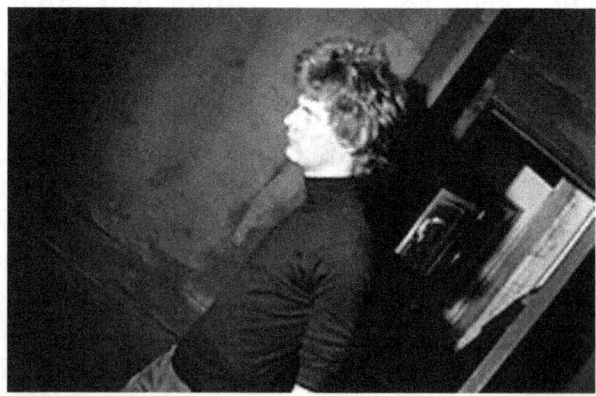

Billy Name in the White Factory, self-portrait

Billy snaps Paul Morrissey as he enters the picture.

Geraldine Smith, star of 'Flesh and 'Trash'', remembered Paul as always being "very attentive to Andy." It would seem a natural progression for his heir apparent to pick up the directing reins, which he'd pretty much already done, if 'Lonesome Cowboys' and the footage we'd seen from 'San Diego Surf' were any indication. Speaking of which, that film was finally "unearthed" and premiered to a select audience at 2011's Art Basel, Miami ('Mardi Gras for rich people'). I don't think any of the old stars were invited. . . As far as Warhol's other art was concerned, his longtime dealers Leo Castelli and Ivan Karp may have shared the same sentiment as Henry Geldzahler, but alas, were almost out of stock thanks to all those movies.

News Interviewer (CBS News, June 4, 1968)
Mr. Castelli, do you feel there will be more years ahead selling Warhol's paintings in your gallery?

Leo Castelli
I'm afraid not, because there are very few left. They're all in the hands of collectors, and he hasn't been producing many lately, except some portraits. He seems to prefer to do filmmaking to painting.

Interviewer
Did either of you gentlemen ever come across the woman said to be his assailant?

Ivan Karp
No, I never saw her personally or knew of her, but there were many people in his circle, in his film world. As I say, he was dealing with curious and eccentric subject matter, and there were strange people moving about his circles. He himself was mostly an observer of this, not so much a participant as a man who watched them and recorded them.

David Croland: When Andy got shot, it changed everything, for Andy and for us. It was traumatic, everyone going insane. No one could have imagined that that would happen to him, in his own studio. No one got over it. Certainly he didn't get over it.

Gerard Malanga: Sooo, it was pretty chaotic. . .

Behind the Flashy Vinyl Facade

By JERRY TALLMER

In his 38 short years, or 39, or 40, or 41, Andy Warhol has succeeded in making Andy Warhol as famous as he is invisible.

Oh, with his shocking silver-sprayed hair and his shock-effect movies and psychedelic acid-rock light shows and his Campbell Soup cans and his crowd of people he has been very visible, on the outside.

It was the carefully guarded inside Andy Warhol that each of his friends had to cling to in separate portions today as Warhol was being treated at Columbus Hospital after being shot in his studio yesterday afternoon by a woman the police say was Valerie Solanas, herself an actress in "I, a Man," one of his films.

He floated above, or through, the wildness around him, with a kind of inner serenity. Yet there was always the possibility,

and sometimes, even before this, the occasion of violence.

"I was stunned when I heard the news but not surprised," said a friend, the writer David Bourdon. "It seems to me he created the environment, the atmosphere, that made situations like this possible. He was very permissive about people, tolerated everything, not only sexual habits but, you know, less popular forms of activity."

Only a few months ago when "The Factory"—Warhol's studio—was located on E. 47th St., an unknown young man entered with a gun, played Russian roulette with it at everyone's head, fired off a few shots, missed, departed.

During the whole incident, according to friends, Warhol was "just very quiet, silent." Partly as a result, The Factory was moved down to its present premises at 33 Union Sq. W.

Then there'd been the time at

the old Factory a few years ago when Andy had had a half-dozen of his paintings of Marilyn Monroe stacked one before the other. Suddenly a girl known to the group as "a part-time junkie" entered "with a revolver that nobody knew was loaded." She aimed it nicely at Marilyn's forehead and blew a hole through the six canvases.

"Andy was kind of upset," says one acquaintance, "but he didn't criticize her, didn't condemn her."

The critics have been variously receptive to Andy Warhol and his various arts. Some have been angered, some have been bored—tantamount to the same thing—and some have been immensely excited. In any event he has never stayed with any one art form for very long.

Originally a display designer and advertising artist for department stores — and a good

one — he overnight in the early 1960s materialized as the crown prince of the new Pop Art derived from comic strips and the like. Forthwith he pronounced Pop Art old hat and moved on into movies — the one form he probably will stay with for a while, if he now survives.

As soon as the hip populace began to enjoy themselves at his swirling-banshee light shows, he'd begin to say: "Change it, change it," and he'd further disjoint the disjointed media so as to make the experiencing of them yet more unendurable.

Also there was his ever-changing stable or "family" of Pop-up glamor girls and instant movie queens stemming, in the words of Elenore Lester, who has a big Warhol piece coming out in the August is-

Continued on Page 33

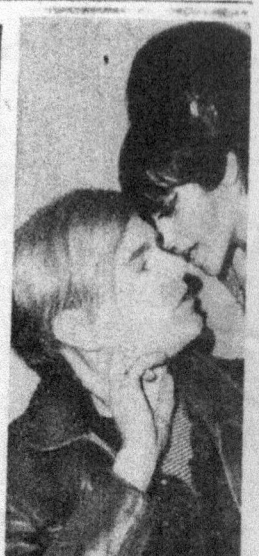

Post Photo by Baxer

Andy Warhol and friend at a recent discotheque party.

Andy Warhol Fighting for Life

By JOSEPH MANCINI

With JOSEPH FEUREY and JAY LEVIN

Pop artist Andy Warhol fought for his life today after being gunned down in his own studio by a woman who had acted in one of his underground films.

The artist-sculptor-film-maker underwent 5½ hours of surgery performed by a four-man team of doctors at Columbus Hospital late last night and was given a "50-50 chance to live."

A hospital spokesman reported late this morning that Warhol was "a little better, perhaps," but still in critical condition.

At 7:30 last night, just three hours and 10 minutes after the shooting, Valerie Solanas, 28, a would-be writer-actress, walked up to a rookie policeman directing traffic in Times Sq. and surrendered.

She reached into her trench coat and handed Patrolman William Schmalix, 22, a .32 automatic and a .22 revolver. The .32 had been fired recently, police said, and Valerie admitted the shooting.

When she apeared in Criminal Court today for arraignment, she insisted she would defend herself, argued with Judge Getzoff, and several times shouted.

She was arraigned on two counts of attempted murder and one count of possessing dangerous weapons. Judge Getzoff ordered her held without bail for another appearance tomorrow. He had sought to have a court psychiatrist talk with her today, but no one was available.

When the Judge asked if she could afford an attorney, she said: "No, I can't. I want to defend myself." The jurist tried to tell her she should have a lawyer for her own protection, but she interupted him to say, "This is going to stay in my own competent hands."

Despite her argument that she didn't want a lawyer, Getzoff assigned Legal Aid Society attor-

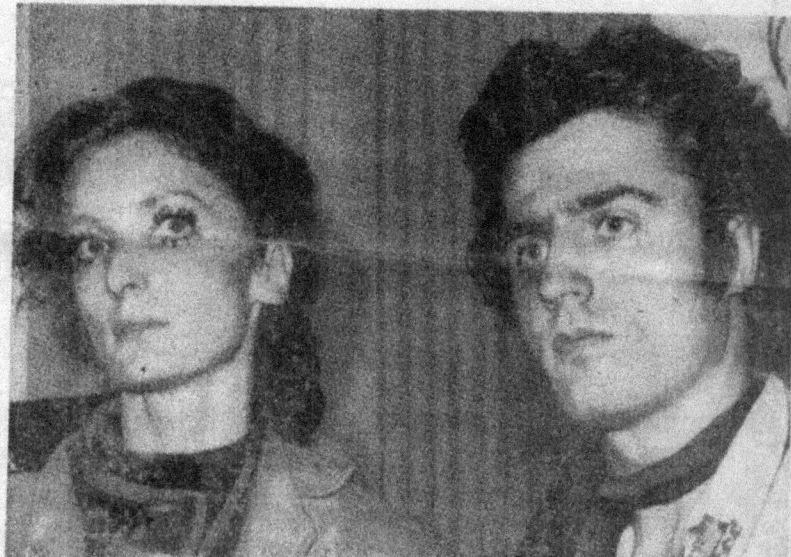

Underground film stars Viva (no last name) and Gerard Malanga wait in Columbus Hospital lobby for word on Andy Warhol's condition.

Associated Press Photo

ney Ronald Veneziano to talk with her. He did, and when he came back to try to set a date for a hearing, she began to shout: "I don't authorize him to do that!"

Conduct Noted

At this point, Judge Getzoff told her: "Because of your conduct and the nature of the charge against you, I'm going to assign the court psychiatrist to make preliminary examination."

When it was learned one was not available, Judge Getzoff told here he would postpone the case for 24 hours, but again, the jurist was interrupted by

her shouting.

"I do not authorize you to do that. Let me have my say."

"Go on," the Judge told her, and she said:

"It was reported in the newspapers that the motive for doing this was because Andy would not produce my play. It was for the opposite reason.

"He has a legal claim to all my works. It's not often that I shoot somebody. I didn't do it for nothing."

Realizing this was a confession that could be used against her, Getzoff ordered the court stenographer to strike her entire outburst from the court record.

then passed through his right lung and out his right side.

A second bullet hit Mario Amaya, 34, an art writer and editor from London, in the hip. The wound was minor and Amaya was released from the hospital after treatment.

The shooting was witnessed by two Warhol assistants, Paul Morrisey and Fred Hughes; by a man called Bill Name, and one other person.

Police today were trying to determine where she obtained the weapons she surrendered to Schmalix. They are saying little about a motive, despite the outburst that the judge struck from the record. But the real

---

Gerard Malanga and Viva were interviewed by reporters at the hospital on June 4th, while Warhol was still undergoing surgery. Amid the constant camera flashes, Malanga looked suave and self-composed, if a tad too pretty, while Viva stared wild-eyed, slack-jawed, and, for once, speechless. . .

Newsman
Gerard, can you account for what happened today? In anything in Andy's life..

Gerard Malanga
Not in anything in connection with Andy's life. And I arrived five minutes or a minute after it had happened, so I missed Valerie in the staircase or the elevator.

Newsman
Did you know the girl who was said to have done this thing?

Gerard Malanga
I just knew her vaguely. I ran into her on the street about two weeks ago one night very late after Max's, and we spoke very briefly. She seemed quite friendly, but she was a very eccentric girl.

Newsman *(to Viva)*
You worked with Andy quite a lot. Did you know this girl?

Viva
Yes, I met her once or twice.

Newsman
How would you describe her?

Viva
Mixed up.

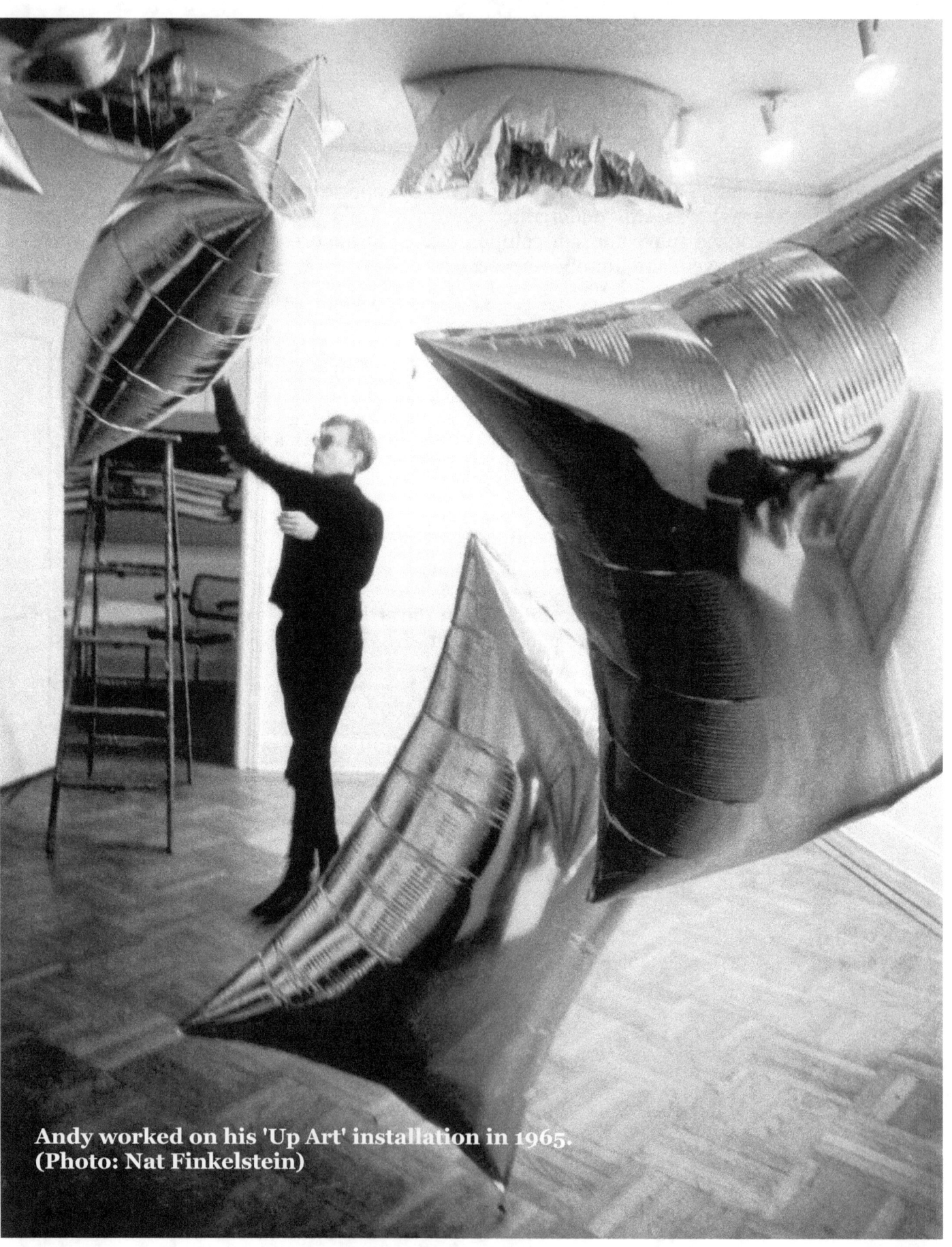

Andy worked on his 'Up Art' installation in 1965.
(Photo: Nat Finkelstein)

SILVER FACTORY FINALE

Andy never said "15 Minutes of Fame." He just adopted it.
He adopted everything. And every one.
—Louis Waldon

Robert Heide: Andy was good for some people and not others. He was maybe helpful to some destructive to others, but maybe some of these would have self-destructed anyway. In other words he was a *conduit*, so he inspired admiration just as he inspired enmity and hatred, and that's sometimes the price of fame. It's no *accident* that Andy is shot. When you become so famous, someone is always lying in wait to possibly. . .

Bob Heide looked woebegone, and left the rest unsaid, but John Lennon was naturally uppermost in our minds. We had just visited with Jonas Mekas, down the street on 2nd Avenue at his Anthology Film Archives. Jonas had made a 'home movie' of Warhol with Lennon at a garden party, as they compared instant Polaroid shots and giggled together like kids in the sunshine, despite Warhol's deep aversion to daylight and Yoko Ono. Here, he looked pale and skeletal, as if in need of a blood transfusion, while Lennon, deleriously happy, devours Japanese food and dances for the camera as Yoko clicks away. It was a private, poignant moment. . . Of course we used the footage. We're filmmakers.

Jonas Mekas: (Martin) Scorsese always credits—I mean, he was *there* at the Film-Maker's Cinematheque, seeing Warhol, seeing all the films. He was inspired and influenced. Influence is a very complex word. Influence can be part of the very climate, the people that you meet, and talk about the same kind of things. Just by talking or seeing what others are doing can clarify your own ideas.

Mary Woronov: Andy was a conduit. He really wasn't interested in the things most people are interested in. The Velvet Underground—the songs were rebellious. The *art* was rebellious. So, you stayed there. But I believe after Warhol was shot, he was afraid, and he didn't want to be so close to the raw kind of insanity that he wanted before. He knew it was different.

David Croland: It was the end of trust, the fear of selfishly thinking it could be me, because I was there that day. . . It was the end of a certain kind of innocent glamour. The glamour got harder, people got harder. They were scared after that.

Mary Woronov: It *was* scary, and so he stepped away. When he stepped away he lost part of his power, and he became the artist that he is. He didn't do any more movies. Well, Paul helped him stop doing movies, because he took over.

Paul Morrissey *(from 'Superstar in a Housedress'):* So I mentioned it to Andy—I said, "I think they (Holly Woodlawn and Jacke Curtis) should play women's libbers," like that ridiculous Valerie Solanas, who had shot him. Andy was very brave about it. He said, "That's a good idea."

Nat Finkelstein: Who walked away from that scene better than when they entered? People like Paul Morrissey, maybe Danny Fields. They were used, and then when they were used up, they were gone. . . Now Nico was different. She was self-sufficient, she was her own person. And she wasn't going to be swayed by those people. I knew her past then. She visited me in Amsterdam. She was still pretty badly strung out. We had a discussion about if I were to rent a larger place in Amsterdam she could stay with me and I would help her. I never was into heroin.

Nat's close friend Nico would always be into heroin, with side trips of LSD, and his love for her would remain unrequited. No longer part of The Velvet Underground, Nico left for the West Coast and the Monterey Pop Festival—and legendary rock star/poet Jim Morrison of The Doors, with whom she would have an intense affair.

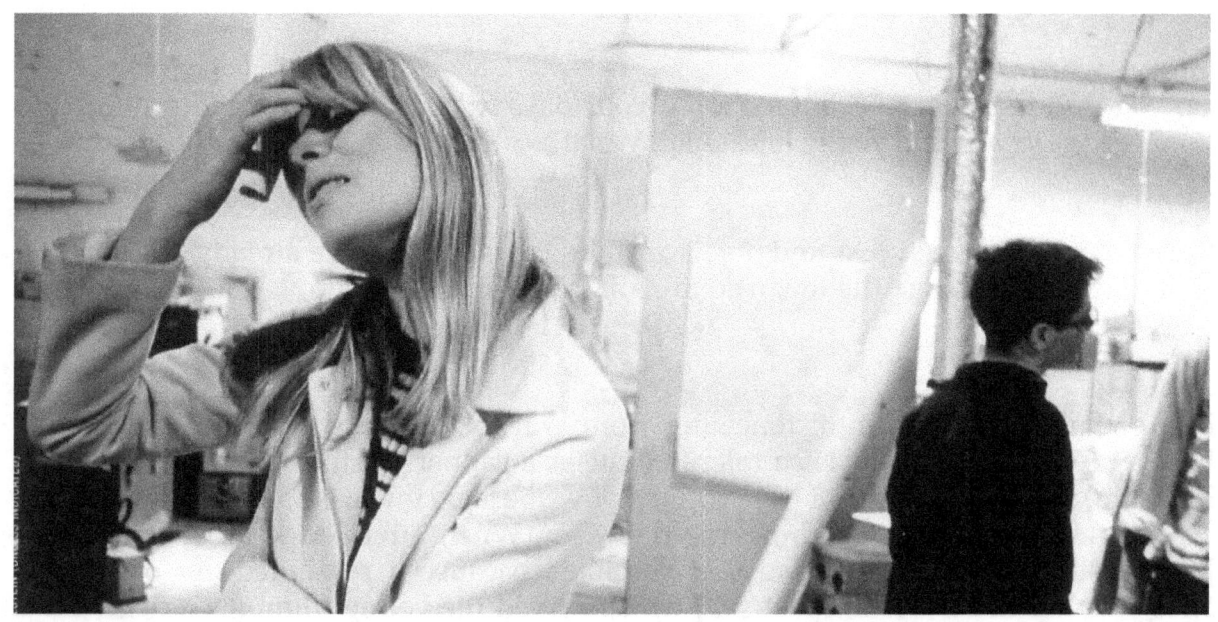

Upon her return from Cannes and the 'Chelsea Girls' non-screening in 1967, Nico had found herself dropped from the Velvet Underground. (Photo: Nat Finkelstein)

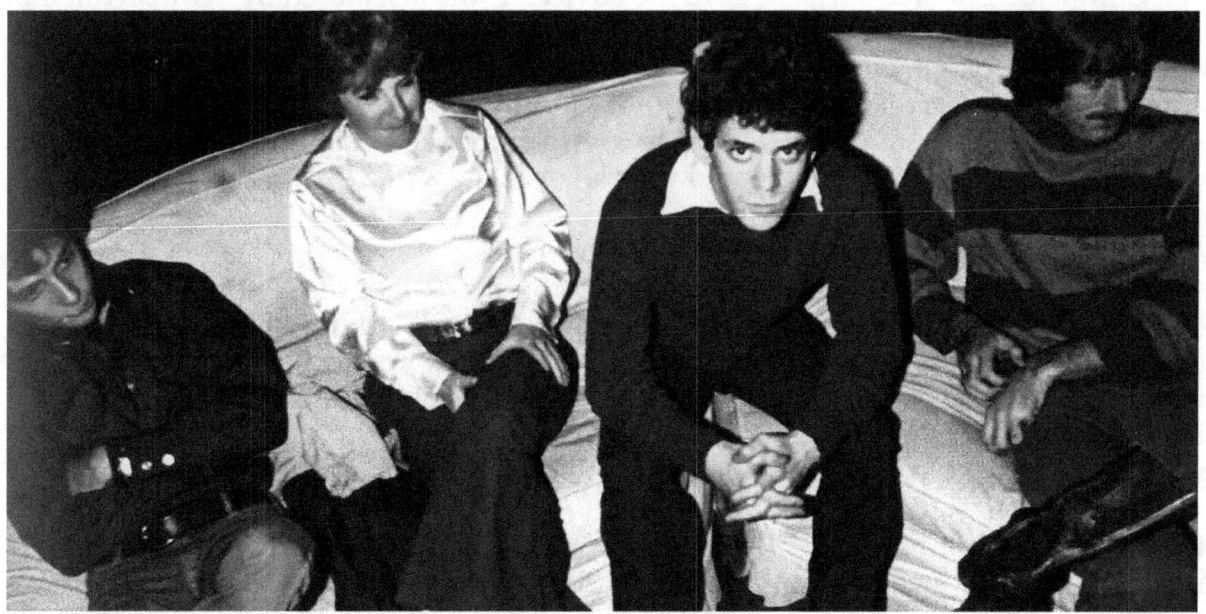

The Velvets prepae to pack it in at the Factory. (Photo: Billy Name)

Interviewer (to Nico)
Do you find that you're swamped a lot, your days with the Velvet Underground and Lou Reed. Do you find you're harassed by that?

Nico
I can't say harassed. I just find it very tasteless, really. Because already that I'm still alive. I'm one amongst the few who are still alive, because I know that the audience likes clichés.

Nico's drug use tended to distance her from Warhol, since he preferred talkers like Edie and Brigid and Viva. Nico tolerated me as a yapper, perhaps because I was also into acid, so long stretches of time could go by where no one would talk, but the brain synapses would be flying with no one the wiser. When interviewed at her concert in Manchester (an industrial town that she liked because it reminded her of Berlin), Nico was her usual circumspect self, which served the young filmmaker right, since his sound recording quality was god-awful.

Ivy Nicholson: I don't think I communicated with any of the other actresses. Oh, Nico I really liked; she was the only one. We saw one another in Paris. She was like me, European. She was a friend, gave me advice. I was fascinated by her apartments. They were all magic, so weird—one totally black with only ashtrays. No paintings, nothing. Can you imagine? The only decor were ashtrays full of horrible cigarettes— a very elegant apartment with nothing in it. I think there might have been a mattress somewhere; I hope so. She lived there with (filmmaker) Phillipe Garell. Another was Moroccan, with different colored veils all over the walls. But again, no furniture.

Allen Midgette: In reality, much of the Silver Factory was a bit leaden more than silver. The toilet of course was also silver, but on the wall of the toilet, Ivy Nicholson had printed, "I'm in Paris once more with no money." It's those kinds of little things that you would want to capture, the fact that the windows are just factory windows looking out on the street, and not so clean—kind of dusty, kind of Mrs. Haversham from 'Great Expectations'. Great expectations were part of what the Factory was, what all these people had, what made you think of it as more glittering, and silvery.

Ultra Violet: You have to belong to somewhere, so that's what held these people together, because we were all rebellious in our own way, rebelling against an establishment that is never right. Nothing is right in the world anyway, so the kids are trying to find an alternative, and that was part of the success of the Factory.

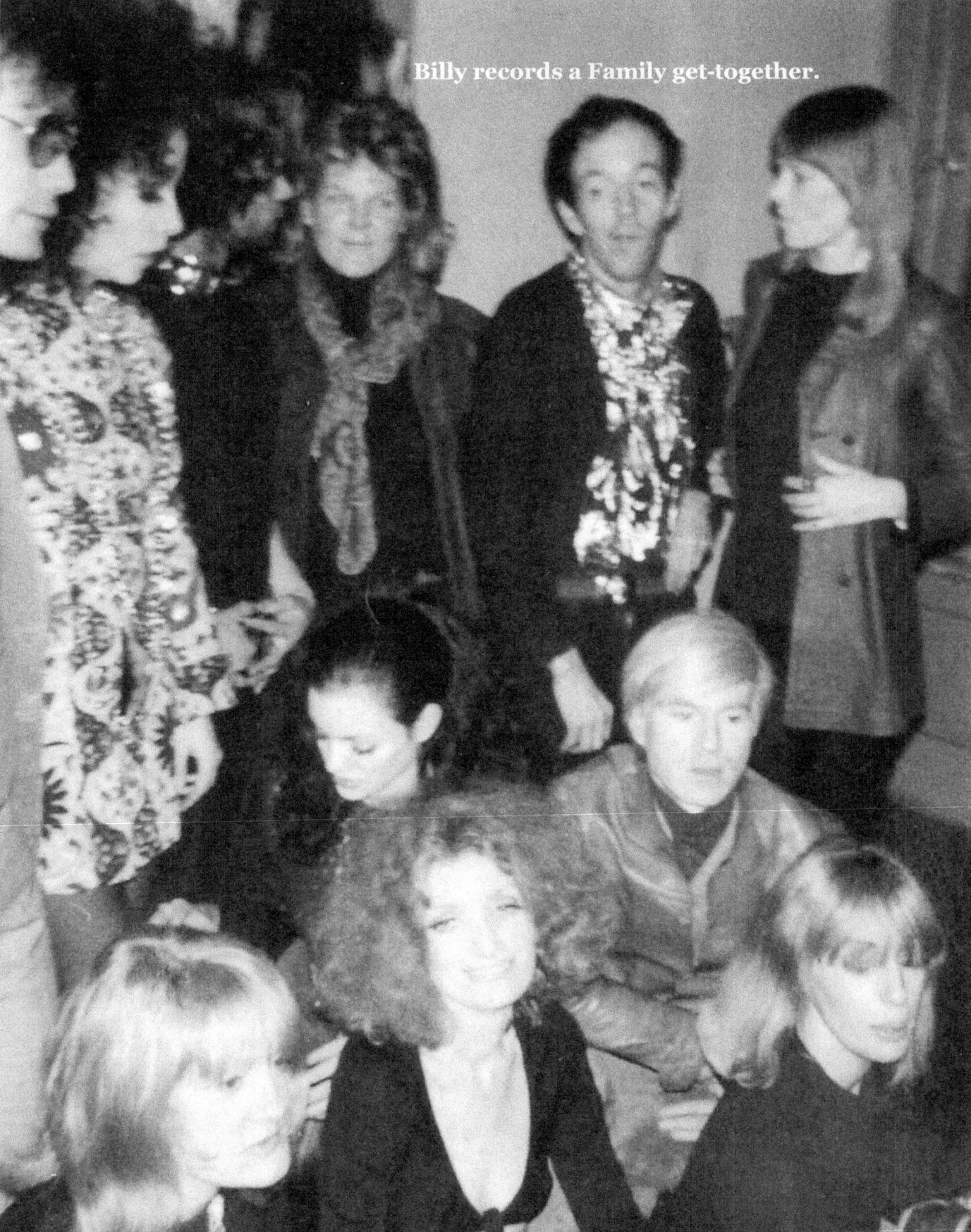

Billy records a Family get-together.

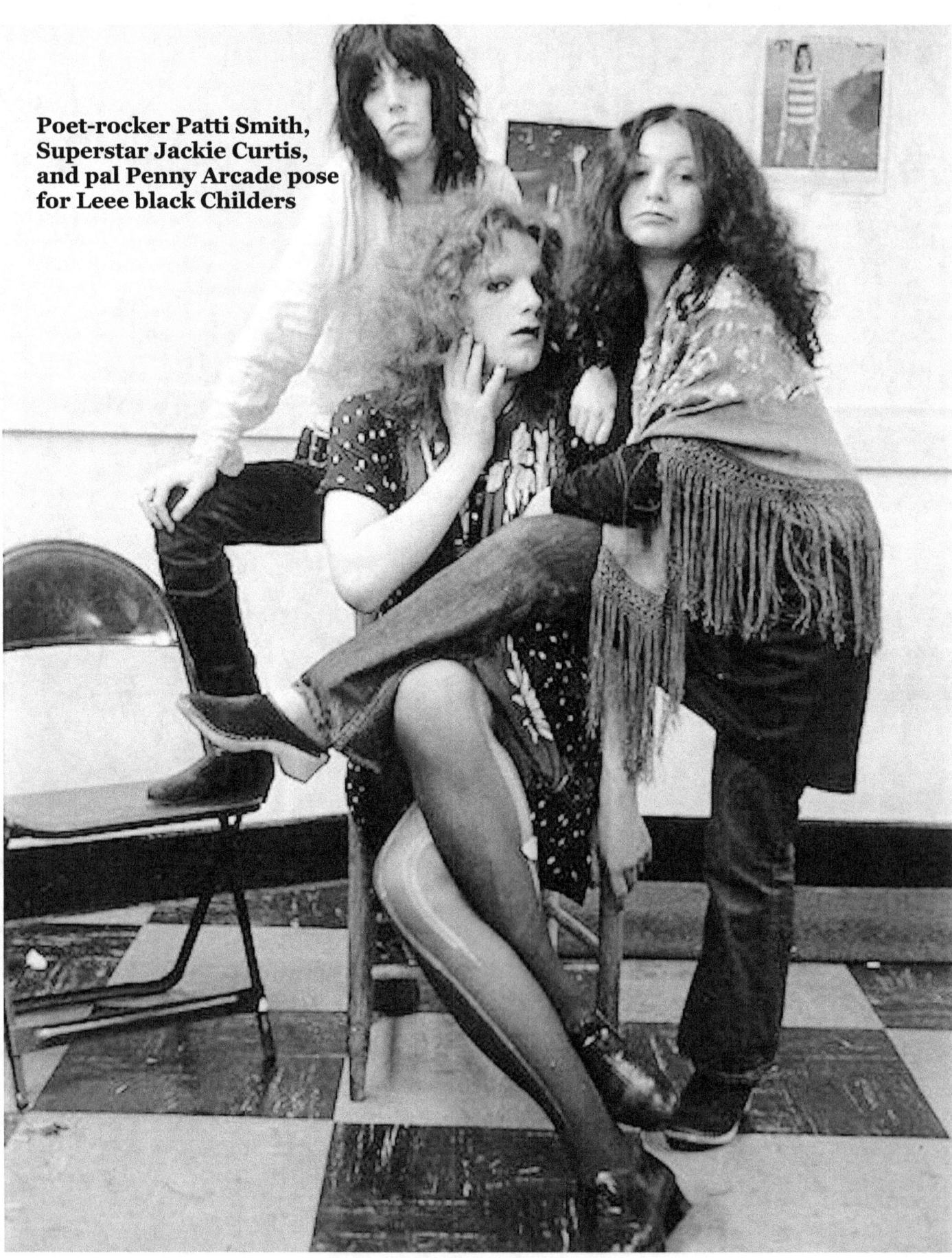

**Poet-rocker Patti Smith,
Superstar Jackie Curtis,
and pal Penny Arcade pose
for Leee black Childers**

Geraldine Smith: We were all younger than Viva and Ultra and Brigid. We were fifteen, sixteen. It was the most fun I ever had, I don't regret anything. The parties! It wasn't a party unless Andy was there. He was like one of these great puppeteers. Everyone wanted to perform for him. I really liked him; he was always nice to me. People blame him for not paying them, or for their mistakes, but they're too negative. A lot of people think he exploited us, but others think it's a stepping stone.

Ultra Violet: Tragedy happened, so things changed. Andy took risks, and he was pretty brave, I guess. And he only realised too late that this kind of thing had to stop if you wanted to stay alive. So, I think that belonging to the Factory. . . Factory is a powerful word. You manufacture things in a factory. We were being manufactured, or we self-manufactured ourselves.

Vincent Fremont: It got very dangerous when it almost took his life. Then, he changed, about who could get close to him. He was still very accessible. . . The craziness he was always attracted to, because he equated it with creativity. People think, "Oh, he got shot and now he can't do anything anymore. He doesn't want any crazy people around." Well, they were just a different kind of crazy people. They looked different; they dressed differently. That was the beginning, where the drag queens and transvestites started coming to visit Andy—when you had Candy Darling, and the very talented Jackie Curtis, and Holly Woodlawn. So, it was a whole different era.

Leee Black Childers: The most beautiful young men on the planet were flocking to the Warhol Factory, where they could be made to feel more like men. Most of them were gay, so they had Jackie Curtis and Candy Darling to be their *dates*, covered in glitter, outrageous clothes . . . stuff they stole from dead people or out of garbage cans, stuck together with safety pins so they wouldn't fall off. It all really did come off as very glamorous. It looked fabulous when they walked in a room, and they always had these beautiful boys with them. Andy loved that. The only problem was very few of them had any talent other than just wearing garbage on their back and getting out on the streets. They couldn't act. They didn't *want* to.

Leee's ribald Chaucerian Canterbury tales of his exotic roommates would have made wonderful little period movies all by themselves, because the drag queens really sparkled in those early Paul Morrissey films. And, thanks to Andy, the serious actresses who'd found themselves out of favor at the Factory, would also become cult queens. . .

Mary Waronov: After Warhol, I got very, very strange roles—'Eating Raoul' where I was a mass murderer, or 'Rock n' Roll High School,' where I was this aging, viciously unsexual school principal. I got a following because I am a good little camp actress, and so now I am a cult queen as you would put it, in Hollywood terms. Well, maybe not Hollywood terms—they do not like cults—but I am an aging cult queen.

Mary, still working on her doc, is in demand on the lecture circuit and was honored with a retrospective of her films and a lifetime achievment award in Hollywood. We shared dinner and a good bottle of wine, so I guess her liver has fully recovered from her feckless youth with Warhol. . . According to Louis Waldon, she'd married and moved to Italy: "Like most people, she didn't want to have anything to do with Andy. Nobody wanted to be identified with Andy. They thought it was bad karma." Out of loyalty, Louis stuck around for a bit longer before he, too, eventually decamped.

Louis Waldon: I made Andy's last movie. He got out of the hospital and we made that movie. He just really wanted to be a famous personality. But this dread that hung over Andy—people really hated him! Because of Pop art. Here were these people struggling to make a new art movement in New York City. The last art movement (Abstract Expressionism) had been Jackson Pollack and those other guys, Yves Kline, all them. They hated him! He was menaced by a lot of crazy people. He got shot at several times. Then he got shot for real, and he told me he died. He said, "I died, Louis. The light at the end of the tunnel went out."

The light had indeed gone out for a while. Warhol had been pronounced clinically dead six minutes after arriving in the emergency room of Columbus Hospital. According to Louis Waldon, surgeon Giuseppe Rossi had to cut open Warhol's chest and literally massage the heart to get a beat. Outside the surgery, Louis tried futilely to keep Ivy Nicholson from holding her own tribal last rites, dancing and screaming for Warhol at the top of her lungs. For all we know, she may have actually had something to do with his miraculous rally—if only to get away from her. . . The last movie Louis made with Warhol was 'Blue Movie'. As Billy Name told us, "We were pre-porn, but we did the first 'fuck movie' with Viva and Louis Waldon actually fucking in the movie. But it was shown and seized by the City of New York." The film was Viva's idea, and consisted of the couple meeting, having sex, and enjoying a lengthy post-coital conversation. 'Blue Movie' would turn out to be Viva's swan song at the Factory. She left New York for Paris and French actor Pierre Clementi. . .

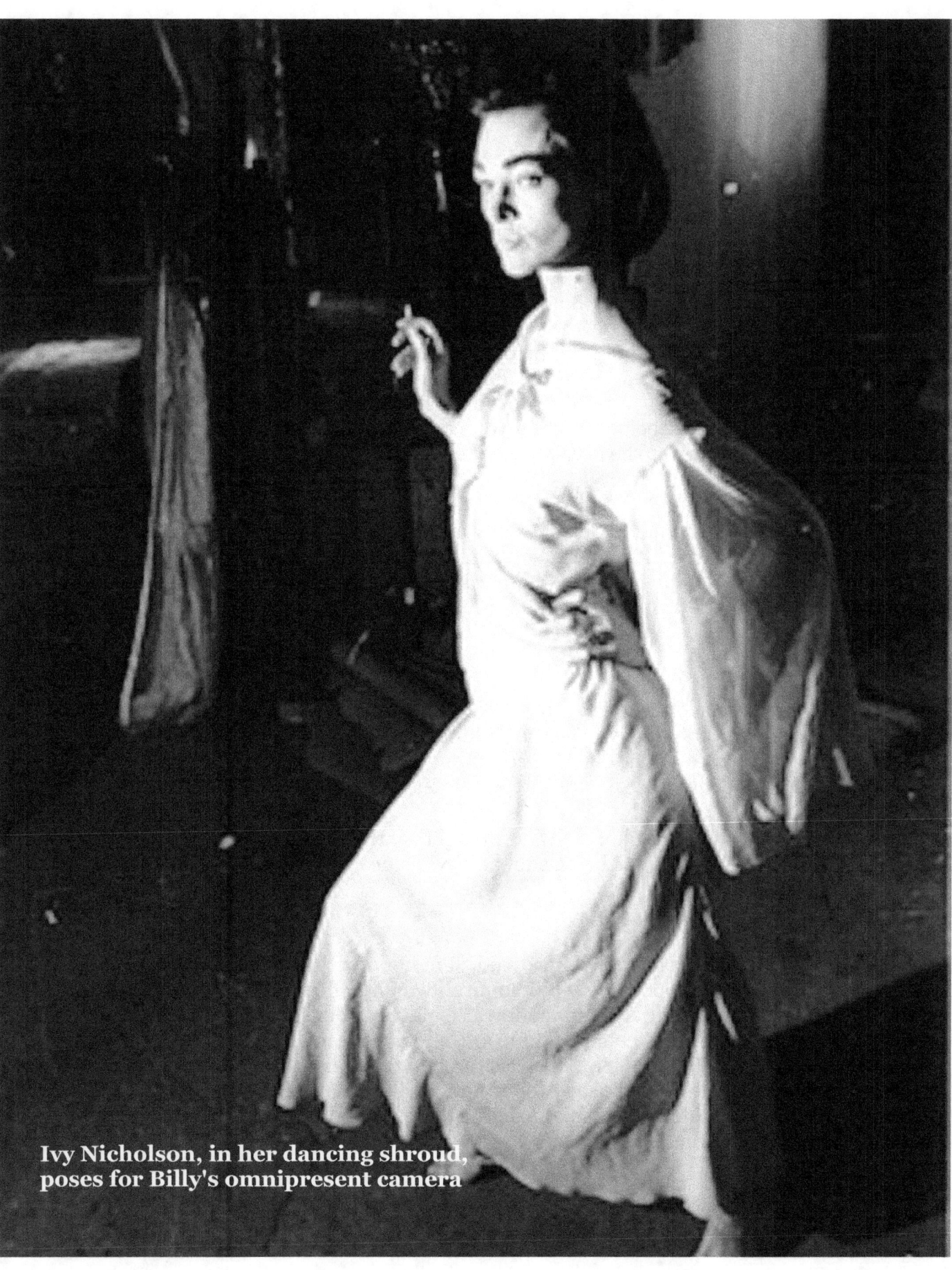

Ivy Nicholson, in her dancing shroud,
poses for Billy's omnipresent camera

Viva: Timothy Leary loved 'Blue Movie'. . . Gene Youngblood *(L. A. film critic)* did, too. He said I was better than Vanessa Redgrave, and it was the first time a real movie star had made love on the screen. It was a real breakthrough.

According to biographer Victor Bockris, Viva had been initially appalled by the rushes for 'Blue Movie', especially the sex scene, but not for the obvious reasons. She had thought the scene "flat and perfunctory," though she and Louis did, indeed, do the deed. Warhol had to plead with her for a release. Viva also recalled that after Warhol was shot, "He was very much changed toward me. Much cooler. He was sexually afraid of women before, I mean you couldn't touch him. He would cringe. But afterwards he seemed to be deeply afraid."

Victor Bockris: After Valerie Solanas shot him, Andy became frightened of crazy women, and he remained frightened of crazy women for the rest of his life. His mother was a crazy woman in a way—there was a lot of craziness in the female side of his family. So Valerie just really scared him. Still, he was worried that after the shooting he wouldn't be able to have ideas, because he depended so much on crazy people for ideas.

Billy Name: You couldn't expect him to be the same Andy that he was before the shooting. I felt the trauma of this whole thing so much that I stayed in my dark room, and I only came out at night. I could not be light-hearted. And Andy made believe he was. . . It was a cardboard Andy. It wasn't a real Andy anymore.

Andy Warhol: Before I got shot, I always thought . . . that I was watching TV instead of living life. Right when I was being shot and ever since, I *knew* that I was watching television.

Billy Name mentioned that Warhol once said, "I'm not afraid to die. I just don't want to be around when it happens.". . . Billy himself would not be around for that much longer to worry about his friend and mentor. He had been cloistered in his dark room for over a year, studying Tibetan Buddhism (one of us!) and meditating, living on take-out and Campbell's soup. Since he was rarely sighted, he'd achieved near mythic status, and was spoken of in hushed tones around the spiffy new 'Black and White' Factory by those who feared he might die in there, and the headlines would read, 'Andy Warhol Locks Man In Toilet'.

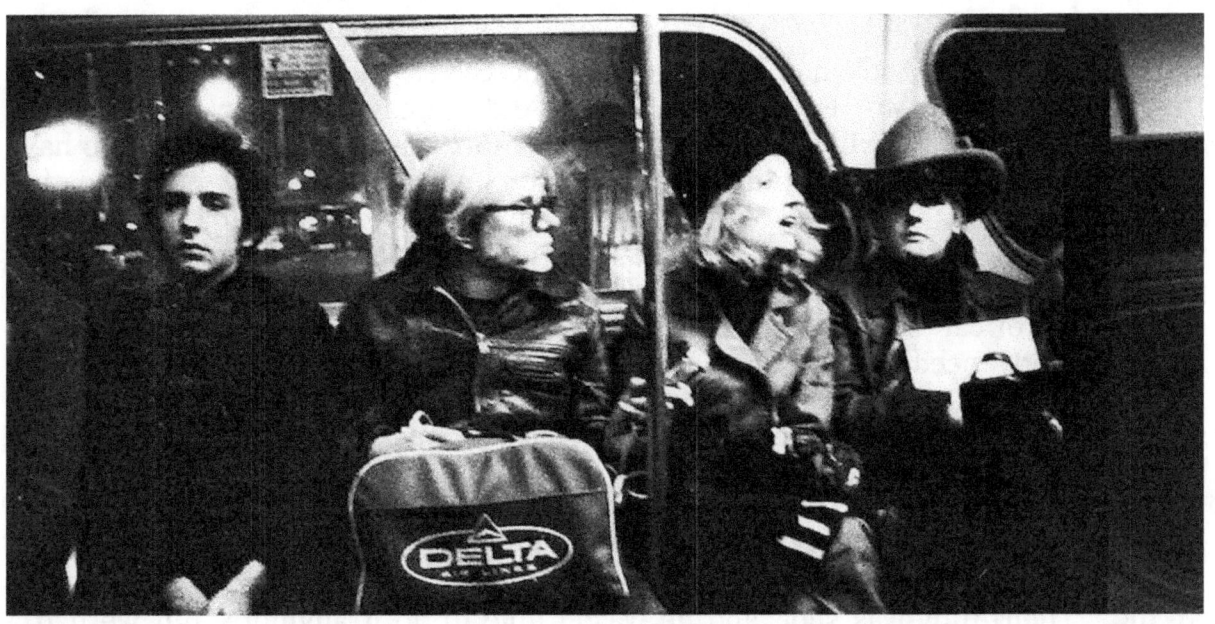

Fred Hughes, Andy, Viva, and Brigid Berlin take (gasp!) public transportation.   Or is it a plug for Delta Airlines?

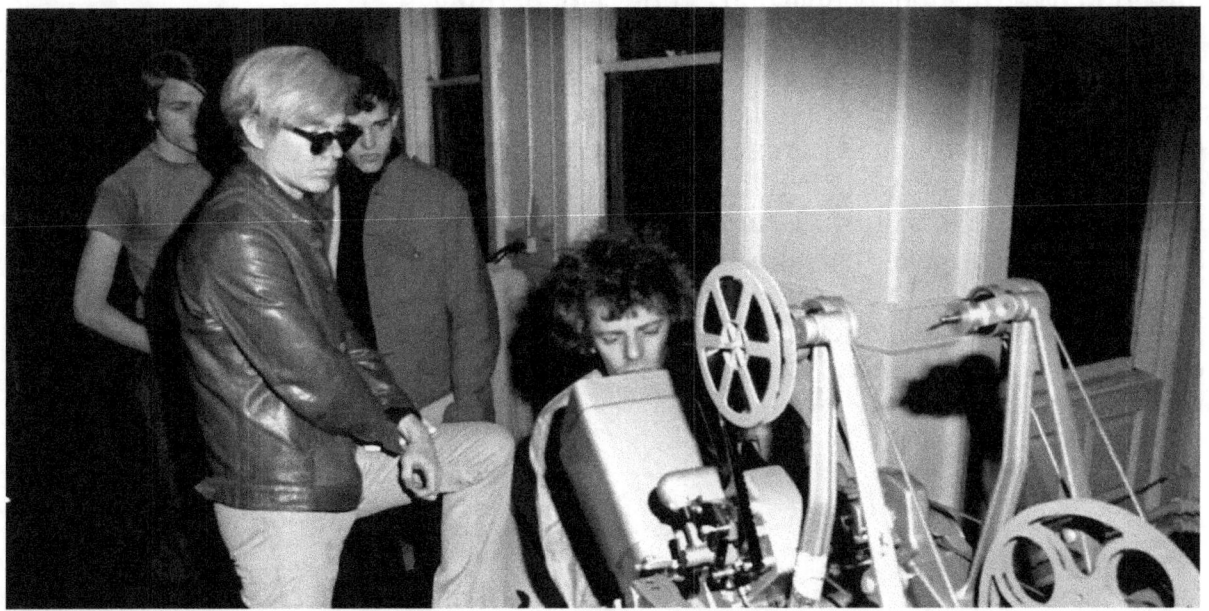

Andy and Paul in the Union Square Factory putting finishing touches on a film, using our old editing favorite, a moviola. Twins Jed and Jay Johnson in B.G. (Photos: Billy Name)

Gerard Malanga: Andy had moved out of the Silver Factory toward the end of December '67. Paul Morrissey wanted to give Andy's image a cleaner look, and one of the things was to convince Andy we had to be more business-like. We had to have desks and a clean space and shiny floors, and, you know, no more silver dust floating around. And we had to get rid of the freaks. Paul was the instigator for getting rid of Ondine, getting rid of Barbara Rubin, getting rid of Billy Name, ultimately probably getting rid of me! I mean, I am still friends with Paul, but let's keep history, let's keep the historical thing in context. Paul saw Andy's potential, rightfully so, but he felt that Andy needed a new image, so it was, basically it was a make-over, a Hollywood make-over. And Andy went along with it. Andy had a good sense and scent for money, and he smelled money, or at least he was dreaming about money. So he probably said, "Well, let's give it a try."

Billy Name: We had a contract to provide a new soft-core porn 'art film' each month for the Hudson Theater on Times Square. 'Bike Boy', starring Viva, was one which we did. Then Andy was shot, and he wasn't able to do it anymore. But we had a contract, so Paul started making his Joe Dallesandro pictures—'Flesh' and 'Trash' and all these things. If Andy hadn't been shot it never would have happened. . . Andy would have continued making Andy Warhol Films, but because he was incapacitated, and we had the contract, Paul took over the camerawork and direction. Well, a lot of people don't know a lot of things.

Geraldine Smith: Paul. Paul. Paul. I loved him, he's a character, a really smart, talented guy. He's very opinionated, he's very loyal, and I like his movies. They're different from anything else, really controversial. I had a crush on Paul as a kid. We all had crushes on Paul. We all thought he was fabulous. When I starred in 'Flesh' opposite Joe Dallessandro, I said, "Paul, where's the script?" He said,"There *is* no script." I had to make the whole thing up! So, I just improvised. I was going to be married to Joe and I had this lesbian girlfriend. And I wanted him to go out and hustle to bring some money home for us. We were friends, we hung out together, we didn't think for one second about anything. Just did it. We did the whole movie on improvisation.

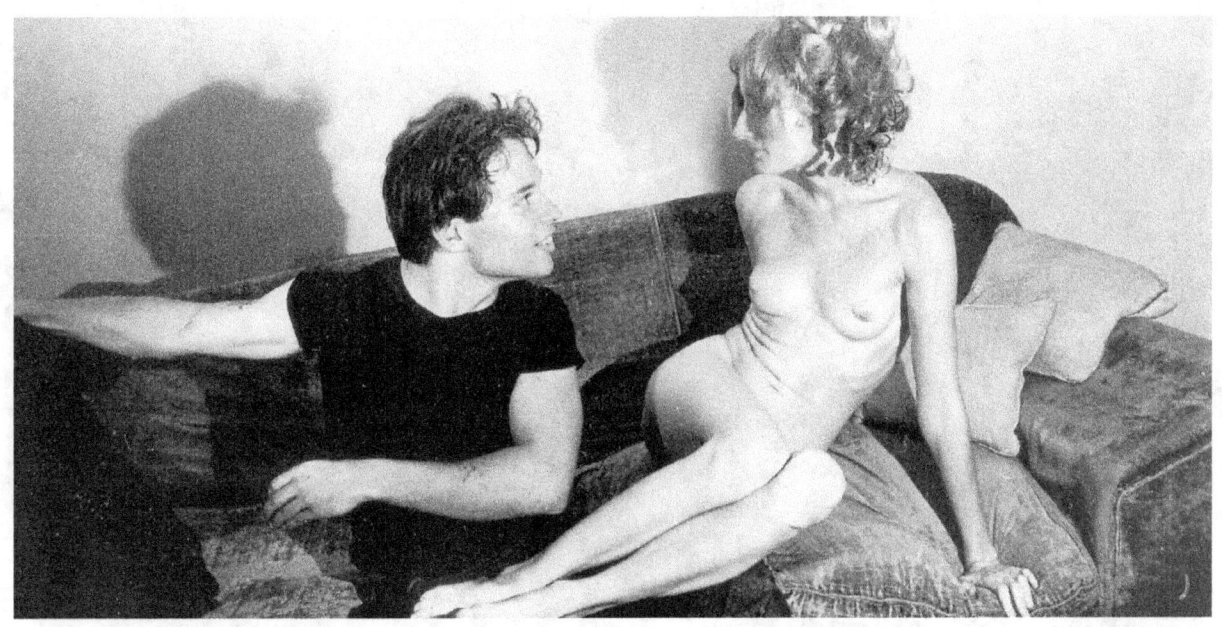

Foreplay. . .   Viva, vivacious star of 'Bike Boy', gets Joe Spencer in the mood.

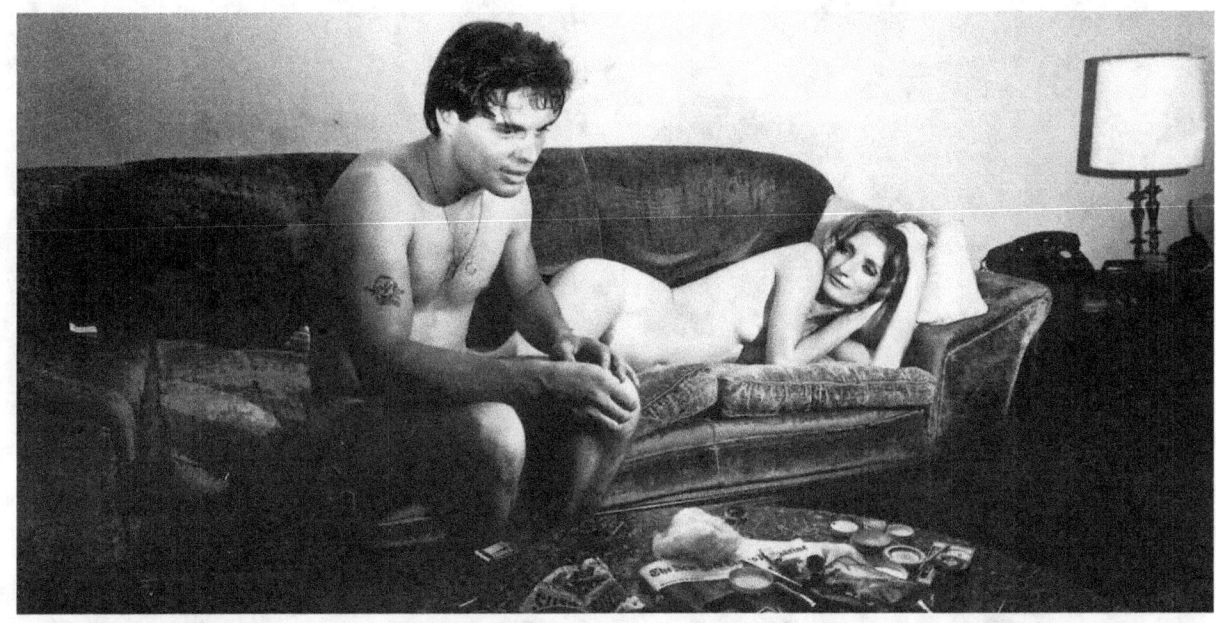

Post-coital regrets? . . .   The couch seems to have taken a direct hit.   Part of a series shot by Billy
Name during filming of 'Bike Boy'.

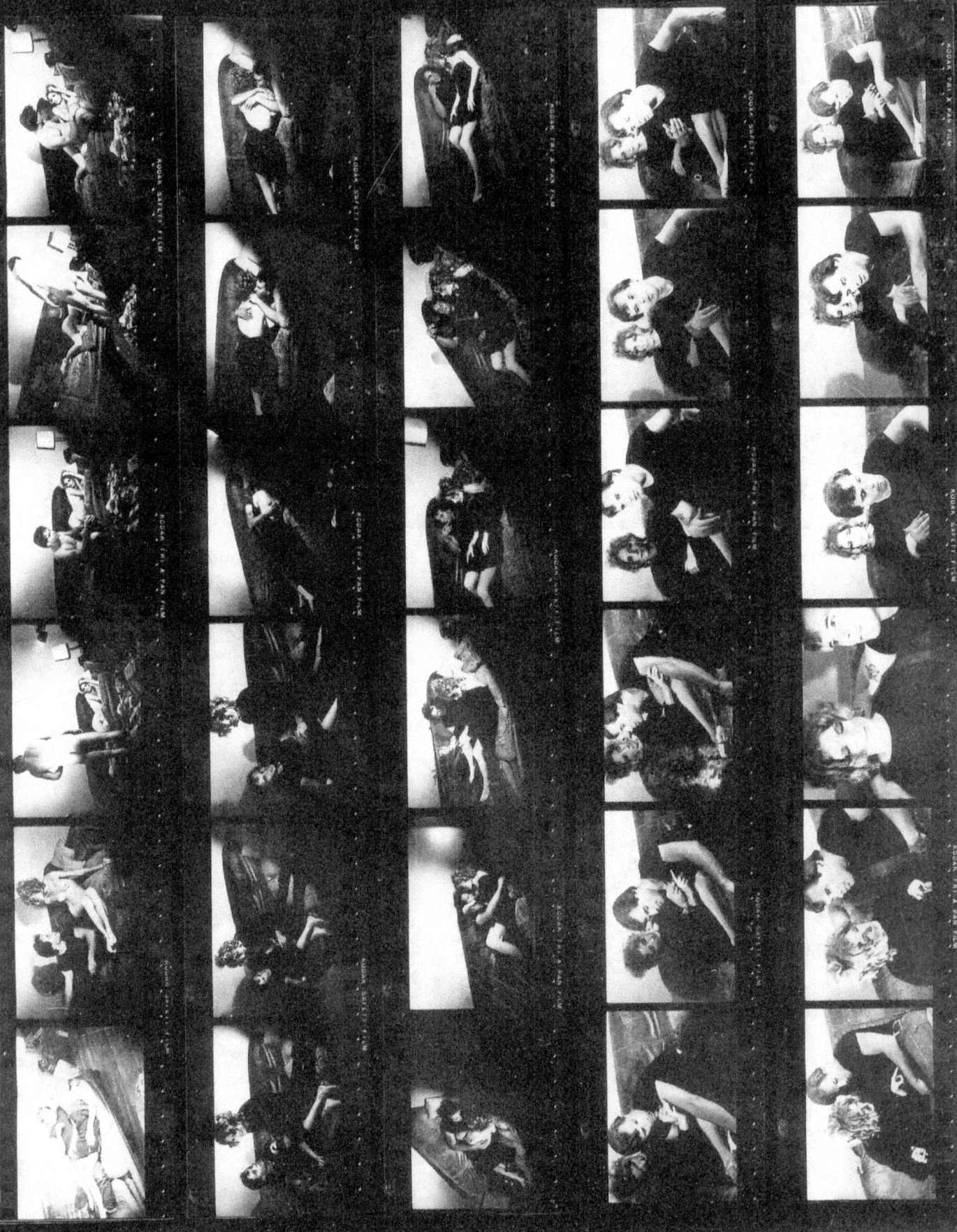

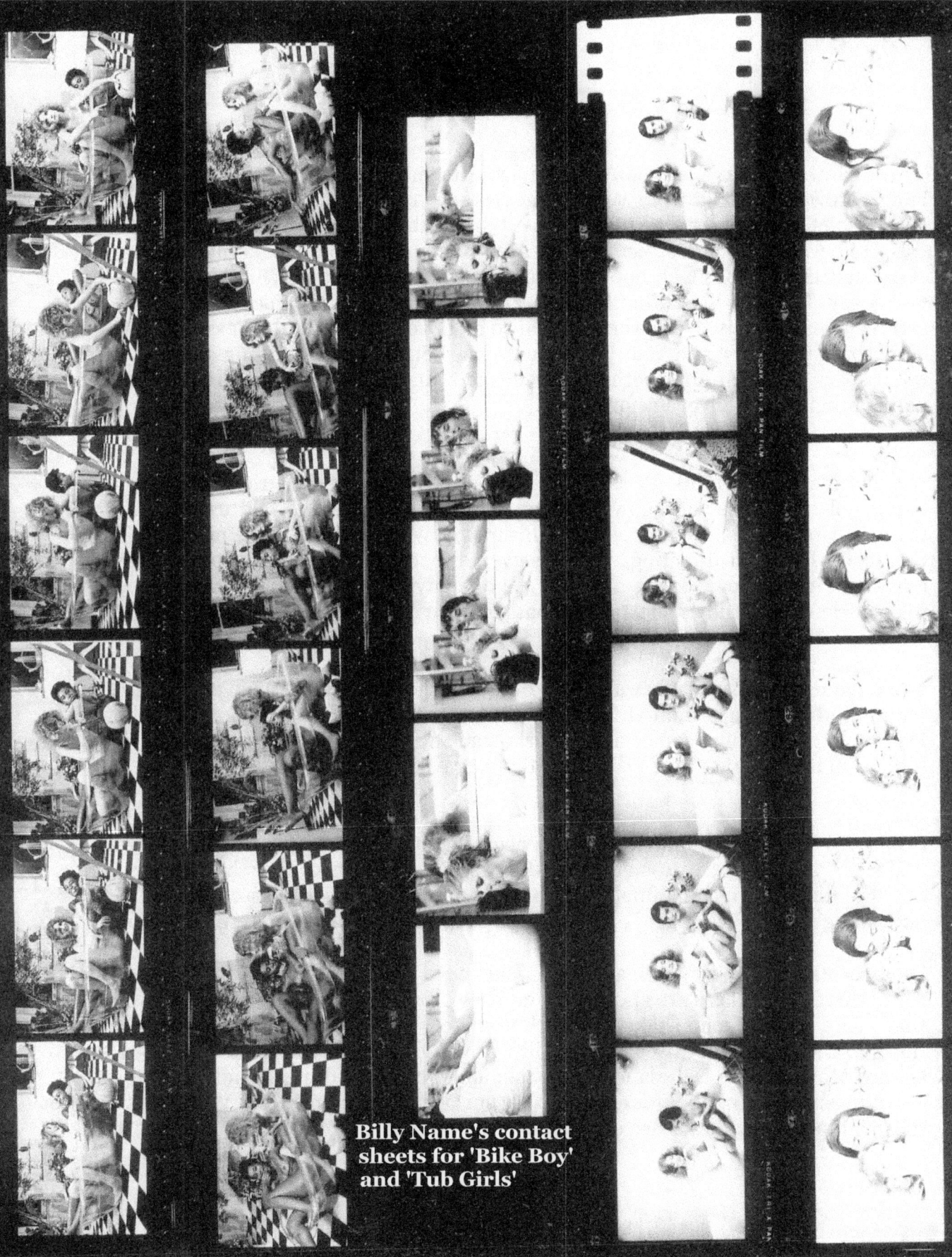

Billy Name's contact
sheets for 'Bike Boy'
and 'Tub Girls'

'Flesh' came about as a reaction to John Schlesinger's film 'Midnight Cowboy', which had borrowed liberally from Warhol movies, even using his people, like Viva and Ultra Violet, for a party scene to represent life in the Factory. Warhol was flattered that Hollywood was at last being influenced by his films, but also a bit envious. He suggested that they "make another 'Hustler' movie." The film, 'Flesh', directed by Morrissey, featured Geraldine Smith, Patti D'Arbanville, and Joe Dallesandro, an eighteen-year-old discovery whose presence in 'Loves of Ondine' had assured roles in 'Lonesome Cowboys' and 'San Diego Surf'. Warhol, slowly recovering and happy to take a back seat, felt safer with these teenagers than with the dangerous divas that had dominated the Silver Factory years.

Ivy Nicholson: Everything was unusual with Andy. One of the strangest things that happened—of course you know that I am in love with him—he told us to go to the prison. Paul chose the courtroom for this movie, which wound up being called 'Love On Trial'. I started directing, having never directed in my entire life! I invented different kinds of love for the actors. Like one guy, Rene Ricard, did self-love while my boyfriend and Andy's ghost would pass in front of the judge wearing underwear.

Louis Waldon felt that Andy was weary of the histrionics. But his own experiences of fending off the tempermental flora and fauna that thrived in the Factory hothouse led Louis to a startling conclusion: Warhol, so shy about his looks that he preferred hiding "in the shadows" and watching others, craved that spotlight himself. . .

Louis Waldon: Andy wanted to be an actor, wanted to be in the movies—he was a real fan. Paul Morrissey wasn't. Paul Morrissey was in to take over the Factory, take over the filming, which he finally did. Paul went into transsexuals and transvestites, and young people. He got rid of all us older people. We all left and went to Europe.

Dave Croland: People get in a corner. They have this life, up there, then they move somewhere else. There are ghosts around New York. People come back who were in that scene, and become shaky—the dichotomy of what it was, and what their life is now. So they lead quiet lives. I am still living a glamorous life in New York. I see Gerard Malanga, Joe Dallesandro. We talk about cerebral things. Andy used to say, "If you want to know about me, look at the surface of my paintings." What does that mean? I look with the surface of my eyes. One can see if I'm telling the truth or not.

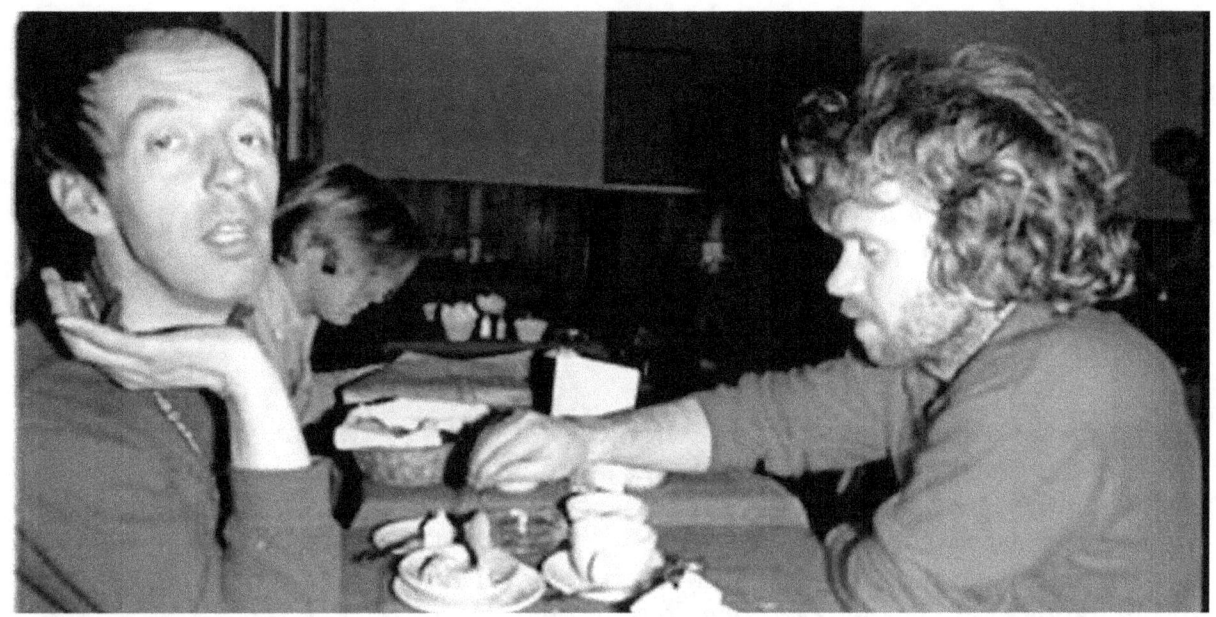

Taylor Mead and Louis Waldon, off to Europe once again, share a meal at Max's Kansas City. The two longtime friends and co-stars died of strokes in 2013,

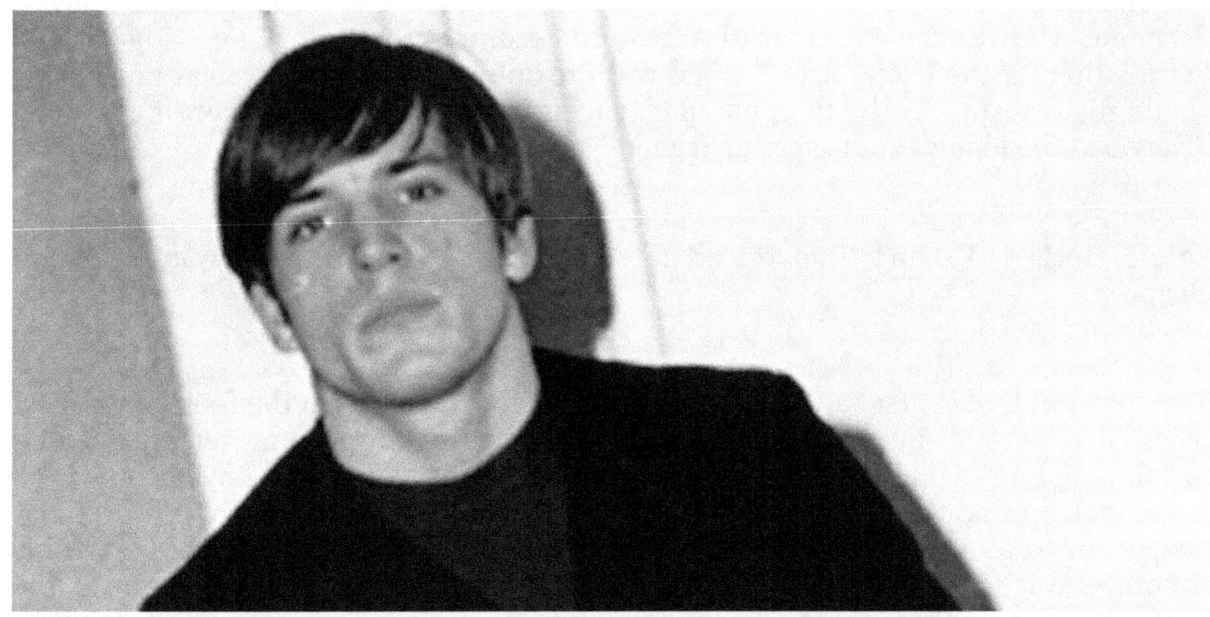

The new kid in town,' Little Joe' Dallesandro, had already worked with Taylor and Louis in 'Lonesome Cowboys' and 'San Diego Surf' when he moved into starring roles in Paul Morrissey's 'Flesh', 'Trash', and 'Heat'. (Photos: Billy Name)

Interviewer *(to Warhol)*
You said all people are the same and that you wanted to be a machine in your painting, is that true?

Andy Warhol *(to Brigid Berlin)*
Uh, is it true, Brigid?

Brigid Berlin
No, he just wishes it were all *easier*.

Taylor Mead: After he was shot the energy level went somewhere else. Then, Brigid was keeping books. Brigid Berlin was his secretary. I made a couple of movies with her where she was fantastic, but I think she had her party list, and we were all off the list. She was controlling all that. So, we were off the list of Andy's parties and dinners and stuff, and I think that it had to do with Brigid. But Andy would just let this all happen. He just let everyone do their own thing.

Perhaps Warhol could continue that laissez-faire illusion because he had Brigid Berlin running interference. Although many women had tried to coax Warhol into the marital bed, Brigid was the wife figure in Warhol's life. According to Vincent Fremont, who worked closely with Andy and became director for The Andy Warhol Foundation for the Visual Arts, "Brigid was the only one who could yell at him. They would really torture each other, but like a loving married couple." According to Viva, "They had the longest running marriage in New York."

Brigid Berlin: I didn't want his art for Christmas. What I wanted was a vacuum cleaner.

Warhol would, of course, always have a soft spot for the lads. In the footage we used from Torbet's 'Andy Superartist', Warhol was interviewed by a youngster who wanted to "play a game" with him, and Warhol cheerfully went along. The boy began with a statement: "I find that people are— " Warhol, cracking a rare smile, said, "I find that people are—fantastic." The last question asked of him, recorded years before his shooting, was: "The most wonderful thing about living. . ." Warhol finished the sentence. His jaunty reply shocked many. But was not a bit surprising to those who knew him. . .

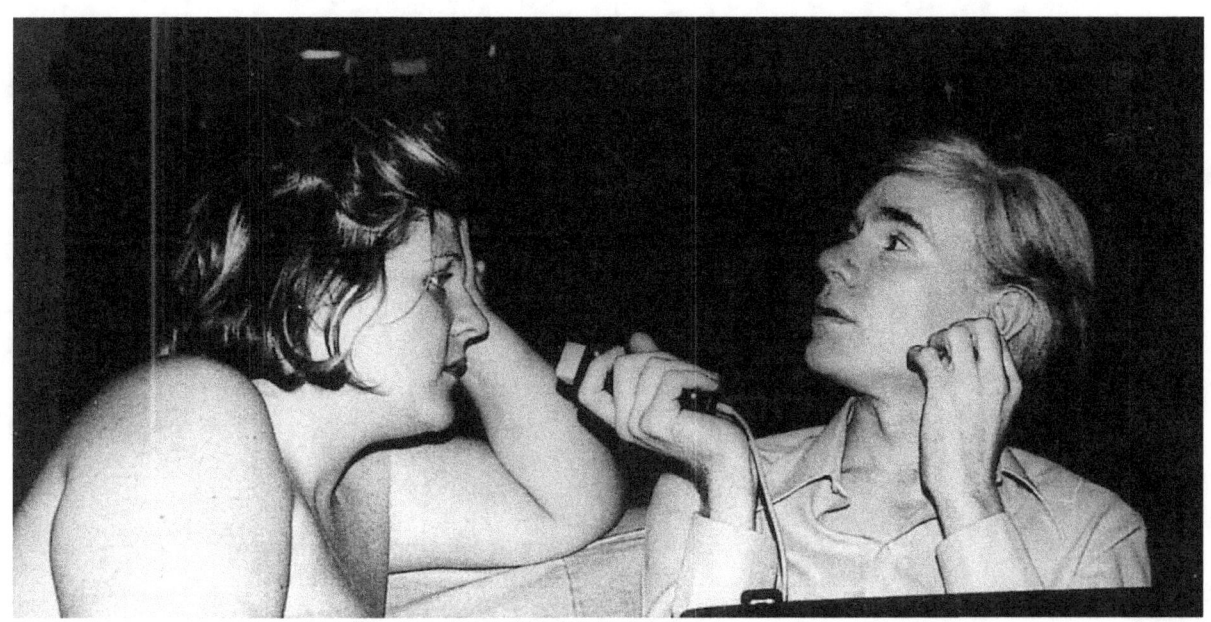

Brigid Berlin and the only person who ever gave her a job.   (Photos: Billy Name)

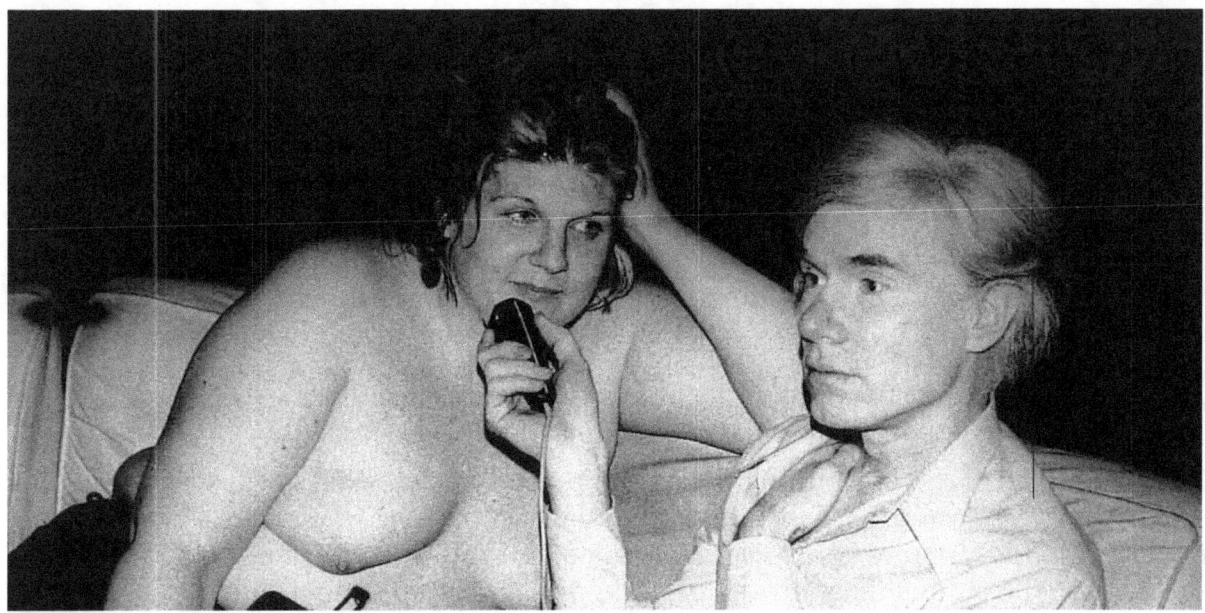

Best friends forever. Brigid and Andy gossiped about everything, every day, and their mutual insights would eventually wind their way into books, films, and history.

AFTER THE FACTORY ... EPILOGUE

The most wonderful thing about living is to be dead.
–Andy Warhol

Victor Bockris: Somebody said about Warhol that "Great artists make art out of what creates the most distress for them." I think that's very true, and a very good point. You can really follow Warhol's work and see how he is facing the things that cause him the most distress. And ultimately his theme is death... The death of his father when he was twelve, the near death of his mother when he was thirteen, left indelibly imprinted on him the horror of hospitals and how quickly someone can just disappear. Also, the horror of death in the religious tradition, where you bring the body back to the house for three days and everybody sits around crying. So it was a very big thing to him, a big thing in his life, death.

Henry Geldzahler: He wouldn't fall asleep until dawn cracked because sleep equals death... Andy was a Catholic and I think he had a sense of evil. His position was not a profoundly moral one—he surrounded himself with all kinds of things that society and the church disapproved of. And perhaps, finally, *he* disapproved of. That was one of the fascinating and repelling aspects of his films and life at the Factory.

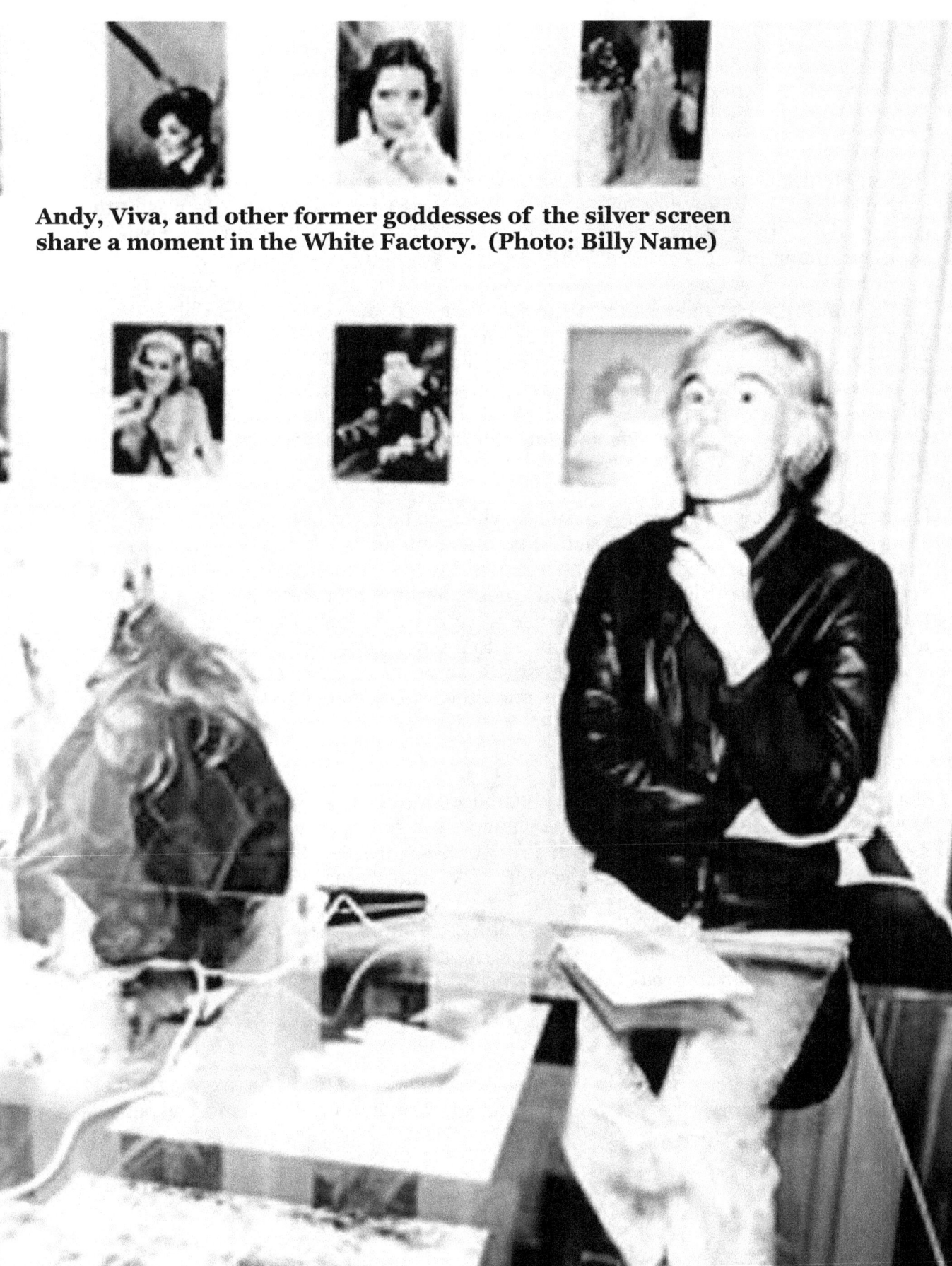

Andy, Viva, and other former goddesses of the silver screen share a moment in the White Factory. (Photo: Billy Name)

Robert Heide: After he was shot, I met him on Macdougal Street. He was very frail at that point. Andy was not just super cool, he was very vulnerable. He was at the cutting edge of the age that we live in now, of technology. . . In the future we will not want our fifteen minutes of fame. We'll pay dearly for our anonymity.

Louis Waldon: I came back from Europe after I hit the cover of the Village Voice with Viva and Brigid Berlin. At a book opening, I walked into the author's bar at the Lion's Head with a buddy of mine. We ordered a drink, and a bartender came out, who was a writer I had known for years. He poured a drink, then he poured himself a drink—and spat it in my face. I said, "What the hell is this about?" My buddy says, "Let's get out of here. These people don't like you, Louis." It was because I was on the cover with Andy Warhol.

Ivy Nicholson: I would have been Andy's wife. He had a long time to think about it. That was during my homeless period. I got more publicity when I became homeless than when I lived in my first husband's castle! I was a countess, married to Regis Du Poleon—not much publicity there. But when I became homeless, it was covered by the Washington Post, The Times. People were flying in from all over to try to find me, a homeless woman! Someone wanted to be my agent, but I was still homeless. So I said, "Okay, I'll show up if you invite some of my homeless friends to the Fairchild." They would! I'd drag in some other homeless guy who was a starving artist, as they say.

It's Ironic that Ivy in the sixties made much more money than Warhol did selling art. When we interviewed her in Paris, she came with a retinue, including her charming son, the Viscount Darius Du Poleon (Yes, those stories of her castle were true). Young Darius had appeared in a couple of Warhol films, but Ivy was hardly a hovering stage mom. Also along for the Paris visit were her adult twins by another former husband, the filmmaker John Palmer ('Empire', 'Ciao Manhattan!'). We drank red wine while she recounted her escapades, sometimes a bit incoherently, reminding one of an unpredictable, very bright bag lady. Then, she decided she'd like to spend the night, and I realized Ivy was homeless once more. . .

Ivy Nicholson: When you live in the street and you don't always have enough to eat it's a real thrill going to have a wonderful meal. You can order the most expensive wine with the most expensive food!

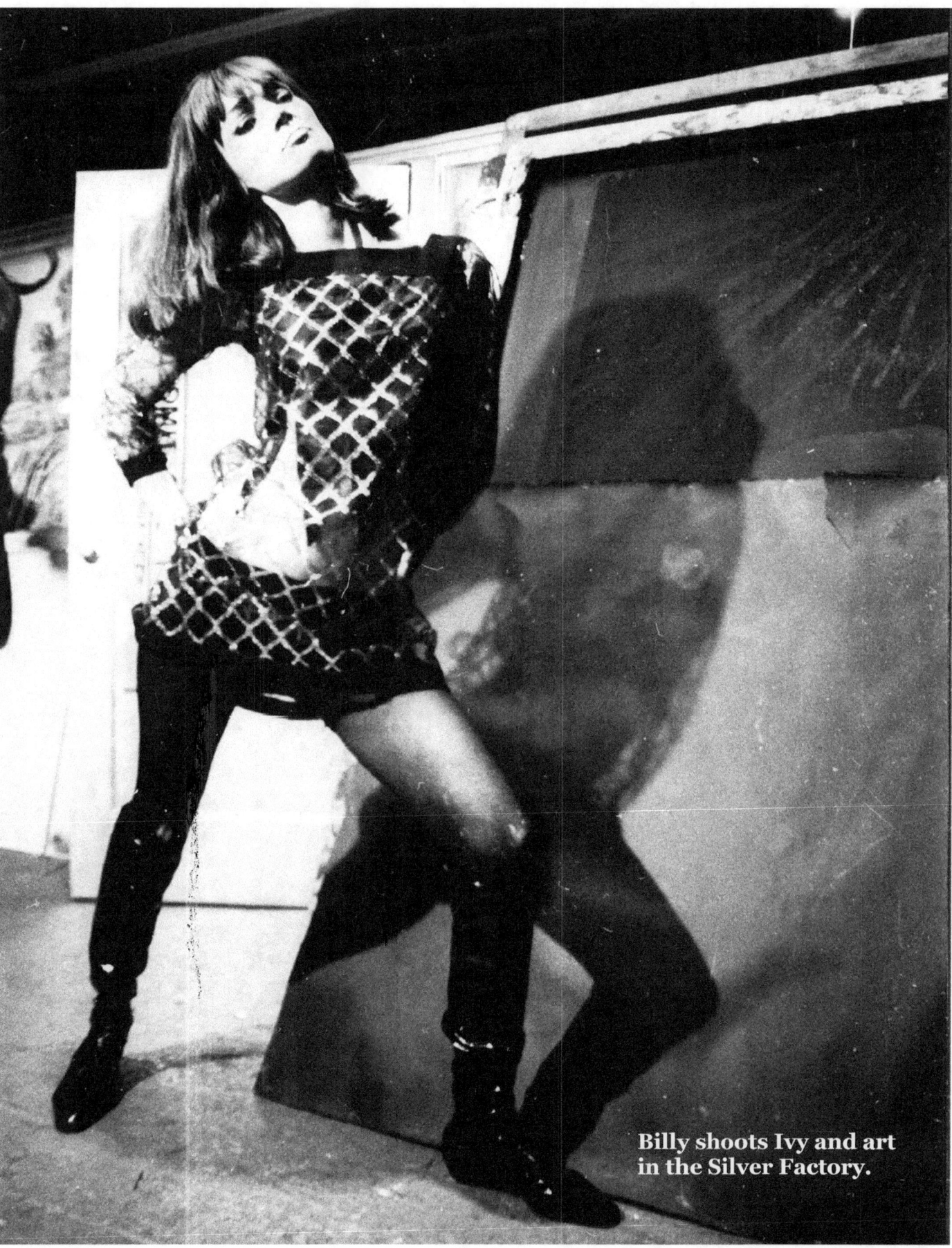

Billy shoots Ivy and art
in the Silver Factory.

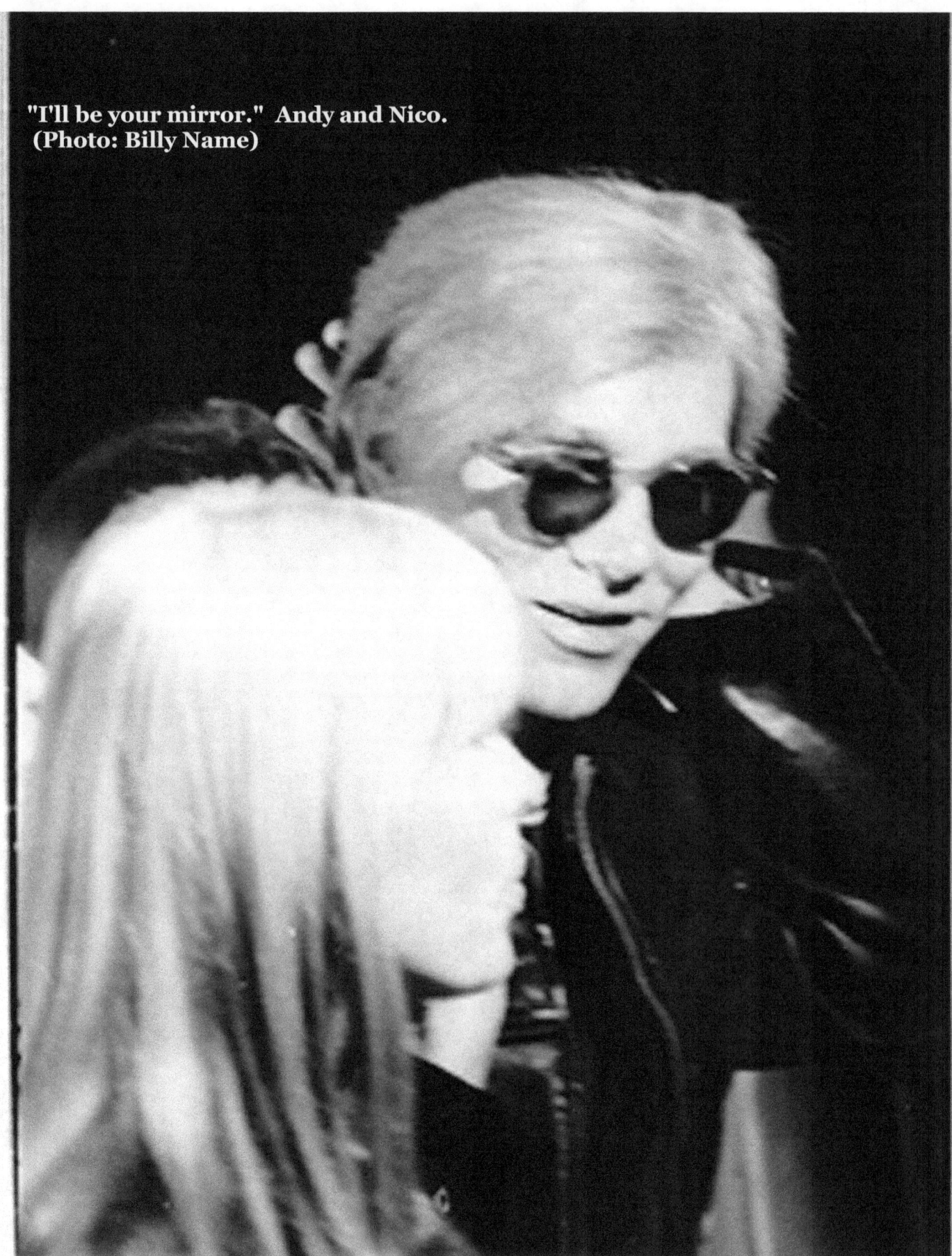

"I'll be your mirror." Andy and Nico.
(Photo: Billy Name)

... Ivy is still a whirilgig of manic energy, but manages to somehow hold it together, and has recently (relatively speaking) directed a film starring her twins, who are supposedly schizophrenic, but very sweet. We also talked about our mutual friend Nico, and the last time we'd seen her before her untimely demise in 1988 at the age of 5. She'd apparently had a heart attack, and had fallen from her bike and hit her head, suffering a brain hemorrhage by the side of a dusty road in Ibiza, Spain. After the Velvets, Nico had done a solo album, 'Chelsea Girl'. She and John Cale also created the wonderous 'The Marble Index'. But I will always think of her (and Andy) when I hear 'All Tomorrow's Parties'. Warhol also adored the haunting 'I'll Be Your Mirror', since he'd so wanted to be Nico, his Nordic goddess Girl of the Year. He'd compared her to the prow of a Viking ship. Nico clearly wanted calmer waters.

Nico: Regrets? I have no regrets, no, except that I was born a man instead of a woman. That's my only regret. *(She laughs and inhales her unfiltered cigarette.)*

Lou Reed: *(strums his guitar in studio)* "It's such a perfect day, you made me forget myself, made me feel I was someone else, someone good. . ."

In 1967 Lou Reed dedicated his song 'European Son' to Syracuse University mentor Delmore Schwartz, who had died the year before at age 52, a sad alcoholic. The Velvets made their last group appearance at Max's in 1970. I remember them playing 'Perfect Day' in the upstairs room. . . Warhol had already lost them. His involvement and interest had waned by 1967, when their album, 'The Velvet Underground and Nico' was finally released by MGM-Verve. In 'Sergeant Pepper's Summer of Love', their dark, edgy compositions lent a discordant note. Even Warhol's cheerful peel-off banana on the cover could not help. Nico had left, John Cale had left, and Lou Reed was ready for the solo career that would take him all over the world. In 1991, struggling with our own version of nihilism, we trudged to the Fondation Cartier in Paris to see Lou and John play together again, reunited thanks to Billy Name. They sang 'Songs for Drella'. *C'était incroyable.* Almost 20 years after that we saw Lou Reed once again in Paris performing 'Berlin' to an oversold house. He looked pretty much the same. Come to think of it, so did we. Time stands still in Paris.

Lou Reed: (Andy) made it all possible, one, by his backing, and two, before we went into the studio, he said, "Use all the dirty words. Don't let them clean a thing."

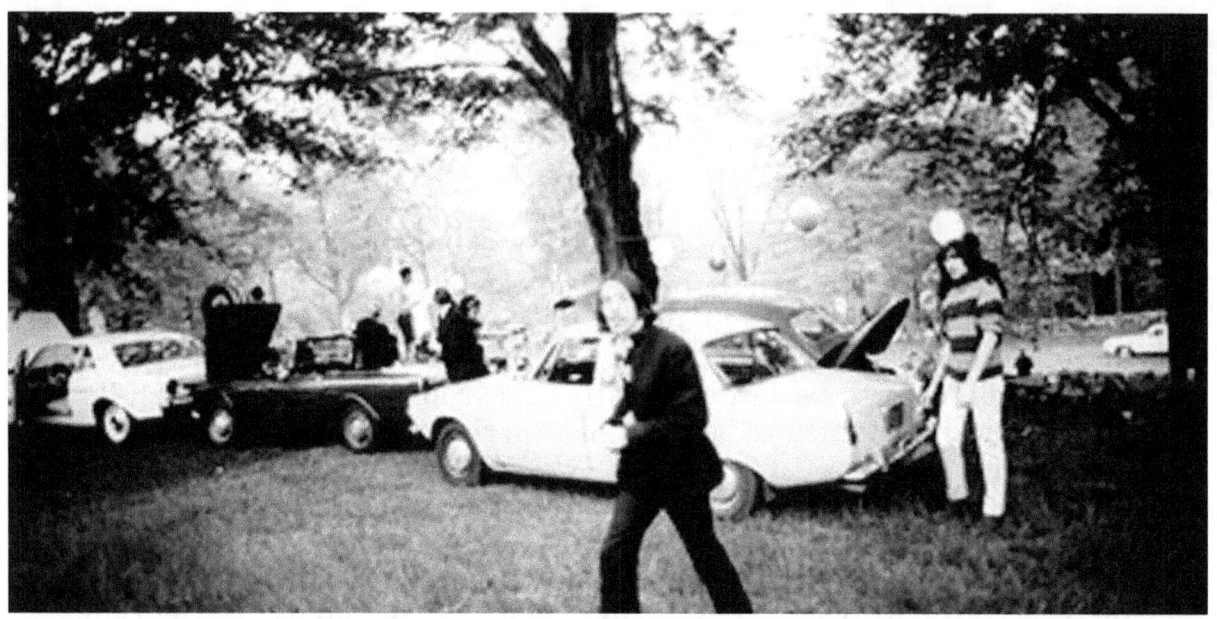

The Velvet Underground arrives for their performance at the famous Philip Johnson 'Glass House', built in 1949, in New Canaan, Connecticut on 47 acres.

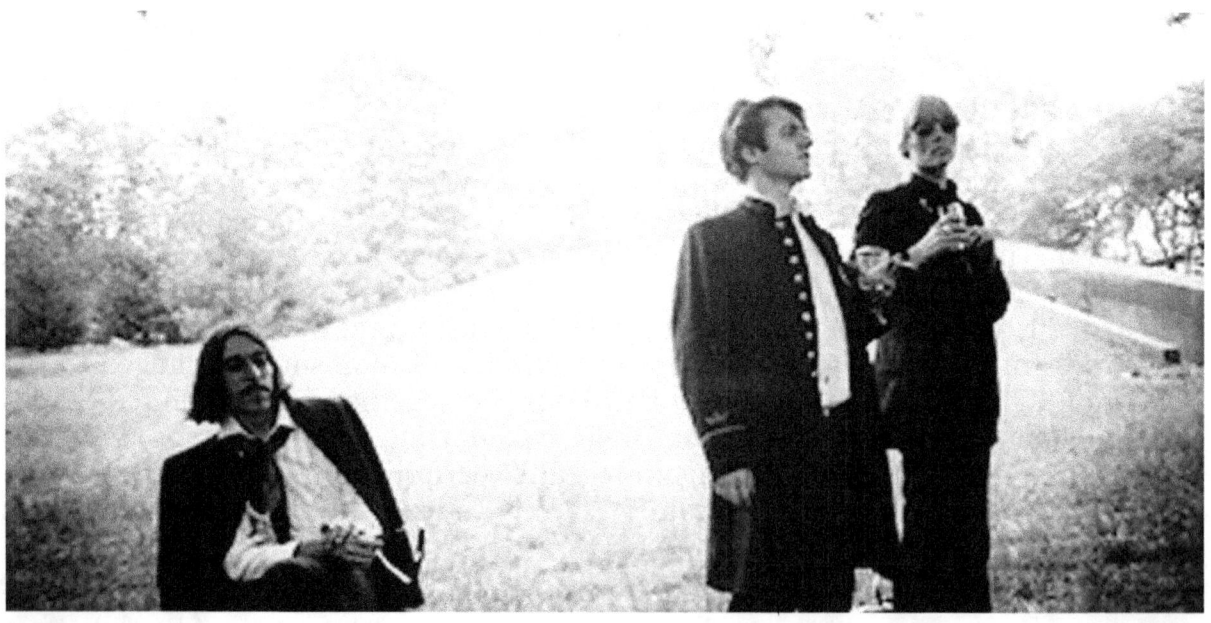

"Such a perfect day." John Cale enjoying a bit of bucolic in the Connecticut woods with Gerard and Nico. (Photos: Billy Name)

Bibbe Hansen: We all lived in loft buildings. They were old factories. Growing up in the art world, to a certain extent art isn't anything special. It's what you do everyday. One time, I was in my father's loft, starving to death, and I went down and found some soup. Al came home a little while later and asked me if I was hungry. I said, "No, I just had some soup." He fished the cans out of the garbage and said, "Do you know what this is?" I said, "Yeah, Campbell's Tomato soup." . . . "No! That was an Andy Warhol signature. You just ate two cans of soup signed by Andy Warhol." So, they say when you are really, really hungry food tastes great. Let me tell you, it tastes even better when you are really, really hungry. And, it is art.

Mary Woronov: I don't care for Pop art. I mean, when I was there I thought it was gold. I thought it was fabulous, and I didn't understand what was going on. I was just one of the little flies on the wall going, "Oh this is fabulous, oh wow, a *soup can, ha ha ha!*" I hate it now.

Gerard Malanga: Andy did something really interesting, although some of the other Pop artists did the same thing to a certain extent, had similar ideas. There was a convergence of those ideas, and that was because of the media. In a sense, the media created Pop art—it became a mirror to the media. The story of Pop art is really the story of the media looking at itself.

Gerard might agree that it could also be Warhol looking at himself—he was fond of self-portraits. The first one he ever made, in 1963, went in 2011 for $38.4 million in a bidding war. As art critic Peter Schjaldahl wrote in the May 2000 issue of The New Yorker: "In Warhol's case, we should acknowledge just how right he got the big changes, and, no less, the big continuities of life on a media-revolutionized planet. His best works of the early sixties flag the exact moment when it was no longer possible to regard mass culture as a sphere of kitsch, remote form the values of serious folk." . . . Bob Heide concurs, since he shopped a *lot* with Warhol. When we visited a friend who had bought Warhol's townhouse, the word "Hoarder" came up.

Robert Heide: Andy *was* cultured. We'd go to flea markets together. Of course, Holly Woodlawn would also be selling at the market with stubble on her face, hung-over *(laugh)*. I had a sign in my apartment from 1947, Betty the Coke girl, with her bright red lips and brown hair—Drink Coca Cola! Andy said, "That's the real Pop art." People call it nostalgia. I think it's classic Americana. Everything is art, when you're dead and gone. Andy and me, we were archeologists. We weren't about the money.

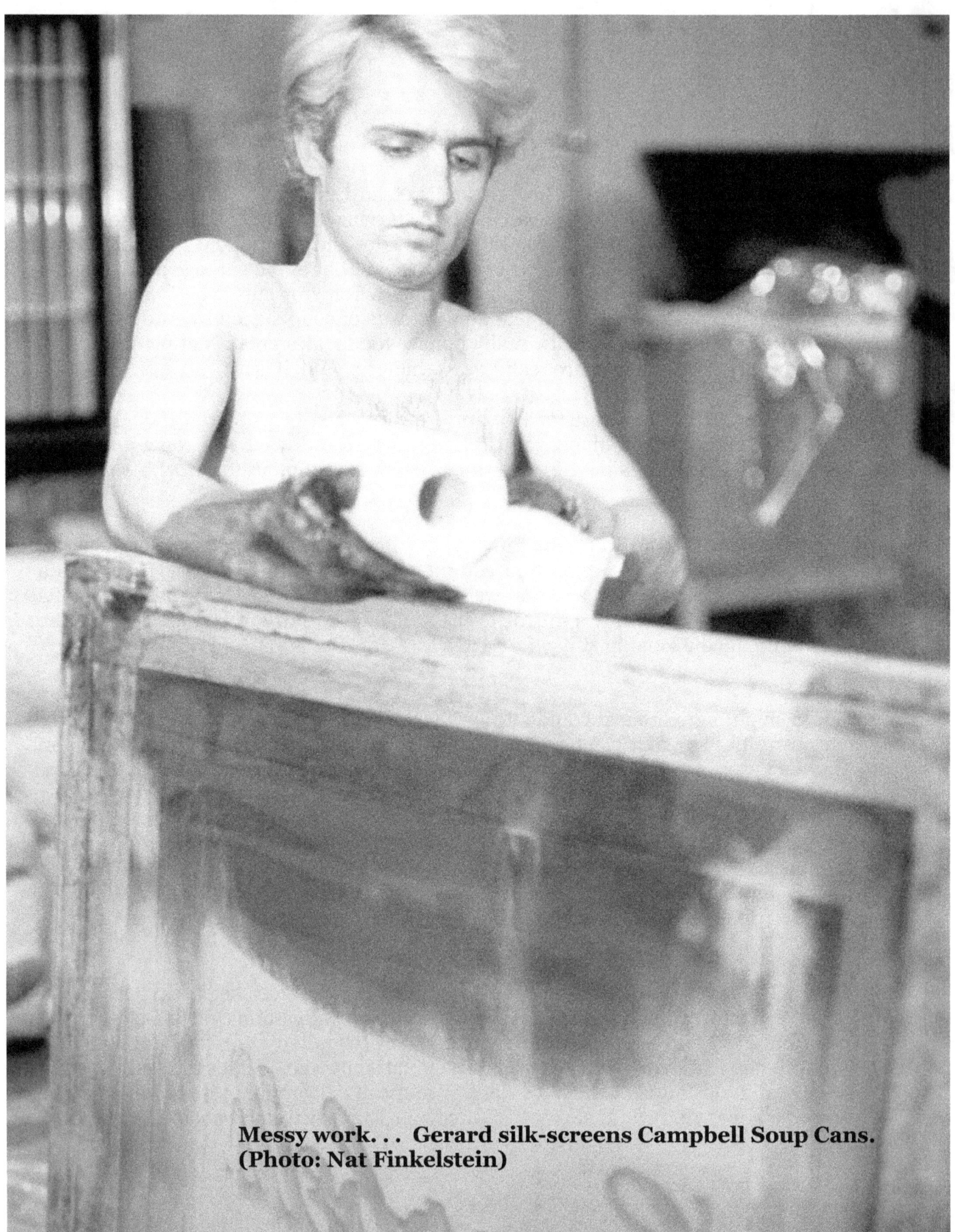

**Messy work. . . Gerard silk-screens Campbell Soup Cans.
(Photo: Nat Finkelstein)**

Vincent Fremont: Andy was the center. He was the force. He said he was just there paying the rent, watching other people do things. That is again the opposite. He was like a huge magnet of ideas and exchange of ideas. That is what life is about, and Andy understood this.

Nat Finkelstein: Whoa, whoa, another kind of Andy Warhol? When you look at it, society in general, what effect did Andy really have? The people around Warhol were a facade, salesmen of toys and titillation. They were a safety valve for society. Think about all the photographs you've seen taken around the Factory, and think about how many people of color you saw before 1969. None.* Sure, there were blacks around, but they didn't get into the Factory—there was only one water fountain. So what effect did Andy have, aside from being just a large rock which was thrown into a pool and made a lot of ripples? The structure remains intact.

---

*Actually, there were a couple of blacks (of course, beautiful) in Warhol's coterie, dancer Rufus Collins (of 'Couch' fame) being one. Finkelstein photographed the striking Donyale Luna, a willowy model I once knew, who worked in a few Warhol movies, including 'Camp' in 1965 with a cast that included Baby Jane Holzer, Jack Smith, Mario Montez and Gerard Malanga. Luna's own 'Donyale Luna' debuted in 1967. She succumbed to an overdose at 39. . . Another unconventional beauty, who prided herself on being "a self-made" woman, Candy Darling succeeded in achieving true Warholian superstardom, but lost the battle with leukemia at 29, achieving underground immortality. A film of her life, 'Beautiful Darling', came out in 2011. Heartbreaking. . . Nobody made a movie about poor old 'Nat the Hat' when he died in 2009 of emphysema (though there were some sighs of relief). He left a legacy of provocative pictures, a peon to the sixties. The New York Times gave him a two-page obit, and suddenly all his stories about Warhol had the ring of truth about them. . .

Andy Warhol: I'd asked around ten or fiveteen people for suggestions. Finally one lady friend asked the right question, "Well, what do you love most?" That's how I started painting money.

A close Warhol pal with little interest in money is still working well into his eighties. Jonas Mekas championed Warhol's movies, and today his Anthology Film Archives is one of the world's largest and most important repositories of avant-garde films. I wish he could find the time to teach a film course at NYU's graduate film school. . .

Jonas Mekas: People think, "Why should we see those films?" Consider, in the old days people used to go and make dangerous long trips into the Orient and bring back spices to enrich the kitchens of Europe, something special they could not find at home. And the same purpose is to show films. They don't have to be great, but they each contain something special and local that we don't have. Every country has cinema, but it's very specific, related to their country, and we should be interested in them. That is what we are all about here at Anthology (Film Archives). We show films that nobody else would show. They don't have to be masterpieces. It's like if you just eat a steak every day and no salad. You sometimes need salad. You cannot live on masterpieces alone! So, that said, you go to Eisenstein, to Renoir, to Rossellini, and nobody can make films like Renoir, nobody can make films like Eisenstein, and *nobody* can make films like Andy. He used everybody around him to produce that whole body of work, that cannot be repeated. It cannot be repeated.

Interviewer *(to Warhol)*
When they tried to explain your film, they said "This was a peek into Hell." For me, William Burroughs' 'Naked Lunch' is like a peek into Hell.

Henry Geldzahler
Andy goes to Church every Sunday, and he probably has his own idea about Hell. . .
(turns to Warhol) Does Chelsea Girls remind you of Hell?

Andy Warhol
Uh, no.

Henry Geldzahler
Were you surprised when critics wrote that?

Andy Warhol
Uh, yes.

A note on a real peek into Hell: Award-winning docu filmmaker and pal of William Burroughs, Jean-Francois Valee (yes, he's French) made a must-see movie that gets under your skin as effectively as a plunged needle. For the above interview we used a hallucinatory clip of Burroughs unearthing his heroin stash from the bathroom of a wretched Mexican hotel room. The film features an interview with extraordinary musician/performance artist Laurie Anderson (widow of Lou Reed), who elegantly waltzes with Burroughs, snappily attired in identical white linen suits.

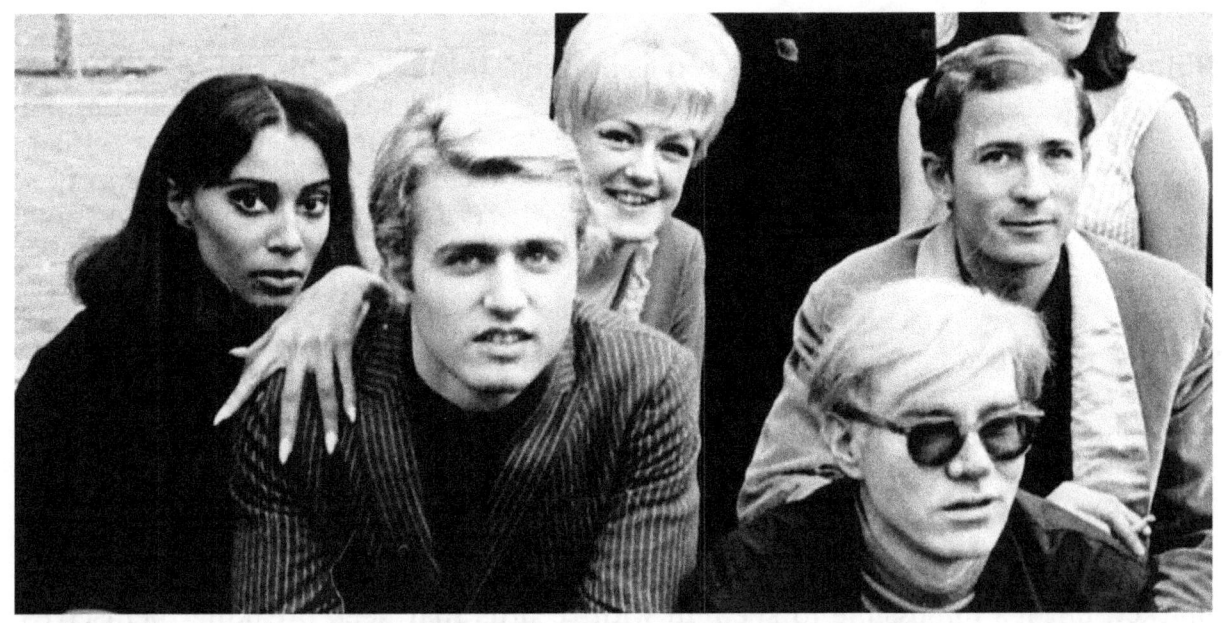

Donyale Luna (the first black 'Supermodel', Gerard, Ingrid Superstar, Danny Williams, and Andy Warhol pose for Nat Finkelstein's camera.

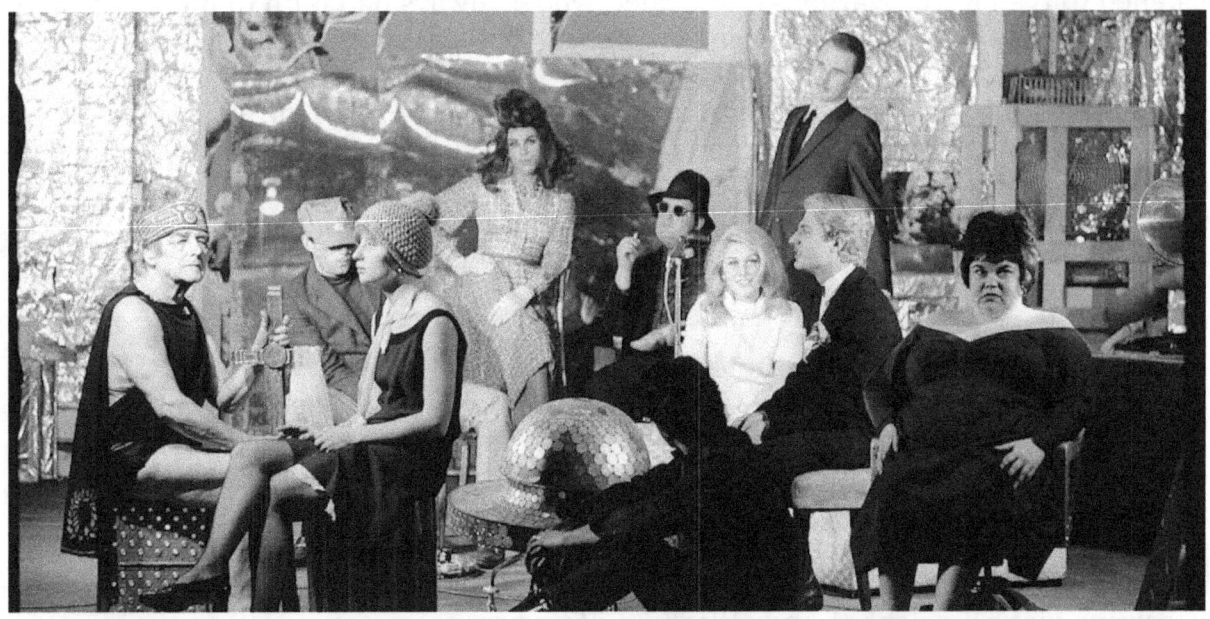

Actor Paul Swann stars in 'Camo (1965) with Gerard Malanga. Other cast members included Tally Brown, Fu Fu Smith, Tosh Carillo, Jack Smith, Mario Montez, Baby Jane Holzer, Judie Babs. (Photo: Steve Schapiro)

Vincent Fremont: Andy was attacked as an artist throughout his career. He would get a showing in the Leo Castelli Gallery, but Leo didn't really understand him. He was more focused on Jasper Johns, Lichenstein and Rauchenberg. Andy actually started creating his own gallery—the Studio. Fred Hughes comes into his life in 1967 and turns it into what he wants to be done, where they are working with various dealers. Leo was a New York dealer, but there were others in Europe.

Gallery owner Leo Castelli said that his job consisted, on a daily basis, of contributing to "the myth-making of myth material." His first wife Ileana Sonnabend had been an early champion of Warhol, with shows at her galleries in Paris and Soho. A year after her death in 2007, the heirs got hit with a 50% estate tax, so they sold off $600 million worth of her $1 billion dollar art collection, including 4 Warhol Marilyns, 3 from his Death and Disaster series, 2 Elizabeth Taylors, and a partridge in a pear tree. . . I have made some small attempt here to note the Warholian flurries in the market, but it's impossible to keep up with records that keep breaking themselves. He reigns as the biggest auction seller from 2012 to 2014. Warhols are for sale everywhere, though some art critics wonder "how long his magic will last," the question no one dares answer. It's a pity that all those Factory People we interviewed decided back then to "take the hundred dollars" and not his art. If only they had listened to Ivan Karp, Warhol's first dealer, who'd always had faith in him. But then, they'd have had no time for us, being too busy with their investment portfollios.

Nat Finkelstein: Andy was broke until the seventies. He would complain. When Fred (Hughes) came in he commercialized it and gave Andy a direction where he could be financially enabled. But as far as the sixties were concerned, that Andy was just sort of evolving? No. There were three different corporations formed under his name, at least three that I know of, so he wasn't evolving.

Fredrick W. Hughes was to become the most important person in Warhol's life. Then a dapper self-possessed twenty-two year old, Hughes had been working since a teenager for the powerful de Menil family, the greatest art collectors in America. (Warhol often filmed on their lavish estate, including, 'Loves of Ondine'). So, he was absolutely all about Warhol's art, selling off the stockpile and getting him into portraits. Another staff member, nineteen-year old Vincent Fremont, would soon replace Billy Name as the (White) Factory foreman, running 'the business' and becoming vice-president of Andy Warhol Enterprise.

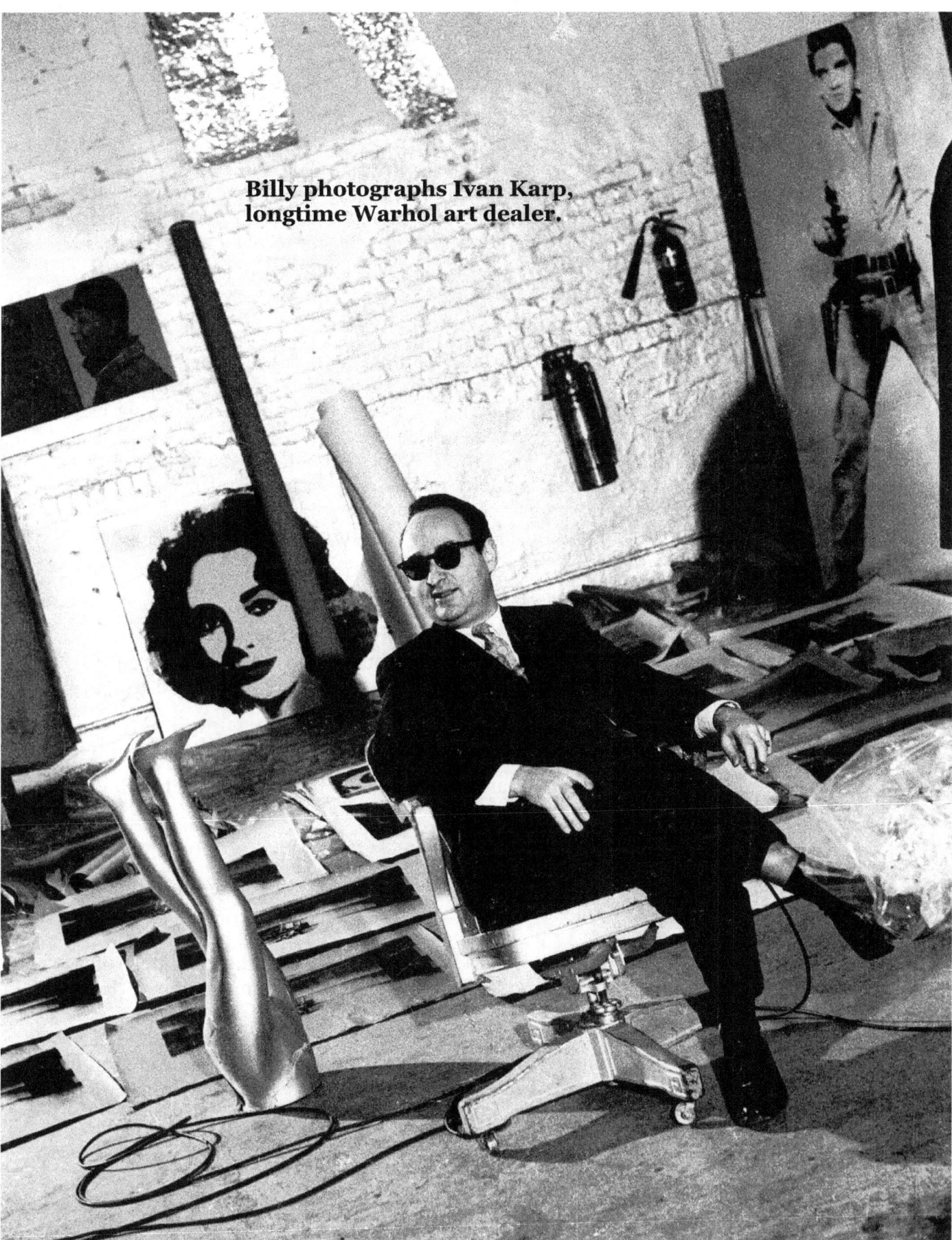

**Billy photographs Ivan Karp,
longtime Warhol art dealer.**

Vincent Fremont: Andy ran his own business. . . I didn't go to college—I went to the University of Andy Warhol. You learned a lot. What was the most important thing I learned from Andy? I don't think there is just one thing. It's multiple life lessons, being close to an artist that way. He was the godfather to my first daughter. As far as working, even though he was a workaholic, he made it fun, at least for himself, and every day was not a walk in the park.

For those exciting turbulent years, according to most of our interview subjects, Warhol had indeed made it fun for himself and his Factory Family. But when it stopped being fun, maybe it was time to 'step out of the picture' and go for a walk in Washington Square Park, and just keep going—which is exactly what Billy Name did. He had valued his time with Andy Warhol, and it shows in all those candid, fly-on-the-wall photographs. A few others we spoke to made me want to say, "Hey, you with the airs. . . Sooner or later, we gotta understand how old we've gotten. It's all gone, the glamour, glory, and silver glitter. And youuuu didn't treasure it." Neither did I.

Billy Name: There was not really a place for me anymore. It was simply an art scene. So I left one day and I left a note on the darkroom door: *"Dear Andy, I am not here anymore, but I am fine, love Billy."* And I went out into the world to see what the planet Earth was doing.

While Billy had quietly lived in his little darkroom, the only person to visit him had been Lou Reed. Apparently, Warhol had gotten used to the situation. . .

Andy Warhol: I had no idea what made him go in, so how could I get him to come out?

Gerard Malanga: *(to Billy Name)* You don't know what happened the day after you moved out? Paul and I went into your room. You know what Paul started doing? He started dancing an Irish jig.

Billy Name: Oh, I know. He didn't want me to be back there from the beginning of the second Factory in Union Square. He would tell Andy things like "Oh, Billy can't stay there because he'll paint the whole place silver." So, I left the note, and just left.

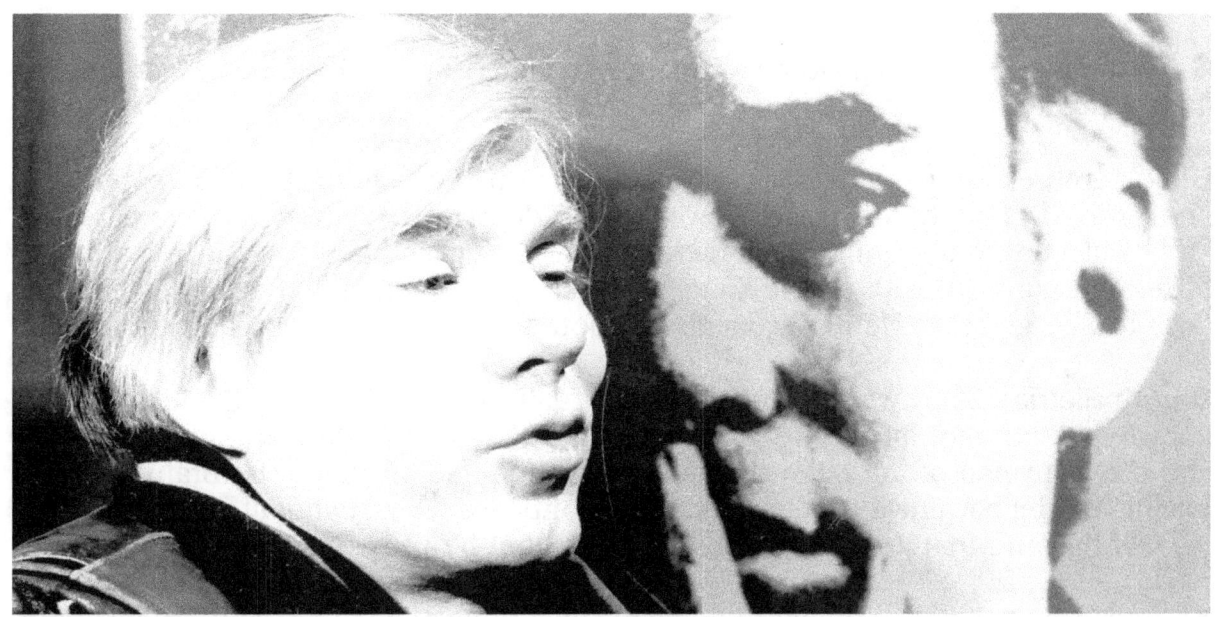

In the Silver Factory, Andy communes with his famous self-portrait. Billy Name's impromtu shots of Andy gave us insight into two complex personalities.

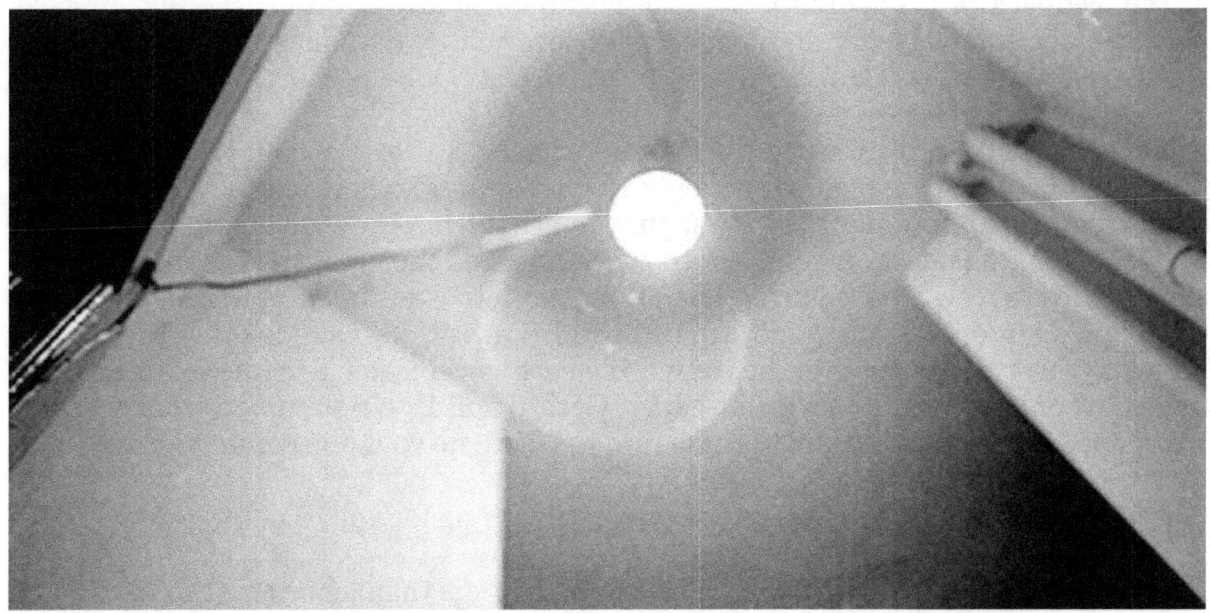

Billy channels William Eggleston in he stark darkroom where he lived for eighteen months, in the Black and White Factory.

Gerard Malanga *(to Billy Name):* Paul was so elated and thrilled at the fact that you had vacated, his albatross.

Billy Name: I never came back. I was living in the streets in the Village, but they knew me at the Paradox on the Lower East Side, and they always let me eat there free. But I enjoyed staying out in the park, and I slept in hallways and in cardboard boxes and hung out with people living in the streets. Eventually, I went down to this farm in Georgia, then New Orleans, then Colorado, then San Francisco, then. . .

Danny Fields: They were too much, really full of moxie, forcing Billy out. But you know what, he went into a lovely life in upstate New York, and he became the mayor and the chairman of the Beaver Dam Commission and all that. He totally changed his life and he became a country boy and a political ecologist and all kinds of things. A lot of the stuff that I'm telling you, excuse me, but he's alive and Andy's dead.

Andy Warhol: I always thought I'd like my own tombstone to be blank. No epitaph, and no name. Well, actually, I'd like it to say 'figment'.

According to art critic Peter Schjeldahl, "Wahol's greatest moment was brief. Caught in the feedback of his own influence, he declined rapidly as an artist. But his peak performance stands higher and higher, while everything that once seemed to contest it falls away."

Billy Name: We were aware at the Factory what we were. We could feel the power, the dynamic of the whole thing, being in the hot spot of the art world. I didn't really have an intent to document . . . I was just an artist who Andy gave a camera to. But we were of the avant-garde mindset, too. We admired the poets in the late fifties and early sixties in New York culture. Then it moved into experimental music, with John Cage and La Monte Young, and experimental film with Jonas Mekas. Andy didn't know that world. He got into the commercial art world when he came to Manhattan, but we were in the legitimate avant-garde, Gerard and I. We stemmed from there, so we opened roadways for Andy to come into it, where he could be comfortable.

Gerard Malanga: Well, it became an interesting thing for you to photograph.

Billy Name: Yeah, but it was more like a dance for me than an attempt to document. I would shoot on the sets; do shots of Nico for the album cover. Or the Velvet Underground. Otherwise, it was dancing all of the time with the camera in my hand.

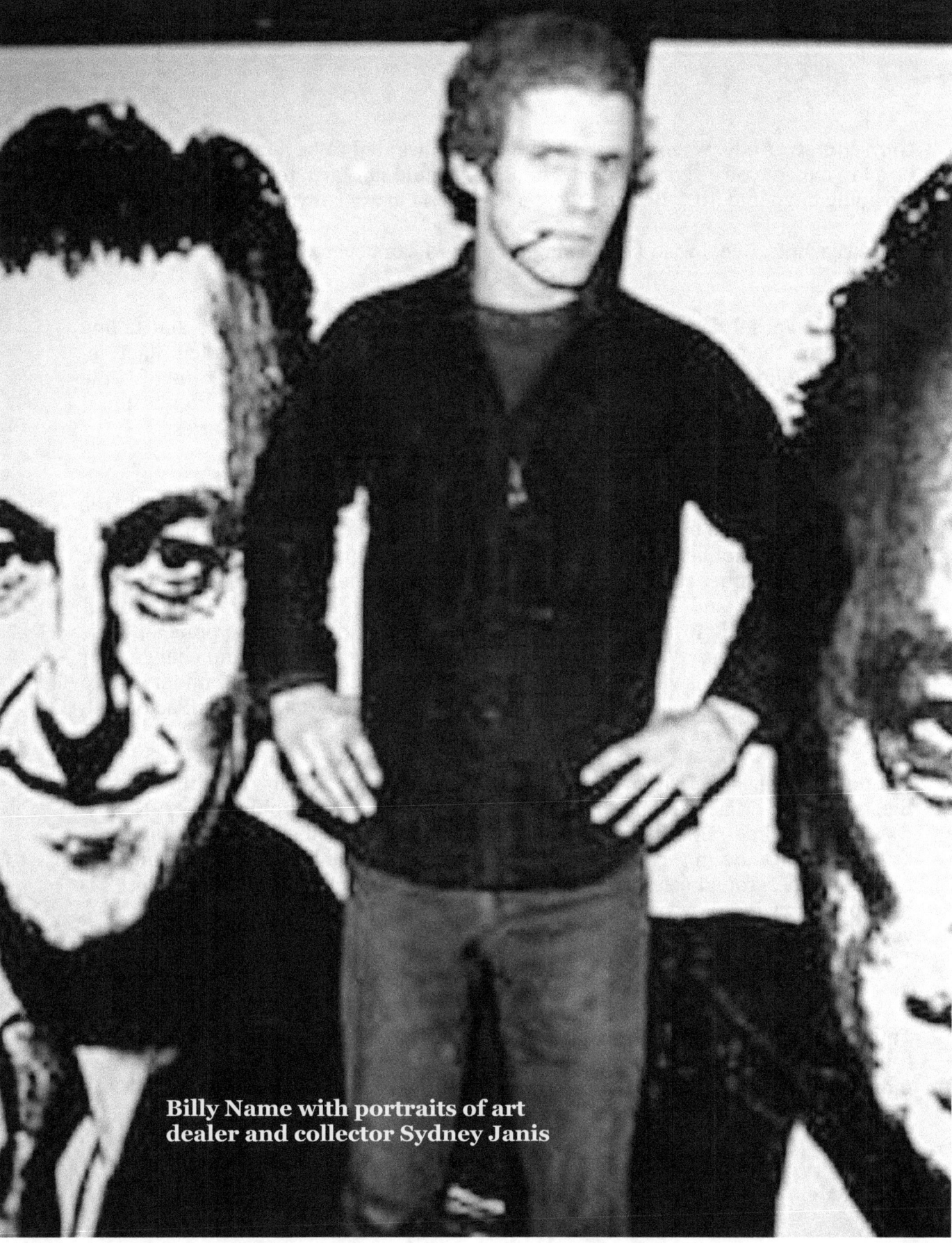

Billy Name with portraits of art dealer and collector Sydney Janis

Ultra Violet: Andy, when he was much younger, wanted to be a tap dancer. And to be a tap dancer you've got to levitate, and Andy could not levitate. So he said, "Gee, I am going to go into art." Because there's no criteria in art. Anything goes.*

Andy Warhol: Gee, I wish I could sing, or hum. I can't even whistle.

Nor could Warhol dance a step, but before the canvases of car crashes and falling bodies came the whimsical life-sized blow-ups of dancing feet in detailed diagram, showing one how to Fox Trot. We choreographed the pictures to the tune of *Cole Porter's classic 'Anything Goes'. Mysteriously, the Warhol Foundation did not find it funny. Well, there was a whole lot they didn't find amusing about our series.

Ultra Violet: Today as an artist I rack my violet brain to find out what shall I be doing, because it's so transient. It's going to last five minutes, or fifteen, if I'm lucky. When I met Warhol he said, "Oh, we have to change your name, nobody could spell it." And I remember reading an article in Scientific American on light—I saw that word 'Ultraviolet', and though it intriguing. I told him, "my name is Ultra Violet," and he just laughed. It proved to be a good name. I would have never done all those things if I had not met Warhol, and he had not said "Let's do a film and change your name." I went into this violet era where everything was violet, from my underwear to my teeth. I am Ultra Violet, still here. I am the only survivor of the Silver Factory.

Not quite, Ultra. Other survivors are still out there, but they always did think outside the box: Billy, Mary, Gerard, Bob, Bibbe, Ivy, Allen, Jane, John, Jonas, Danny, David, Susan, Paul, Brigid, Holly, Vincent, and Viva, who will always be a superstar, as long as she stays in seclusion. . . Taylor Mead may have left us, but he continues to be an underground celebrity. We saw Warhol's favorite Beat poet, just before his hilarious show in a Bowery bar, and wound up using it over our end titles. By now, you're thinking 'Andy Warhol's Factory People' should have been subtitled 'How Not To Make A Documentary'. It's okay, Taylor loved us, or was it the scotch?

Taylor Mead: Andy made them all famous, semi-famous. . . I am one of the most semi-famous people in the world, except for Ultra of course. But If I'd been rich and famous, I would have had AIDS by now. I would have bought every hustler in Hollywood. I had all the numbers. . .

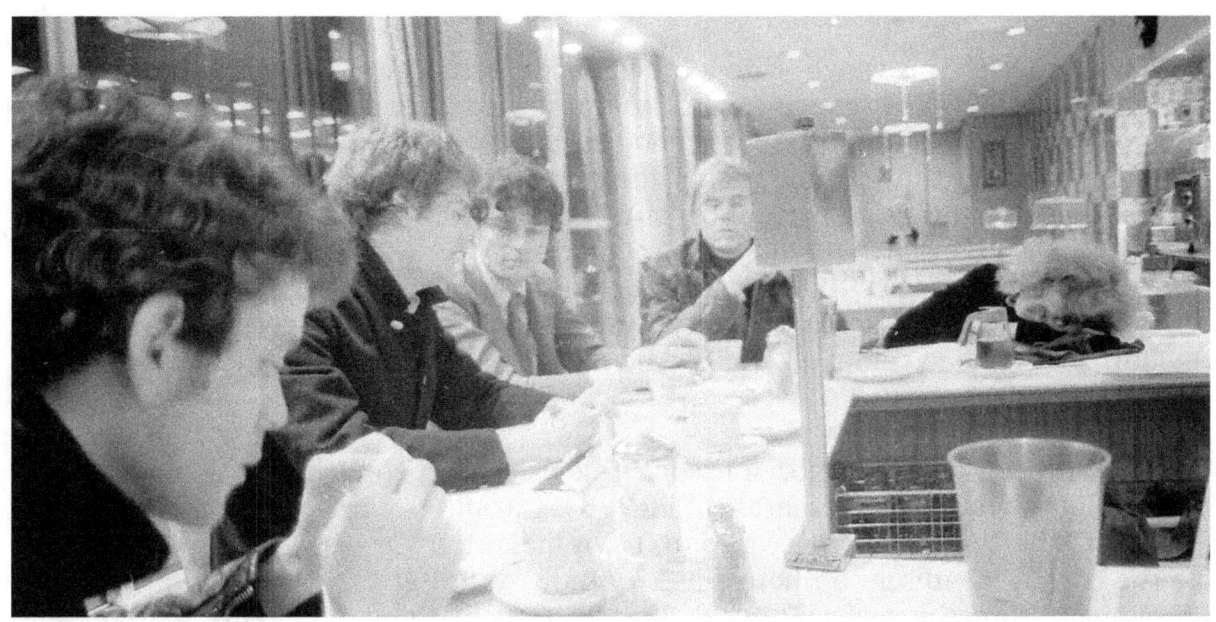

Lou Reed, Paul Morrissey, a friend, and Andy, enjoying the end of a late night, and ignoring, at right, a sleeping Viva.

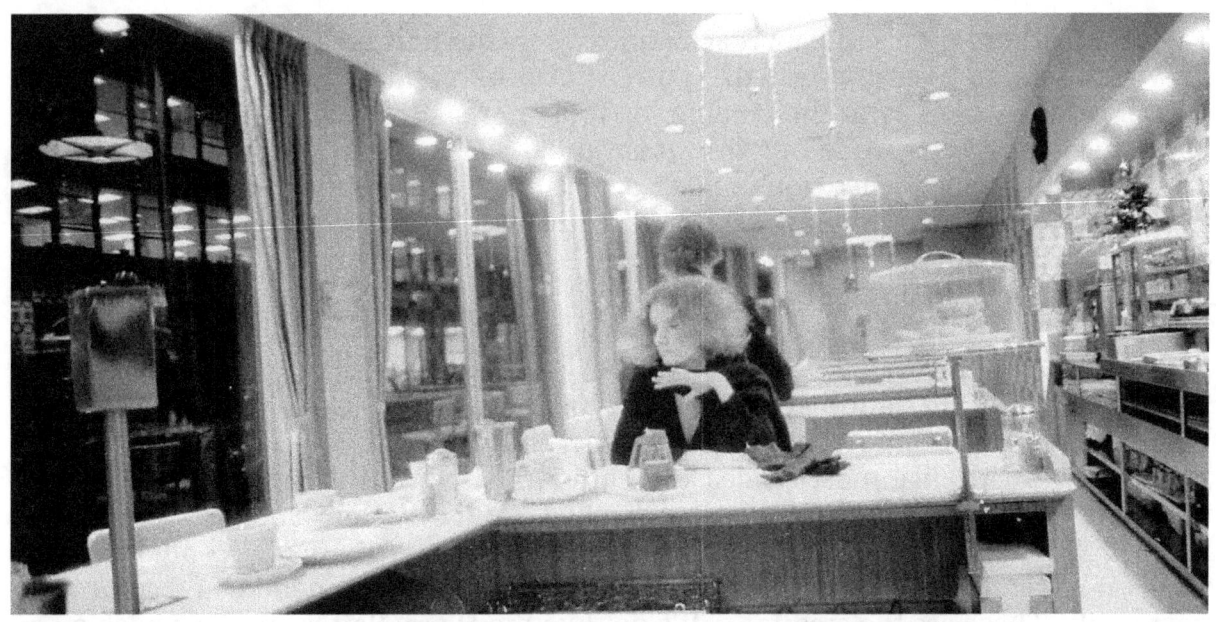

Viva wakes up in a nearly deserted diner (Paul in B.G.), as Billy Name channels Edward Hopper's 'Nighthawks'.

. . . Taylor checked his watch with a touch of consternation. "Now see, I'm way past my time, actually. They're waiting for me to go onstage. I have to prepare for my public. I have to appear for the three people that showed up." Well, he'd forgotten to reset his watch for the fall time change, and was an hour early. More people showed up soon enough, including a couple of curators from the Whitney Museum who were preparing a retrospective of Taylor's many films. He claims to be "buried alive in museums', but his fans still turn out. In some marvelous strange way, Taylor sums up the spirit of Lenny Bruce, the advent of the sixties, and the decadal mayhem on the horizon. We had come full circle. And now it was time for . . . Taylor's Show!

--

Taylor Mead: Okay. In honor of French Television, or people in Paris, or whoever is here tonight—you got the cameras rolling? . . . I would like to do an homage to the Statue of Liberty, which France gave to us, reluctantly. Or we were reluctant to pay for the trip over—misers on both sides. Finally, it got erected. So my poem is,:"Is Lesbianism Something New?" God, I'm slurring like crazy. Fucking whiskey and drugs. . . "Is lesbianism something new?" Well, there has been a very masculine woman carrying a torch for someone, standing conspicuously in New York harbor for over a hundred years. Here's to Lady Liberty. Boy, is she tough looking, too. . .

Taylor pulled out a ragged paperback and read us his first poem from his first book, for which he was "nearly arrested." I'd reprint it here, but he deserves to sell a few, even posthumously. After the reading, he took a break to play his radio and sip his 'prop' glass of scotch while our titles continued. Okay, they did go on for awhile. This tends to happen when you've gone over budget and are now begging for money from assorted sources, who expect a plug in the credits, even though we know those credits on TV zip by as quickly as transvestite ripping off five o'clock shadow. Luckily, Taylor went on and on. . .

Taylor Mead: Here's another fairy tale by Taylor fucking Mead: Once upon a time, but there's no such thing as once upon a time. *(Taylor holds up his sketch pad).* In a large castle—with, like most castles and cathedrals, penises all over the place while outlawing them—In a castle, a monster dwelled. Andy Warhol. Though I think Andy is paying for this reading, so I better be carefull. *Wonderful* Andy. Wonderful Andy was a monster. *(flips a page)* Can anybody see this? Is it too anemic? I'll color it for next week. These are the credits. . . It's not like the Harry Potter credits, which go on for twenty minutes. Was the movie that good? Loved the dragons.

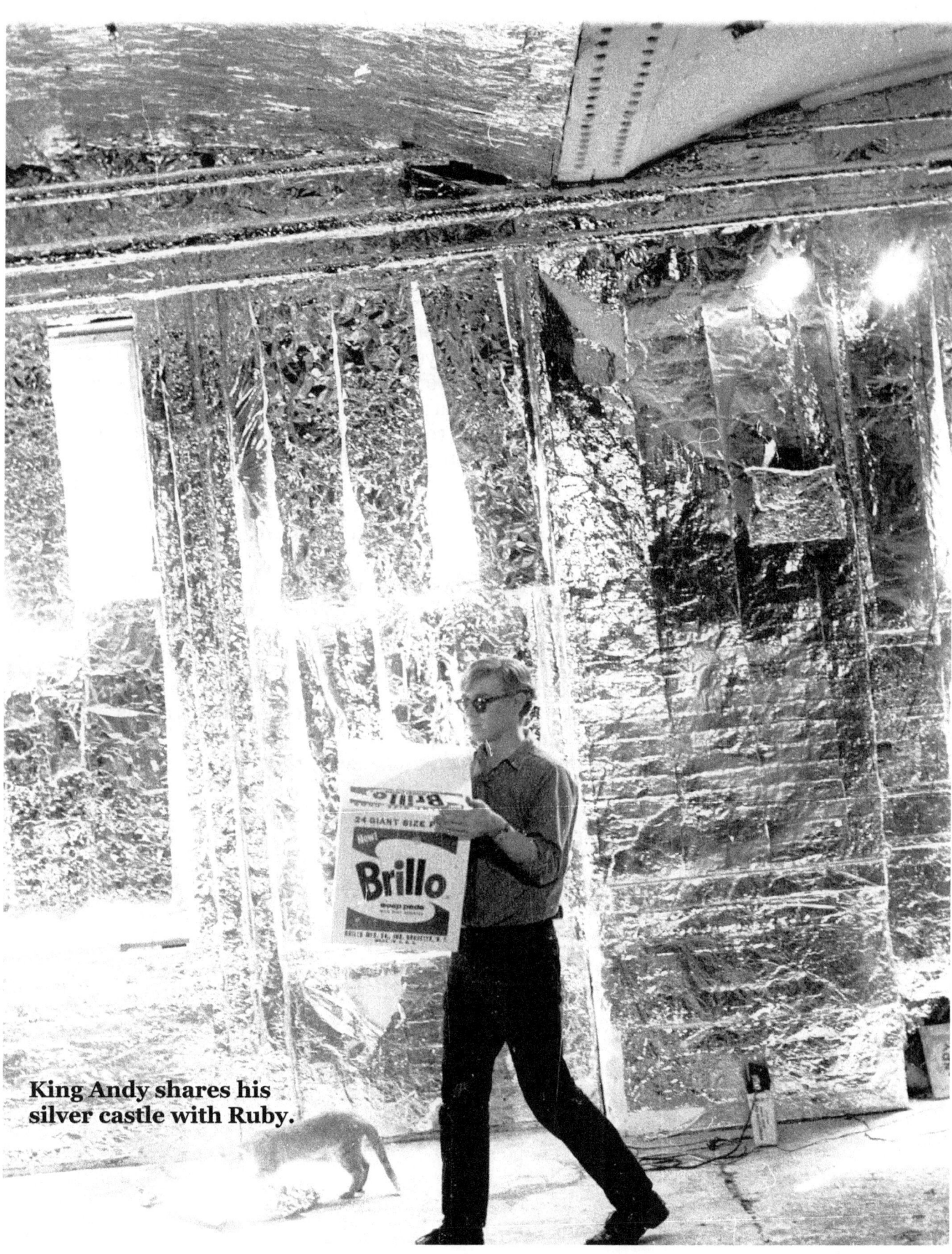

King Andy shares his
silver castle with Ruby.

Young child *(to Warhol)*
Would you like to add something to that?

Andy Warhol
No.

And neither would we, except to add a sincere footnote of gratitude to all our Factory People, even the difficult ones (You know who you are), to the patient folks whose footage we licensed, even the difficult ones (You know who you are), and to our workaholic editors and technical experts (You're all difficult). Thank you Victor Bockris, for writing the best biography I ever read about Warhol. Though I expect there will be more, I don't expect to read them. Thanks Edie and Nico, for the memories. Thank you to the late Lou Reed and to Bob Dylan, for being good sports and for being more relevant than ever. The big subjects of the sixties are back with a vengeance, and that's why everybody remembers, even the ones who weren't there.

So, thank you to former WCBS TV news correspondent and present novelist Mary Pangalos Manilla, and to former filmmaker and present day columnist Diana Colson, who were there in the sixties, and remembered it all differently.

A final shower of Buddhist blessings on Billy Name for his iconic photographs, his benevolent friendship, his stories, and his unique insight. . . Billy did not see his trunk, which held all those negatives (and Valerie Solanas' script) until 1987. When Andy Warhol died, on Billy's birthday (!), the trunk was returned to him. . . Sadly, those negatives have recently been 'lost' to the ages once again, thanks to a thieving, nefarious erstwhile agent, but that is another tale.

Warhol, too, had his work "stolen left and right." Ever Zen, he shrugged his shoulders, like Billy, and expected matters to eventually resolve themselves (with a platoon of busy lawyers). However, he did once complain that "The Campbell's Soup Company has not sent me a single can of soup." . . . So thanks again, Andy, ironic until the end, for a truly Warholian experience. By the time I had gone through my piles of research and newspaper clippings, I came to the same conclusion as your multitude of fans and foes: You reached the public as no other artist has before you, except maybe Picasso, which has made you the most collected (and protected) artist on the planet. Therefore, rather than encourage any more legal attention from the keepers of your flame, we have wisely decided not to do the sequel.

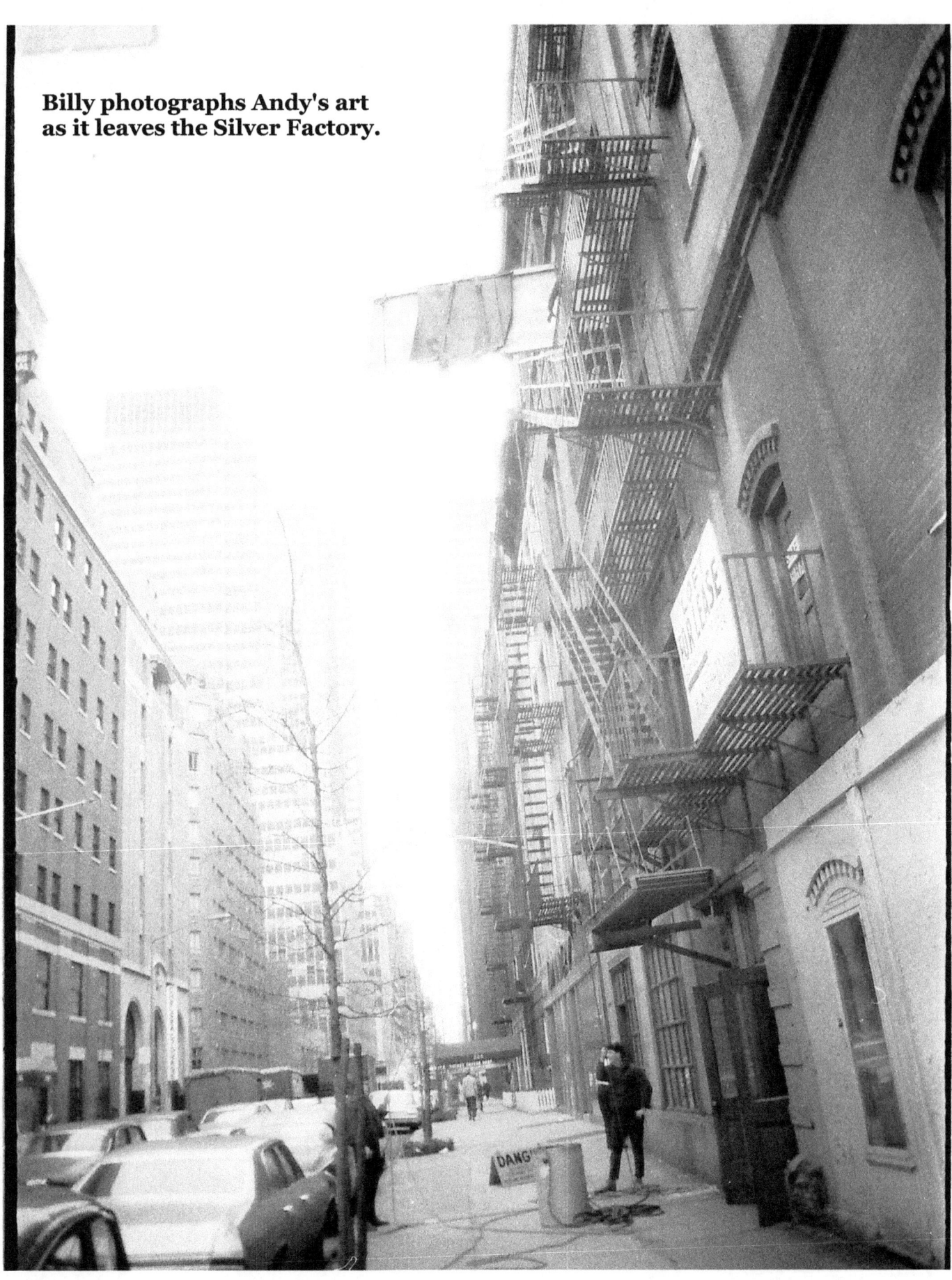

Billy photographs Andy's art as it leaves the Silver Factory.